DAN-22   DANTES SUBJECT STANDARDIZED TESTS (DSST)

This is your
PASSBOOK for...

Introduction to Education (Foundations of)

Test Preparation Study Guide
Questions & Answers

COPYRIGHT NOTICE

This book is SOLELY intended for, is sold ONLY to, and its use is RESTRICTED to individual, bona fide applicants or candidates who qualify by virtue of having seriously filed applications for appropriate license, certificate, professional and/or promotional advancement, higher school matriculation, scholarship, or other legitimate requirements of education and/or governmental authorities.

This book is NOT intended for use, class instruction, tutoring, training, duplication, copying, reprinting, excerption, or adaptation, etc., by:

1) Other publishers
2) Proprietors and/or Instructors of "Coaching" and/or Preparatory Courses
3) Personnel and/or Training Divisions of commercial, industrial, and governmental organizations
4) Schools, colleges, or universities and/or their departments and staffs, including teachers and other personnel
5) Testing Agencies or Bureaus
6) Study groups which seek by the purchase of a single volume to copy and/or duplicate and/or adapt this material for use by the group as a whole without having purchased individual volumes for each of the members of the group
7) Et al.

Such persons would be in violation of appropriate Federal and State statutes.

PROVISION OF LICENSING AGREEMENTS – Recognized educational, commercial, industrial, and governmental institutions and organizations, and others legitimately engaged in educational pursuits, including training, testing, and measurement activities, may address request for a licensing agreement to the copyright owners, who will determine whether, and under what conditions, including fees and charges, the materials in this book may be used them. In other words, a licensing facility exists for the legitimate use of the material in this book on other than an individual basis. However, it is asseverated and affirmed here that the material in this book CANNOT be used without the receipt of the express permission of such a licensing agreement from the Publishers. Inquiries re licensing should be addressed to the company, attention rights and permissions department.

All rights reserved, including the right of reproduction in whole or in part, in any form or by any means, electronic or mechanical, including photocopying, recording, or by any information storage and retrieval system, without permission in writing from the Publisher.

Copyright © 2025 by
National Learning Corporation

212 Michael Drive, Syosset, NY 11791
(516) 921-8888 • www.passbooks.com
E-mail: info@passbooks.com

PASSBOOK® SERIES

THE *PASSBOOK® SERIES* has been created to prepare applicants and candidates for the ultimate academic battlefield – the examination room.

At some time in our lives, each and every one of us may be required to take an examination – for validation, matriculation, admission, qualification, registration, certification, or licensure.

Based on the assumption that every applicant or candidate has met the basic formal educational standards, has taken the required number of courses, and read the necessary texts, the *PASSBOOK® SERIES* furnishes the one special preparation which may assure passing with confidence, instead of failing with insecurity. Examination questions – together with answers – are furnished as the basic vehicle for study so that the mysteries of the examination and its compounding difficulties may be eliminated or diminished by a sure method.

This book is meant to help you pass your examination provided that you qualify and are serious in your objective.

The entire field is reviewed through the huge store of content information which is succinctly presented through a provocative and challenging approach – the question-and-answer method.

A climate of success is established by furnishing the correct answers at the end of each test.

You soon learn to recognize types of questions, forms of questions, and patterns of questioning. You may even begin to anticipate expected outcomes.

You perceive that many questions are repeated or adapted so that you can gain acute insights, which may enable you to score many sure points.

You learn how to confront new questions, or types of questions, and to attack them confidently and work out the correct answers.

You note objectives and emphases, and recognize pitfalls and dangers, so that you may make positive educational adjustments.

Moreover, you are kept fully informed in relation to new concepts, methods, practices, and directions in the field.

You discover that you are actually taking the examination all the time: you are preparing for the examination by "taking" an examination, not by reading extraneous and/or supererogatory textbooks.

In short, this PASSBOOK®, used directedly, should be an important factor in helping you to pass your test.

NONTRADITIONAL EDUCATION

Students returning to school as adults bring more varied experience to their studies than do the teenagers who begin college shortly after graduating from high school. As a result, there are numerous programs for students with nontraditional learning curves. Hundreds of colleges and universities grant degrees to people who cannot attend classes at a regular campus or have already learned what the college is supposed to teach.

You can earn nontraditional education credits in many ways:
- Passing standardized exams
- Demonstrating knowledge gained through experience
- Completing campus-based coursework, and
- Taking courses off campus

Some methods of assessing learning for credit are objective, such as standardized tests. Others are more subjective, such as a review of life experiences.

With some help from four hypothetical characters – Alice, Vin, Lynette, and Jorge – this article describes nontraditional ways of earning educational credit. It begins by describing programs in which you can earn a high school diploma without spending 4 years in a classroom. The college picture is more complicated, so it is presented in two parts: one on gaining credit for what you know through course work or experience, and a second on college degree programs. The final section lists resources for locating more information.

Earning High School Credit

People who were prevented from finishing high school as teenagers have several options if they want to do so as adults. Some major cities have back-to-school programs that allow adults to attend high school classes with current students. But the more practical alternatives for most adults are to take the General Educational Development (GED) tests or to earn a high school diploma by demonstrating their skills or taking correspondence classes.

Of course, these options do not match the experience of staying in high school and graduating with one's friends. But they are viable alternatives for adult learners committed to meeting and, often, continuing their educational goals.

GED Program

Alice quit high school her sophomore year and took a job to help support herself, her younger brother, and their newly widowed mother. Now an adult, she wants to earn her high school diploma – and then go on to college. Because her job as head cook and her family responsibilities keep her busy during the day, she plans to get a high school equivalency diploma. She will study for, and take, the GED tests. Every year, about half a million adults earn their high school credentials this way. A GED diploma is accepted in lieu of a high school one by more than 90 percent of employers, colleges, and universities, so it is a good choice for someone like Alice.

The GED testing program is sponsored by the American Council on Education and State and local education departments. It consists of examinations in five subject areas: Writing, science, mathematics, social studies, and literature and the arts. The tests also measure skills such as analytical ability, problem solving, reading comprehension, and ability to understand and apply information. Most of the questions are multiple choice; the writing test includes an essay section on a topic of general interest.

Eligibility rules for taking the exams vary, but some states require that you must be at least 18. Tests are given in English, Spanish, and French. In addition to standard print, versions in large print, Braille, and audiocassette are also available. Total time allotted for the tests is 7 1/2 hours.

The GED tests are not easy. About one-fourth of those who complete the exams every year do not pass. Passing scores are established by administering the tests to a sample of graduating high school seniors. The minimum standard score is set so that about one-third of graduating seniors would not pass the tests if they took them.

Because of the difficulty of the tests, people need to prepare themselves to take them. Often, they start by taking the Official GED Practice Tests, usually available through a local adult education center. Centers are listed in your phone book's blue pages under "Adult Education," "Continuing Education," or "GED." Adult education centers also have information about GED preparation classes and self-study materials. Classes are generally arranged to accommodate adults' work schedules. National Learning Corporation publishes several study guides that aim to thoroughly prepare test-takers for the GED.

School districts, colleges, adult education centers, and community organizations have information about GED testing schedules and practice tests. For more information, contact them, your nearest GED testing center, or:

GED Testing Service
One Dupont Circle, NW, Suite 250
Washington, DC 20036-1163
1(800) 62-MY GED (626-9433)
(202) 939-9490

Skills Demonstration

Adults who have acquired high school level skills through experience might be eligible for the National External Diploma Program. This alternative to the GED does not involve any direct instruction. Instead, adults seeking a high school diploma must demonstrate mastery of 65 competencies in 8 general areas: Communication; computation; occupational preparedness; and self, social, consumer, scientific, and technological awareness.

Mastery is shown through the completion of the tasks. For example, a participant could prove competency in computation by measuring a room for carpeting, figuring out the amount of carpet needed, and computing the cost.

Before being accepted for the program, adults undergo an evaluation. Tests taken at one of the program's offices measure reading, writing, and mathematics abilities. A take-home segment includes a self-assessment of current skills, an individual skill evaluation, and an occupational interest and aptitude test.

Adults accepted for the program have weekly meetings with an assessor. At the meeting, the assessor reviews the participant's work from the previous week. If the task has not been completed properly, the assessor explains the mistake. Participants continue to correct their errors until they master each competency. A high school diploma is awarded upon proven mastery of all 65 competencies.

Fourteen States and the District of Columbia now offer the External Diploma Program. For more information, contact:
External Diploma Program
One Dupont Circle, NW, Suite 250
Washington, DC 20036-1193
(202) 939-9475

Correspondence and Distance Study
Vin dropped out of high school during his junior year because his family's frequent moves made it difficult for him to continue his studies. He promised himself at the time he dropped out that he would someday finish the courses needed for his diploma. For people like Vin, who prefer to earn a traditional diploma in a nontraditional way, there are about a dozen accredited courses of study for earning a high school diploma by correspondence, or distance study. The programs are either privately run, affiliated with a university, or administered by a State education department.

Distance study diploma programs have no residency requirements, allowing students to continue their studies from almost any location. Depending on the course of study, students need not be enrolled full time and usually have more flexible schedules for finishing their work. Selection of courses ranges from vo-tech to college prep, and some programs place different emphasis on the types of diplomas offered. University affiliated schools, for example, allow qualified students to take college courses along with their high school ones. Students can then apply the college credits toward a degree at that university or transfer them to another institution.

Taking courses by distance study is often more challenging and time consuming than attending classes, especially for adults who have other obligations. Success depends on each student's motivation. Students usually do reading assignments on their own. Written exercises, which they complete and send to an instructor for grading, supplement their reading material.

A list of some accredited high schools that offer diplomas by distance study is available free from the Distance Education and Training Council, formerly known as the National Home Study Council. Request the "DETC Directory of Accredited Institutions" from:
The Distance Education and Training Council
1601 18th Street, NW.
Washington, DC 20009-2529
(202) 234-5100

Some publications profiling nontraditional college programs include addresses and descriptions of several high school correspondence ones. See the Resources section at the end of this article for more information.

Getting College Credit For What You Know
Adults can receive college credit for prior coursework, by passing examinations, and documenting experiential learning. With help from a college advisor, nontraditional students should assess their skills, establish their educational goals, and determine the number of college credits they might be eligible for.

Even before you meet with a college advisor, you should collect all your school and training records. Then, make a list of all knowledge and abilities acquired through experience, no matter how irrelevant they seem to your chosen field. Next, determine your educational goals: What specific field do you wish to study? What kind of a degree do you want? Finally, determine how your past work fits into the field of study. Later on, you will evaluate educational programs to find one that's right for you.

People who have complex educational or experiential learning histories might want to have their learning evaluated by the Regents Credit Bank. The Credit Bank, operated by Regents College of the University of the State of New York, allows people to consolidate credits earned through college, experience, or other methods. Special assessments are available for Regents College enrollees whose knowledge in a specific field cannot be adequately evaluated by standardized exams. For more information, contact the Regents Credit Bank at:

Regents College
7 Columbia Circle
Albany, NY 12203-5159
(518) 464-8500

Credit For Prior College Coursework

When Lynette was in college during the 1970s, she attended several different schools and took a variety of courses. She did well in some classes and poorly in others. Now that she is a successful business owner and has more focus, Lynette thinks she should forget about her previous coursework and start from scratch. Instead, she should start from where she is.

Lynette should have all her transcripts sent to the colleges or universities of her choice and let an admissions officer determine which classes are applicable toward a degree. A few credits here and there may not seem like much, but they add up. Even if the subjects do not seem relevant to any major, they might be counted as elective credits toward a degree. And comparing the cost of transcripts with the cost of college courses, it makes sense to spend a few dollars per transcript for a chance to save hundreds, and perhaps thousands, of dollars in books and tuition.

Rules for transferring credits apply to all prior coursework at accredited colleges and universities, whether done on campus or off. Courses completed off campus, often called extended learning, include those available to students through independent study and correspondence. Many schools have extended learning programs; Brigham Young University, for example, offers more than 300 courses through its Department of Independent Study. One type of extended learning is distance learning, a form of correspondence study by technological means such as television, video and audio, CD-ROM, electronic mail, and computer tutorials. See the Resources section at the end of this article for more information about publications available from the National University Continuing Education Association.

Any previously earned college credits should be considered for transfer, no matter what the subject or the grade received. Many schools do not accept the transfer of courses graded below a C or ones taken more than a designated number of years ago. Some colleges and universities also have limits on the number of credits that can be transferred and applied toward a degree. But not all do. For example, Thomas Edison State College, New Jersey's State college for adults, accepts the transfer of all 120 hours of credit required for a baccalaureate degree – provided all the credits are transferred from regionally accredited schools, no more than 80 are at the junior college level, and the student's grades overall and in the field of study average out to C.

To assign credit for prior coursework, most schools require original transcripts. This means you must complete a form or send a written, signed request to have your transcripts released directly to a college or university. Once you have chosen the schools you want to apply to, contact the schools you attended before. Find out how much each transcript costs, and ask them to send your transcripts to the ones you are applying to. Write a letter that includes your name (and names used during attendance, if different) and dates of attendance, along with the names and addresses of the schools to which your transcripts should be sent. Include payment and mail to the registrar at the schools you have attended. The registrar's office will process your request and send an official transcript of your coursework to the colleges or universities you have designated.

Credit For Noncollege Courses

Colleges and universities are not the only ones that offer classes. Volunteer organizations and employers often provide formal training worth college credit. The American Council on Education has two programs that assess thousands of specific courses and make recommendations on the amount of college credit they are worth. Colleges and universities accept the recommendations or use them as guidelines.

One program evaluates educational courses sponsored by government agencies, business and industry, labor unions, and professional and voluntary organizations. It is the Program on Noncollegiate Sponsored Instruction (PONSI). Some of the training seminars Alice has participated in covered topics such as food preparation, kitchen safety, and nutrition. Although she has not yet earned her GED, Alice can earn college credit because of her completion of these formal job-training seminars. The number of credits each seminar is worth does not hinge on Alice's current eligibility for college enrollment.

The other program evaluates courses offered by the Army, Navy, Air Force, Marines, Coast Guard, and Department of Defense. It is the Military Evaluations Program. Jorge has never attended college, but the engineering technology classes he completed as part of his military training are worth college credit. And as an Army veteran, Jorge is eligible for a service that takes the evaluations one step further. The Army/American Council on Education Registry Transcript System (AARTS) will provide Jorge with an individualized transcript of American Council on Education credit recommendations for all courses he completed, the military occupational specialties (MOS's) he held, and examinations he passed while in the Army. All Army and National Guard enlisted personnel and veterans who enlisted after October 1981 are eligible for the transcript. Similar services are being considered by the Navy and Marine Corps.

To obtain a free transcript, see your Army Education Center for a 5454R transcript request form. Include your name, Social Security number, basic active service date, and complete address where you want the transcript sent. Mail your request to:
AARTS Operations Center
415 McPherson Ave.
Fort Leavenworth, KS 66027-1373

Recommendations for PONSI are published in *The National Guide to Educational Credit for Training Programs;* military program recommendations are in *The Guide to the Evaluation of Educational Experiences in the Armed Forces.* See the Resources section at the end of this article for more information about these publications.

Former military personnel who took a foreign language course through the Defense Language Institute may request course transcripts by sending their name, Social Security number, course title, duration of the course, and graduation date to:

Commandant, Defense Language Institute
Attn: ATFL-DAA-AR
Transcripts
Presidio of Monterey
Monterey, CA 93944-5006

Not all of Jorge's and Alice's courses have been assessed by the American Council on Education. Training courses that have no Council credit recommendation should still be assessed by an advisor at the schools they want to attend. Course descriptions, class notes, test scores, and other documentation may be helpful for comparing training courses to their college equivalents. An oral examination or other demonstration of competency might also be required.

There is no guarantee you will receive all the credits you are seeking – but you certainly won't if you make no attempt.

Credit By Examination

Standardized tests are the best-known method of receiving college credit without taking courses. These exams are often taken by high school students seeking advanced placement for college, but they are also available to adult learners. Testing programs and colleges and universities offer exams in a number of subjects. Two U.S. Government institutes have foreign language exams for employees that also may be worth college credit.

It is important to understand that receiving a passing score on these exams does not mean you get college credit automatically. Each school determines which test results it will accept, minimum scores required, how scores are converted for credit, and the amount of credit, if any, to be assigned. Most colleges and universities accept the American Council on Education credit recommendations, published every other year in the 250-page *Guide to Educational Credit by Examination*. For more information, contact:

The American Council on Education
Credit by Examination Program
One Dupont Circle, Suite 250
Washington, DC 20036-1193
(202) 939-9434

Testing programs:

You might know some of the five national testing programs by their acronyms or initials: CLEP, ACT PEP: RCE, DANTES, AP, and NOCTI. (The meanings of these initialisms are explained below.) There is some overlap among programs; for example, four of them have introductory accounting exams. Since you will not be awarded credit more than once for a specific subject, you should carefully evaluate each program for the subject exams you wish to take. And before taking an exam, make sure you will be awarded credit by the college or university you plan to attend.

CLEP (College-Level Examination Program), administered by the College Board, is the most widely accepted of the national testing programs; more than 2,800 accredited schools award credit for passing exam scores. Each test covers material taught in basic undergraduate courses. There are five general exams – English composition, humanities, college mathematics, natural sciences, and social sciences and history – and many subject exams. Most exams are entirely multiple-choice, but English composition exams may include an essay section. For more information, contact:

CLEP
P.O. Box 6600
Princeton, NJ 08541-6600
(609) 771-7865

ACT PEP: RCE (American College Testing Proficiency Exam Program: Regents College Examinations) tests are given in 38 subjects within arts and sciences, business, education, and nursing. Each exam is recommended for either lower- or upper-level credit. Exams contain either objective or extended response questions, and are graded according to a standard score, letter grade, or pass/fail. Fees vary, depending on the subject and type of exam. For more information or to request free study guides, contact:

ACT PEP: Regents College Examinations
P.O. Box 4014
Iowa City, IA 52243
(319) 337-1387
(New York State residents must contact Regents College directly.)

DANTES (Defense Activity for Nontraditional Education Support) standardized tests are developed by the Educational Testing Service for the Department of Defense. Originally administered only to military personnel, the exams have been available to the public since 1983. About 50 subject tests cover business, mathematics, social science, physical science, humanities, foreign languages, and applied technology. Most of the tests consist entirely of multiple-choice questions. Schools determine their own administering fees and testing schedules. For more information or to request free study sheets, contact:

DANTES Program Office
Mail Stop 31-X
Educational Testing Service
Princeton, NJ 08541
1(800) 257-9484

The AP (Advanced Placement) Program is a cooperative effort between secondary schools and colleges and universities. AP exams are developed each year by committees of college and high school faculty appointed by the College Board and assisted by consultants from the Educational Testing Service. Subjects include arts and languages, natural sciences, computer science, social sciences, history, and mathematics. Most tests are 2 or 3 hours long and include both multiple-choice and essay questions. AP courses are available to help students prepare for exams, which are offered in the spring. For more information about the Advanced Placement Program, contact:

Advanced Placement Services
P.O. Box 6671
Princeton, NJ 08541-6671
(609) 771-7300

NOCTI (National Occupational Competency Testing Institute) assessments are designed for people like Alice, who have vocational-technical skills that cannot be evaluated by other tests. NOCTI assesses competency at two levels: Student/job ready and teacher/experienced worker. Standardized evaluations are available for occupations such as auto-body repair, electronics, mechanical drafting, quantity food preparation, and upholstering. The tests consist of multiple-choice questions and a performance component. Other services include workshops, customized assessments, and pre-testing. For more information, contact:

NOCTI
500 N. Bronson Ave.
Ferris State University
Big Rapids, MI 49307
(616) 796-4699

Colleges and universities:

Many colleges and universities have credit-by-exam programs, through which students earn credit by passing a comprehensive exam for a course offered by the institution. Among the most widely recognized are the programs at Ohio University, the University of North Carolina, Thomas Edison State College, and New York University.

Ohio University offers about 150 examinations for credit. In addition, you may sometimes arrange to take special examinations in non-laboratory courses offered at Ohio University. To take a test for credit, you must enroll in the course. If you plan to transfer the credit earned, you also need written permission from an official at your school. Books and study materials are available, for a cost, through the university. Exams must be taken within 6 months of the enrollment date; most last 3 hours. You may arrange to take the exam off campus if you do not live near the university.

Ohio University is on the quarter-hour system; most courses are worth 4 quarter hours, the equivalent of 3 semester hours. For more information, contact:

Independent Study
Tupper Hall 302
Ohio University
Athens, OH 45701-2979
1(800) 444-2910
(614) 593-2910

The University of North Carolina offers a credit-by-examination option for 140 independent study (correspondence) courses in foreign languages, humanities, social sciences, mathematics, business administration, education, electrical and computer engineering, health administration, and natural sciences. To take an exam, you must request and receive approval from both the course instructor and the independent studies department. Exams must be taken within six months of enrollment, and you may register for no more than two at a time. If you are not near the University's Chapel Hill campus, you may take your exam under supervision at an accredited college, university, community college, or technical institute. For more information, contact:

Independent Studies
CB #1020, The Friday Center
UNC-Chapel Hill
Chapel Hill, NC 27599-1020
1(800) 862-5669 / (919) 962-1134

The Thomas Edison College Examination Program offers more than 50 exams in liberal arts, business, and professional areas. Thomas Edison State College administers tests twice a month in Trenton, New Jersey; however, students may arrange to take their tests with a proctor at any accredited American college or university or U.S. military base. Most of the tests are multiple choice; some also include short answer or essay questions. Time limits range from 90 minutes to 4 hours, depending on the exam. For more information, contact:

Thomas Edison State College
TECEP, Office of Testing and Assessment
101 W. State Street
Trenton, NJ 08608-1176
(609) 633-2844

New York University's Foreign Language Program offers proficiency exams in more than 40 languages, from Albanian to Yiddish. Two exams are available in each language: The 12-point test is equivalent to 4 undergraduate semesters, and the 16-point exam may lead to upper level credit. The tests are given at the university's Foreign Language Department throughout the year.

Proof of foreign language proficiency does not guarantee college credit. Some colleges and universities accept transcripts only for languages commonly taught, such as French and Spanish. Nontraditional programs are more likely than traditional ones to grant credit for proficiency in other languages.

For an informational brochure and registration form for NYU's foreign language proficiency exams, contact:

New York University
Foreign Language Department
48 Cooper Square, Room 107
New York, NY 10003
(212) 998-7030

Government institutes:
The Defense Language Institute and Foreign Service Institute administer foreign language proficiency exams for personnel stationed abroad. Usually, the tests are given at the end of intensive language courses or upon completion of service overseas. But some people – like Jorge, who knows Spanish – speak another language fluently and may be allowed to take a proficiency exam in that language before completing their tour of duty. Contact one of the offices listed below to obtain transcripts of those scores. Proof of proficiency does not guarantee college credit, however, as discussed above.

To request score reports from the Defense Language Institute for Defense Language Proficiency Tests, send your name, Social Security number, language for which you were tested, and, most importantly, when and where you took the exam to:

Commandant, Defense Language Institute
Attn: ATFL-ES-T
DLPT Score Report Request
Presidio of Monterey
Monterey, CA 93944-5006

To request transcripts of scores for Foreign Service Institute exams, send your name, Social Security number, language for which you were tested, and dates or year of exams to:

Foreign Service Institute
Arlington Hall
4020 Arlington Boulevard
Rosslyn, VA 22204-1500
Attn: Testing Office (Send your request to the attention of the testing office of the foreign language in which you were tested)

Credit For Experience

Experiential learning credit may be given for knowledge gained through job responsibilities, personal hobbies, volunteer opportunities, homemaking, and other experiences. Colleges and universities base credit awards on the knowledge you have attained, not for the experience alone. In addition, the knowledge must be college level; not just any learning will do. Throwing horseshoes as a hobby is not likely to be worth college credit. But if you've done research on how and where the sport originated, visited blacksmiths, organized tournaments, and written a column for a trade journal – well, that's a horseshoe of a different color.

Adults attempting to get credit for their experience should be forewarned: Having your experience evaluated for college credit is time-consuming, tedious work – not an easy shortcut for people who want quick-fix college credits. And not all experience, no matter how valuable, is the equivalent of college courses.

Requesting college credit for your experiential learning can be tricky. You should get assistance from a credit evaluations officer at the school you plan to attend, but you should also have a general idea of what your knowledge is worth. A common method for converting knowledge into credit is to use a college catalog. Find course titles and descriptions that match what you have learned through experience, and request the number of credits offered for those courses.

Once you know what credit to ask for, you must usually present your case in writing to officials at the college you plan to attend. The most common form of presenting experiential learning for credit is the portfolio. A portfolio is a written record of your knowledge along with a request for equivalent college credit. It includes an identification and description of the knowledge for which you are requesting credit, an explanatory essay of how the knowledge was gained and how it fits into your educational plans, documentation that you have acquired such knowledge, and a request for college credit. Required elements of a portfolio vary by schools but generally follow those guidelines.

In identifying knowledge you have gained, be specific about exactly what you have learned. For example, it is not enough for Lynette to say she runs a business. She must identify the knowledge she has gained from running it, such as personnel management, tax law, marketing strategy, and inventory review. She must also include brief descriptions about her knowledge of each to support her claims of having those skills.

The essay gives you a chance to relay something about who you are. It should address your educational goals, include relevant autobiographical details, and be well organized, neat, and convey confidence. In his essay, Jorge might first state his goal of becoming an engineer. Then he would explain why he joined the Army, where he got hands-on training and experience in developing and servicing electronic equipment.

This, he would say, led to his hobby of creating remote-controlled model cars, of which he has built 20. His conclusion would highlight his accomplishments and tie them to his desire to become an electronic engineer.

Documentation is evidence that you've learned what you claim to have learned. You can show proof of knowledge in a variety of ways, including audio or video recordings, letters from current or former employers describing your specific duties and job performance, blueprints, photographs or artwork, and transcripts of certifying exams for professional licenses and certification – such as Alice's certification from the American Culinary Federation. Although documentation can take many forms, written proof alone is not always enough. If it is impossible to document your knowledge in writing, find out if your experiential learning can be assessed through supplemental oral exams by a faculty expert.

Earning a College Degree

Nontraditional students often have work, family, and financial obligations that prevent them from quitting their jobs to attend school full time. Can they still meet their educational goals? Yes.

More than 150 accredited colleges and universities have nontraditional bachelor's degree programs that require students to spend little or no time on campus; over 300 others have nontraditional campus-based degree programs. Some of those schools, as well as most junior and community colleges, offer associate's degrees nontraditionally. Each school with a nontraditional course of study determines its own rules for awarding credit for prior coursework, exams, or experience, as discussed previously. Most have charges on top of tuition for providing these special services.

Several publications profile nontraditional degree programs; see the Resources section at the end of this article for more information. To determine which school best fits your academic profile and educational goals, first list your criteria. Then, evaluate nontraditional programs based on their accreditation, features, residency requirements, and expenses. Once you have chosen several schools to explore further, write to them for more information. Detailed explanations of school policies should help you decide which ones you want to apply to.

Get beyond the printed word – especially the glowing words each school writes about itself. Check out the schools you are considering with higher education authorities, alumni, employers, family members, and friends. If possible, visit the campus to talk to students and instructors and sit in on a few classes, even if you will be completing most or all of your work off campus. Ask school officials questions about such things as enrollment numbers, graduation rate, faculty qualifications, and confusing details about the application process or academic policies. After you have thoroughly investigated each prospective college or university, you can make an informed decision about which is right for you.

Accreditation

Accreditation is a process colleges and universities submit to voluntarily for getting their credentials. An accredited school has been investigated and visited by teams of observers and has periodic inspections by a private accrediting agency. The initial review can take two years or more.

Regional agencies accredit entire schools, and professional agencies accredit either specialized schools or departments within schools. Although there are no national accrediting standards, not just any accreditation will do. Countless "accreditation associations" have been invented by schools, many of which have no academic programs and sell phony degrees, to accredit themselves. But 6 regional and about 80 professional accrediting associations in the United States are recognized by the U.S. Department of Education or the Commission on Recognition of Postsecondary Accreditation. When checking accreditation, these are the names to look for. For more information about accreditation and accrediting agencies, contact:

> Institutional Participation Oversight Service Accreditation and State Liaison Division
> U.S. Department of Education
> ROB 3, Room 3915
> 600 Independence Ave., SW
> Washington, DC 20202-5244
> (202) 708-7417

Because accreditation is not mandatory, lack of accreditation does not necessarily mean a school or program is bad. Some schools choose not to apply for accreditation, are in the process of applying, or have educational methods too unconventional for an accrediting association's standards. For the nontraditional student, however, earning a degree from a college or university with recognized accreditation is an especially important consideration. Although nontraditional education is becoming more widely accepted, it is not yet mainstream. Employers skeptical of a degree earned in a nontraditional manner are likely to be even less accepting of one from an unaccredited school.

Program Features

Because nontraditional students have diverse educational objectives, nontraditional schools are diverse in what they offer. Some programs are geared toward helping students organize their scattered educational credits to get a degree as quickly as possible. Others cater to those who may have specific credits or experience but need assistance in completing requirements. Whatever your educational profile, you should look for a program that works with you in obtaining your educational goals.

A few nontraditional programs have special admissions policies for adult learners like Alice, who plan to earn their GEDs but want to enroll in college in the meantime. Other features of nontraditional programs include individualized learning agreements, intensive academic counseling, cooperative learning and internship placement, and waiver of some prerequisites or other requirements – as well as college credit for prior coursework, examinations, and experiential learning, all discussed previously.

Lynette, whose primary goal is to finish her degree, wants to earn maximum credits for her business experience. She will look for programs that do not limit the number of credits awarded for equivalency exams and experiential learning. And since well-documented proof of knowledge is essential for earning experiential learning credits, Lynette should make sure the program she chooses provides assistance to students submitting a portfolio.

Jorge, on the other hand, has more credits than he needs in certain areas and is willing to forego some. To become an engineer, he must have a bachelor's degree; but because he is accustomed to hands-on learning, Jorge is interested in getting experience as he gains more technical skills. He will concentrate on finding schools with strong cooperative education, supervised fieldwork, or internship programs.

Residency Requirements

Programs are sometimes deemed nontraditional because of their residency requirements. Many people think of residency for colleges and universities in terms of tuition, with in-state students paying less than out-of-state ones. Residency also may refer to where a student lives, either on or off campus, while attending school.

But in nontraditional education, residency usually refers to how much time students must spend on campus, regardless of whether they attend classes there. In some nontraditional programs, students need not ever step foot on campus. Others require only a very short residency, such as one day or a few weeks. Many schools have standard residency requirements of several semesters but schedule classes for evenings or weekends to accommodate working adults.

Lynette, who previously took courses by independent study, prefers to earn credits by distance study. She will focus on schools that have no residency requirement. Several colleges and universities have nonresident degree completion programs for adults with some college credit. Under the direction of a faculty advisor, students devise a plan for earning their remaining credits. Methods for earning credits include independent study, distance learning, seminars, supervised fieldwork, and group study at arranged sites. Students may have to earn a certain number of credits through the degree-granting institution. But many programs allow students to take courses at accredited schools of their choice for transfer toward their degree.

Alice wants to attend lectures but has an unpredictable schedule. Her best course of action will be to seek out short residency programs that require students to attend seminars once or twice a semester. She can take courses that are televised and videotape them to watch when her schedule permits, with the seminars helping to ensure that she properly completes her coursework. Many colleges and universities with short residency requirements also permit students to earn some credits elsewhere, by whatever means the student chooses.

Some fields of study require classroom instruction. As Jorge will discover, few colleges and universities allow students to earn a bachelor's degree in engineering entirely through independent study. Nontraditional residency programs are designed to accommodate adults' daytime work schedules. Jorge should look for programs offering evening, weekend, summer, and accelerated courses.

Tuition and Other Expenses

The final decisions about which schools Alice, Jorge, and Lynette attend may hinge in large part on a single issue: Cost. And rising tuition is only part of the equation. Beginning with application fees and continuing through graduation fees, college expenses add up.

Traditional and nontraditional students have some expenses in common, such as the cost of books and other materials. Tuition might even be the same for some courses, especially for colleges and universities offering standard ones at unusual times. But for nontraditional programs, students may also pay fees for services such as credit or transcript review, evaluation, advisement, and portfolio assessment.

Students are also responsible for postage and handling or setup expenses for independent study courses, as well as for all examination and transcript fees for transferring credits. Usually, the more nontraditional the program, the more detailed the fees. Some schools charge a yearly enrollment fee rather than tuition for degree completion candidates who want their files to remain active.

Although tuition and fees might seem expensive, most educators tell you not to let money come between you and your educational goals. Talk to someone in the financial aid department of the school you plan to attend or check your library for publications about financial aid sources. The U.S. Department of Education publishes a guide to Federal aid programs such as Pell Grants, student loans, and work-study. To order the free 74-page booklet, *The Student Guide: Financial Aid from the U.S. Department of Education,* contact:

    Federal Student Aid Information Center
    P.O. Box 84
    Washington, DC 20044
    1 (800) 4FED-AID (433-3243)

Resources

Information on how to earn a high school diploma or college degree without following the usual routes is available from several organizations and in numerous publications. Information on nontraditional graduate degree programs, available for master's through doctoral level, though not discussed in this article, can usually be obtained from the same resources that detail bachelor's degree programs.

National Learning Corporation publishes study guides for all of these exams, for both general examinations and tests in specific subject areas. To order study guides, or to browse their catalog featuring more than 5,000 titles, visit NLC online at www.passbooks.com, or contact them by phone at (800) 632-8888.

Organizations

Adult learners should always contact their local school system, community college, or university to learn about programs that are readily available. The following national organizations can also supply information:

    American Council on Education
    One Dupont Circle
    Washington, DC 20036-1193
    (202) 939-9300

Within the American Council on Education, the Center for Adult Learning and Educational Credentials administers the National External Diploma Program, the GED Program, the Program on Noncollegiate Sponsored Instruction, the Credit by Examination Program, and the Military Evaluations Program.

DANTES Subject Standardized Tests

INTRODUCTION

The DANTES (Defense Activity for Non-Traditional Education Support) subject standardized tests are comprehensive college and graduate level examinations given by the Armed Forces, colleges and graduate schools as end-of-subject course evaluation final examinations or to obtain college equivalency credits in the various subject areas tested.

The DANTES Examination Program enables students to obtain college credit for what they have learned on the job, through self-study, personal interest, correspondence courses or by any other means. It is used by colleges and universities to award college credit to students who demonstrate that they know as much as students completing an equivalent college course. It is a cost-efficient, time-saving way for students to use their knowledge to accomplish their educational goals.

Most schools accept the American Council on Education (ACE) recommendations for the minimum score required and the amount of credit awarded, but not all schools do. Be sure to check the policy regarding the score level required for credit and the number of credits to be awarded.

Not all tests are accepted by all institutions. Even when a test is accepted by an institution, it may not be acceptable for every program at that institution. Before considering testing, ascertain the acceptability of a specific test for a particular course.

Colleges and universities that administer DANTES tests may administer them to any applicant – or they may administer the tests only to students registered at their institution. Decisions about who will be allowed to test are made by the school. Students should contact the test center to determine current policies and schedules for DANTES testing.

Colleges and universities authorized to administer DANTES tests usually do so throughout the calendar year. Each school sets its own fee for test administration and establishes its own testing schedule. Contact the representative at the administering school directly to make arrangements for testing.

Checklist
For Students

✓ Visit **www.getcollegecredit.com** to obtain a list of tests, fact sheets, test preparation materials, participating colleges and universities, and much more.

✓ Contact your school advisor to confirm that the DSST you selected will fit into your curriculum.

✓ Consult the *DSST Candidate Information Bulletin* for answers to specific questions.

✓ Contact the test site to schedule your test.

✓ Prepare for your examination by using the fact sheet as a guide.

✓ Take the test.

If you would like a score report sent to your college or university, it is a good idea to bring the four-digit code with you. You must write the DSST Test Center Code for that institution on your answer sheet at the time of testing. DSST Test Center Codes are noted in the DSST Participating Colleges and Universities listing on the Web site.

If you prefer to send a score report to an institution at a later date, there is a transcript fee of $20 for each transcript ordered.

Thomson Prometric
DSST Program
2000 Lenox Drive, Third Floor
Lawrenceville, NJ 08648

Toll-free: 877-471-9860
609-895-5011

E-mail: pnj-dsst@thomson.com

MAKING A COLLEGE DEGREE WITHIN YOUR REACH

Today, there are many educational alternatives to the classroom—you can learn from your job, your reading, your independent study, and special interests you pursue. You may already have learned the subject matter covered by some college-level courses.

The DSST Program is a nationally recognized testing program that gives you the opportunity to receive college credit for learning acquired outside the traditional college classroom. Colleges and universities throughout the United States administer the program, developed by Thomson Prometric, year-round. Annually, over 90,000 DSSTs are administered to individuals who are interested in continuing their education. Take advantage of the DSST testing program; it speeds the educational process and provides the flexibility adults need, making earning a degree more feasible.

Since requirements differ from college to college, please check with the credit-awarding institution before taking a DSST. More than 1,800 colleges and universities currently award credit for DSSTs, and the number is growing every day. You can choose from 37 test titles in the areas of Social Science, Business, Mathematics, Applied Technology, Humanities, and Physical Science. A brief description of each examination is found on the pages that follow.

Reach Your Career Goals Through DSSTs

Use DSSTs to help you earn your degree, get a promotion, or simply demonstrate that you have college-level knowledge in subjects relevant to your work.

Save Time...

You don't have to sit through classes when you have previously acquired the knowledge or experience for most of what is being taught and can learn the rest yourself. You might be able to bypass introductory-level courses in subject areas you already know.

Save Money...

DSSTs save you money because the classes you bypass by earning credit through the DSST Program are classes you won't have to pay for on your way to earning your degree. You can use the money instead to take more advanced courses that can be more challenging and rewarding.

Improve Your Chances for Admission to College

Each college has its own admission policies; however, having passing scores for DSSTs on your transcript can provide strong evidence of how well you can perform at the college level.

Gain Confidence Performing at a College Level

Many adults returning to college find that lack of confidence is often the greatest hurdle to overcome. Passing a DSST demonstrates your ability to perform on a college level.

Make Up for Courses You May Have Missed

You may be ready to graduate from college and find that you are a few credits short of earning your degree. By using semester breaks, vacation time, or leisure time to study independently, you can prepare to take one or more DSSTs, fulfill your academic requirements, and graduate on time.

If You Cannot Attend Regularly Scheduled Classes...

If your lifestyle or responsibilities prevent you from attending regularly scheduled classes, you can earn your college degree from a college offering an external degree program. The DSST Program allows you to earn your degree by study and experience outside the traditional classroom.

Many colleges and universities offer external degree or distance learning programs. For additional information, contact the college you plan to attend or:

Center for Lifelong Learning
American Council on Education
One DuPont Circle NW, Suite 250
Washington, DC 20036
202-939-9475
www.acenet.edu
(Select "Center for Lifelong Learning" under "Programs & Services"
for more information)

Fact Sheets

For each test, there is a Fact Sheet that outlines the topics covered by each test and includes a list of sample questions, a list of recommended references of books that would be useful for review, and the number of credits awarded for a passing score as recommended by the American Council on Education (ACE). *Please note that some schools require scores that are higher than the minimum ACE-recommended passing score.* It is suggested that you check with your college or university to determine what score they require in order to earn credit. You can obtain Fact Sheets by:
- Downloading them from www.getcollegecredit.com
- E-mailing a request to pnj-dsst@thomson.com
- Completing a Candidate Publications Order Form

DSST Online Practice Tests

DSST online practice tests contain items that reflect a *partial range of difficulty* identified in the Content Outline section on each Fact Sheet. There is an online DSST Practice Test in the following categories:
- Mathematics
- Social Science
- Business
- Physical Science
- Applied Technology
- Humanities

Although the online DSST Practice Test questions do not indicate the full range of difficulty you would find in an actual DSST test, they will help you assess your knowledge level. Each online DSST Practice Test can be purchased by visiting www.getcollegecredit.com and clicking on **DSST Practice Exams.**

TAKING DSST EXAMINATIONS

Earning College Credit for DSST Examinations

To find out if the college of your choice awards credit for passing DSST scores, contact the admissions office or counseling and testing office. The college can also provide information on the scores required for awarding credit, the number of credit hours awarded, and any courses that can be bypassed with satisfactory scores.

It is important that you contact the institution of your choice as early as possible since credit-awarding policies differ among colleges and universities.

Where to Take DSSTs

DSSTs are administered at colleges and universities nationwide. Each location determines the frequency and scheduling of test administrations. To obtain the most current list of participating DSST colleges and universities:
- Visit and download the information from www.getcollegecredit.com
- E-mail pnj-dsst@thomson.com

Scheduling Your Examination

Please be aware that some colleges and universities provide DSST testing services to enrolled students only. After you have selected a college or university that administers DSSTs, you will need to contact them to schedule your test date.

The fee to take a DSST is $60 per test. This fee entitles you to two score reports after the test is scored. One will be sent directly to you and the other will be sent to the college or university that you designate on your answer sheet. You may pay the test fee with a certified check or U.S. money order made payable to Thomson Prometric or you may charge the test fee to your Visa, MasterCard or American Express credit card. Note: The credit card statement will reflect a charge from Thomson Prometric for all DSST examinations. *(Declined credit card charges will be assessed an additional $25 processing fee.)*

In addition, the test site may also require a test administration fee for each examination, to be paid directly to the institution. Contact the test site to determine its administration fee and payment policy.

Other Testing Arrangements

If you are unable to find a participating DSST college or university in your area, you may want to contact the testing office of a local accredited college or university to determine whether a representative from that office will agree to administer the test(s) for you.

The school's representative should then contact the DSST Program at 866-794-3497 to arrange for this administration. If you are unable to locate a test site, contact Thomson Prometric for assistance at pnj-dsst@thomson.com or 866-794-3497.

Testing Accommodations for Students with Disabilities

Thomson Prometric is committed to serving test takers with disabilities by providing services and reasonable testing accommodations as set forth in the provisions of the *Americans with Disabilities Act* (ADA). If you have a disability, as prescribed by the ADA, and require special testing services or arrangements, please contact the test administrator at the test site. You will be asked to submit to the test administrator documentation of your disability and your request for special accommodations. The test administrator will then forward your documentation along with your request for testing accommodations to Thomson Prometric for approval.

Please submit your request as far in advance of your test date as possible so that the necessary accommodations can be made. Only test takers with documented disabilities are eligible for special accommodations.

On the Day of the Examination

It is important to review this information and to have the correct identification present on the day of the examination:
- Arrive on time as a courtesy to the test administrator.
- Bring a valid form of government-issued identification that includes a current photo and your signature (acceptable documents include a driver's license, passport, state-issued identification card or military identification). *Anyone who fails to present valid identification will not be allowed to test.*
- Bring several No. 2 (soft-lead) sharpened pencils with good erasers, a watch, and a black pen if you will be writing an essay.
- Do not bring books or papers.
- Do not bring an alarm watch that beeps, a telephone, or a phone beeper into the testing room.
- The use of nonprogrammable calculators, slide rules, scratch paper and/or other materials is permitted for some of the tests.

DSST SCORING POLICIES

Your DSST examination scores are reported only to you, unless you request that they be sent elsewhere. If you want your scores sent to your college, you must provide the correct DSST code number of the school on your answer sheet at the time you take the test. See the *DSST Directory of Colleges and Universities* on the Web site www.getcollegecredit.com.

If your institution is not listed, contact Thomson Prometric at 866-794-3497 to establish a code number. (Some schools may require a student to be enrolled prior to receiving a score report.)

Receiving Your Score Report

Allow approximately four weeks after testing to receive your score report.

Calling DSST Customer Service before the required four-week score processing time has elapsed will not expedite the processing of your scores. Due to privacy and security requirements, scores will not be reported to students over the telephone under any circumstance.

Scoring of Principles of Public Speaking Speeches

The speech portion of the *Principles of Public Speaking* examination will be sent to speech raters who are faculty members at accredited colleges that currently teach or have previously taught the course. Scores for the *Principles of Public Speaking* examination are available six to eight weeks from receipt by Thomson Prometric. If you take the *Principles of Public Speaking* examination and fail (either the objective, speech portion, or both), you must follow the retesting policy waiting period of six months (180 days) before retaking the entire exam.

Essays

The essays for *Ethics in America* and *Technical Writing* are optional and thus are not scored by raters. The essays are forwarded to the college or university that you designate, along with your score report, for their use in determining the award of credit. Before taking the *Ethics in America* or *Technical Writing* examinations, check with your college or university to determine whether the essay is required.

NOTE: *Principles of Public Speaking* speech topic cassette tapes and essays are kept on file at Thomson Prometric for one year from the date of administration.

How to Get Transcripts

There is a $20 fee for each transcript you request. Payment must be in the form of a certified check, U.S. money order payable to Thomson Prometric, or credit card. Personal checks and debit cards are NOT an acceptable method of payment. One transcript may include scores for one or more examinations taken. To request a transcript, download the Transcript Order Form from www.getcollegecredit.com.

DESCRIPTION OF THE DSST EXAMINATIONS

Mathematics

• **Fundamentals of College Algebra** covers mathematical concepts such as fundamental algebraic operations; linear, absolute value; quadratic equations, inequalities, radials, exponents and logarithms, factoring polynomials and graphing. The use of a nonprogrammable, handheld calculator is permitted.

• **Principles of Statistics** tests the understanding of the various topics of statistics, both qualitatively and quantitatively, and the ability to apply statistical methods to solve a variety of problems. The topics included in this test are descriptive statistics; correlation and regression; probability; chance models and sampling and tests of significance. The use of a nonprogrammable, handheld calculator is permitted.

Social Science

• **Art of the Western World** deals with the history of art during the following periods: classical; Romanesque and Gothic; early Renaissance; high Renaissance, Baroque; rococo; neoclassicism and romanticism; realism, impressionism and post-impressionism; early twentieth century; and post-World War II.

• **Western Europe Since 1945** tests the knowledge of basic facts and terms and the understanding of concepts and principles related to the areas of the historical background of the aftermath of the Second World War and rebuilding of Europe; national political systems; issues and policies in Western European societies; European institutions and processes; and Europe's relations with the rest of the world.

• **An Introduction to the Modern Middle East** emphasizes core knowledge (including geography, Judaism, Christianity, Islam, ethnicity); nineteenth-century European impact; twentieth-century Western influences; World Wars I and II; new nations; social and cultural changes (1900-1960) and the Middle East from 1960 to present.

• **Human/Cultural Geography** includes the Earth and basic facts (coordinate systems, maps, physiography, atmosphere, soils and vegetation, water); culture and environment, spatial processes (social processes, modern economic systems, settlement patterns, political geography); and regional geography.

- **Rise and Fall of the Soviet Union** covers Russia under the Old Regime; the Revolutionary Period; New Economic Policy; Pre-war Stalinism; The Second World War; Post-war Stalinism; The Khrushchev Years; The Brezhnev Era; and reform and collapse.

- **A History of the Vietnam War** covers the history of the roots of the Vietnam War; the First Vietnam War (1946-1954); pre-war developments (1954-1963); American involvement in the Vietnam War; Tet (1968); Vietnamizing the War (1968-1973); Cambodia and Laos; peace; legacies and lessons.

- **The Civil War and Reconstruction** covers the Civil War from presecession (1861) through Reconstruction. It includes causes of the war; secession; Fort Sumter; the war in the east and in the west; major battles; the political situation; assassination of Lincoln; end of the Confederacy; and Reconstruction.

- **Foundations of Education** includes topics such as contemporary issues in education; past and current influences on education (philosophies, democratic ideals, social/economic influences); and the interrelationships between contemporary issues and influences.

- **Life-span Developmental Psychology** covers models and theories; methods of study; ethical issues; biological development; perception, learning and memory; cognition and language; social, emotional, and personality development; social behaviors, family life cycle, extrafamilial settings; singlehood and cohabitation; occupational development and retirement; adjustment to life stresses; and bereavement and loss.

- **Drug and Alcohol Abuse** includes such topics as drug use in society; classification of drugs; pharmacological principles; alcohol (types, effects of, alcoholism); general principles and use of sedative hypnotics, narcotic analgesics, stimulants, and hallucinogens; other drugs (inhalants, steroids); and prevention/treatment.

- **General Anthropology** deals with anthropology as a discipline; theoretical perspectives; physical anthropology; archaeology; social organization; economic organization; political organization; religion; and modernization and application of anthropology.

- **Introduction to Law Enforcement** includes topics such as history and professional movement of law enforcement; overview of the U.S. criminal justice system; police systems in the U.S.; police organization, management, and issues; and U.S. law and precedents.

- **Criminal Justice** deals with criminal behavior (crime in the U.S., theories of crime, types of crime); the criminal justice system (historical origins, legal foundations, due process); police; the court system (history and organization, adult court system, juvenile court, pre-trial and post-trial processes); and corrections.

- **Fundamentals of Counseling** covers historical development (significant influences and people); counselor roles and functions; the counseling relationship; and theoretical approaches to counseling.

Business
- **Principles of Finance** deals with financial statements and planning; time value of money; working capital management; valuation and characteristics; capital budgeting; cost of capital; risk and return; and international financial management. The use of a nonprogrammable, handheld calculator is permitted.

- **Principles of Financial Accounting** includes topics such as general concepts and principles, accounting cycle and classification; transaction analysis; accruals and deferrals; cash and internal control; current accounts; long- and short-term liabilities; capital stock; and financial statements. The use of a nonprogrammable, handheld calculator is permitted.

- **Human Resource Management** covers general employment issues; job analysis; training and development; performance appraisals; compensation issues; security issues; personnel legislation and regulation; labor relations and current issues; an overview of the Human Resource Management Field; Human Resource Planning; Staffing; training and development; compensation issues; safety and health; employee rights and discipline; employment law; labor relations and current issues and trends.

- **Organizational Behavior** deals with the study of organizational behavior (scientific approaches, research designs, data collection methods); individual processes and characteristics; interpersonal and group processes and characteristics; organizational processes and characteristics; and change and development processes.

- **Principles of Supervision** deals with the roles and responsibilities of the supervisor; management functions (planning, organization and staffing, directing at the supervisory level); and other topics (legal issues, stress management, union environments, quality concerns).

- **Business Law II** covers topics such as sales of goods; debtor and creditor relations; business organizations; property; and commercial paper.

- **Introduction to Computing** includes topics such as history and technological generations; hardware/software; applications to information technology; program development; data management; communications and connectivity; and computing and society. The use of a nonprogrammable, handheld calculator is permitted.

- **Management Information Systems** covers systems theory, analysis and design of systems, hardware and software; database management; telecommunications; management of the MIS functional area and informational support.

- **Introduction to Business** deals with economic issues affecting business; international business; government and business; forms of business ownership; small business, entrepreneurship and franchise; management process; human resource management; production and operations; marketing management; financial management; risk management and insurance; and management and information systems.

- **Money and Banking** covers the role and kinds of money; commercial banks and other financial intermediaries; central banking and the Federal Reserve system; money and macroeconomics activity; monetary policy in the U.S.; and the international monetary system.

- **Personal Finance** includes topics such as financial goals and values; budgeting; credit and debt; major purchases; taxes; insurance; investments; and retirement and estate planning. The use of auxiliary materials, such as calculators and slide rules, is NOT permitted.

- **Business Mathematics** deals with basic operations with integers, fractions, and decimals; round numbers; ratios; averages; business graphs; simple interest; compound interest and annuities; net pay and deductions; discounts and markups; depreciation and net worth; corporate securities; distribution of ownership; and stock and asset turnover.

Physical Science
• **Astronomy** covers the history of astronomy, celestial mechanics; celestial systems; astronomical instruments; the solar system; nature and evolution; the galaxy; the universe; determining astronomical distances; and life in the universe.

• **Here's to Your Health** covers mental health and behavior; human development and relationships; substance abuse; fitness and nutrition; risk factors, disease, and disease prevention; and safety, consumer awareness, and environmental concerns.

• **Environment and Humanity** deals with topics such as ecological concepts (ecosystems, global ecology, food chains and webs); environmental impacts; environmental management and conservation; and political processes and the future.

• **Principles of Physical Science I** includes physics: Newton's Laws of Motion; energy and momentum; thermodynamics; wave and optics; electricity and magnetism; chemistry: properties of matter; atomic theory and structure; and chemical reactions.

• **Physical Geology** covers Earth materials; igneous, sedimentary, and metamorphic rocks; surface processes (weathering, groundwater, glaciers, oceanic systems, deserts and winds, hydrologic cycle); internal Earth processes; and applications (mineral and energy resources, environmental geology).

Applied Technology
• **Technical Writing** covers topics such as theory and practice of technical writing; purpose, content, and organizational patterns of common types of technical documents; elements of various technical reports; and technical editing. Students have the option to write a short essay on one of the technical topics provided. Thomson Prometric will not score the essay; however, for determining the award of credit, a copy of the essay will be forwarded to the college or university you've designated along with the score report or transcript.

Humanities
• **Ethics in America** deals with ethical traditions (Greek views, Biblical traditions, moral law, consequential ethics, feminist ethics); ethical analysis of issues arising in interpersonal and personal-societal relationships and in professional and occupational roles; and relationships between ethical traditions and the ethical analysis of situations. Students have the option to write an essay to analyze a morally problematic situation in terms of issues relevant to a decision and arguments for alternative positions. Thomson Prometric will not score the essay; however, for determining the award of credit, a copy of the essay will be forwarded to the college or university you've designated along with the score report or transcript.

• **Introduction to World Religions** covers topics such as dimensions and approaches to religion; primal religions; Hinduism; Buddhism; Confucianism; Taoism; Judaism; Christianity; and Islam.

• **Principles of Public Speaking** consists of two parts: Part One consists of multiple-choice questions covering considerations of Principles of Public Speaking; audience analysis; purposes of speeches; structure/organization; content/supporting materials; research; language and style; delivery; communication apprehension; listening and feedback; and criticism and evaluation. Part Two requires the student to record an impromptu persuasive speech that will be scored.

FREQUENTLY ASKED QUESTIONS ABOUT DSSTs

In order to pass the test, must I study from one of the recommended references?

The recommended references are a listing of books that were being used as textbooks in college courses of the same or similar title at the time the test was developed. Appropriate textbooks for study are not limited to those listed in the fact sheet. If you wish to obtain study resources to prepare for the examination, you may reference either the current edition of the listed titles or textbooks currently used at a local college or university for the same class title. It is recommended that you reference more than one textbook on the topics outlined in the fact sheet. You should begin by checking textbook content against the content outline included on the front page of the DSST fact sheet before selecting textbooks that cover the text content from which to study. Textbooks may be found at the campus bookstore of a local college or university offering a course on the subject.

Is there a penalty for guessing on the tests?

There is no penalty for guessing on DSSTs, so you should mark an answer for each question.

How much time will I have to complete the test?

Many DSSTs can be completed within 90 minutes; however, additional time can be allowed if necessary.

What should I do if I find a test question irregularity?

Continue testing and then report the irregularity to the test administrator after the test. This may be done by asking that the test administrator note the irregularity on the Supervisor's Irregularity Report or you can write to Thomson Prometric, DSST Program, 2000 Lenox Drive, Third Floor, Lawrenceville, NJ 08648, and indicate the form and question number(s) or circumstances as well as your name and address.

When will I receive my score report?

Allow approximately four weeks from the date of testing to receive your score report. Allow six to eight weeks to receive a score report for the *Principles of Public Speaking* examination.

Will my test scores be released without my permission?

Your test score will not be released to anyone other than the school you designate on your answer sheet unless you write to us and ask us to send a transcript elsewhere. Instructions about how to do this can be found on your score report. Your scores may be used for research purposes, but individual scores are never made public nor are individuals identified if research findings are made public.

If I do not achieve a passing score on the test, how long must I wait until I can take the test again?

If you do not receive a score on the test that will enable you to obtain credit for the course, you may take the test again after six months (180 days). Please do not attempt to take the test before six months (180 days) have passed because you will receive a score report marked *invalid* and your test fee will not be refunded.

Can my test scores be canceled?

The test administrator is required to report any irregularities to Thomson Prometric. <u>The consequence of bringing unauthorized materials into the testing room, or giving or receiving help, will be the forfeiture of your test fee and the invalidation of test scores.</u> The DSST Program reserves the right to cancel scores and not issue score reports in such situations.

What can I do if I feel that my test scores were not accurately reported?

Thomson Prometric recognizes the extreme importance of test results to candidates and has a multi-step quality-control procedure to help ensure that reported scores are accurate. If you have reason to believe that your score(s) were not accurately reported, you may request to have your answer sheet reviewed and hand scored.

The fees for this service are:
- $20 fee if requested within six months of the test date
- $30 fee if requested more than six months from the test date
- $30 fee if a re-evaluation of the *Principles of Public Speaking* speech is requested

The fee for this service can be paid by credit card or by certified check or U.S. money order payable to Thomson Prometric. Submit your request for score verification along with the appropriate fee or credit card information (credit card number and expiration date) to Thomson Prometric, DSST Program, 2000 Lenox Drive, Third Floor, Lawrenceville, NJ 08648. Include your full name, the test title, the date you took the test, and your Social Security number. Candidates will be notified if a scoring discrepancy is discovered within four weeks of receipt of the request.

What does ACE recommendation mean?

The ACE recommendation is the minimum passing score recommended by the American Council on Education for any given test. It is equivalent to the average score of students in the DSST norming sample who received a grade of C for the course. Some schools require a score higher than the ACE recommendation.

Who is NLC?

National Learning Corporation (NLC) has been successfully preparing candidates for 40 years for over 5,000 exams. NLC publishes Passbook® study guides to help candidates prepare for all DANTES and CLEP exams and almost every other type of exam from high school through adult career.

Go to our website — www.passbooks.com — or call (800) 632-8888 for information about ordering our Passbooks.

To get detailed information on the DSST program and DSST preparation materials, visit www.getcollegecredit.com.

If you are interested in taking the DSST exams, call 877-471-9860 or e-mail pnj-dsst@thomson.com.

HOW TO TAKE A TEST

You have studied long, hard and conscientiously.

With your official admission card in hand, and your heart pounding, you have been admitted to the examination room.

You note that there are several hundred other applicants in the examination room waiting to take the same test.

They all appear to be equally well prepared.

You know that nothing but your best effort will suffice. The "moment of truth" is at hand: you now have to demonstrate objectively, in writing, your knowledge of content and your understanding of subject matter.

You are fighting the most important battle of your life—to pass and/or score high on an examination which will determine your career and provide the economic basis for your livelihood.

What extra, special things should you know and should you do in taking the examination?

I. YOU MUST PASS AN EXAMINATION

A. WHAT EVERY CANDIDATE SHOULD KNOW
Examination applicants often ask us for help in preparing for the written test. What can I study in advance? What kinds of questions will be asked? How will the test be given? How will the papers be graded?

B. HOW ARE EXAMS DEVELOPED?
Examinations are carefully written by trained technicians who are specialists in the field known as "psychological measurement," in consultation with recognized authorities in the field of work that the test will cover. These experts recommend the subject matter areas or skills to be tested; only those knowledges or skills important to your success on the job are included. The most reliable books and source materials available are used as references. Together, the experts and technicians judge the difficulty level of the questions.
Test technicians know how to phrase questions so that the problem is clearly stated. Their ethics do not permit "trick" or "catch" questions. Questions may have been tried out on sample groups, or subjected to statistical analysis, to determine their usefulness.
Written tests are often used in combination with performance tests, ratings of training and experience, and oral interviews. All of these measures combine to form the best-known means of finding the right person for the right job.

II. HOW TO PASS THE WRITTEN TEST

A. BASIC STEPS

1) Study the announcement

How, then, can you know what subjects to study? Our best answer is: "Learn as much as possible about the class of positions for which you've applied." The exam will test the knowledge, skills and abilities needed to do the work.

Your most valuable source of information about the position you want is the official exam announcement. This announcement lists the training and experience qualifications. Check these standards and apply only if you come reasonably close to meeting them. Many jurisdictions preview the written test in the exam announcement by including a section called "Knowledge and Abilities Required," "Scope of the Examination," or some similar heading. Here you will find out specifically what fields will be tested.

2) Choose appropriate study materials

If the position for which you are applying is technical or advanced, you will read more advanced, specialized material. If you are already familiar with the basic principles of your field, elementary textbooks would waste your time. Concentrate on advanced textbooks and technical periodicals. Think through the concepts and review difficult problems in your field.

These are all general sources. You can get more ideas on your own initiative, following these leads. For example, training manuals and publications of the government agency which employs workers in your field can be useful, particularly for technical and professional positions. A letter or visit to the government department involved may result in more specific study suggestions, and certainly will provide you with a more definite idea of the exact nature of the position you are seeking.

3) Study this book!

III. KINDS OF TESTS

Tests are used for purposes other than measuring knowledge and ability to perform specified duties. For some positions, it is equally important to test ability to make adjustments to new situations or to profit from training. In others, basic mental abilities not dependent on information are essential. Questions which test these things may not appear as pertinent to the duties of the position as those which test for knowledge and information. Yet they are often highly important parts of a fair examination. For very general questions, it is almost impossible to help you direct your study efforts. What we can do is to point out some of the more common of these general abilities needed in public service positions and describe some typical questions.

1) General information

Broad, general information has been found useful for predicting job success in some kinds of work. This is tested in a variety of ways, from vocabulary lists to questions about current events. Basic background in some field of work, such as sociology or economics, may be sampled in a group of questions. Often these are principles which have become familiar to most persons through exposure rather than through formal training. It is difficult to advise you how to study for these questions; being alert to the world around you is our best suggestion.

2) Verbal ability

An example of an ability needed in many positions is verbal or language ability. Verbal ability is, in brief, the ability to use and understand words. Vocabulary and grammar tests are typical measures of this ability. Reading comprehension or paragraph interpretation questions are common in many kinds of civil service tests. You are given a paragraph of written material and asked to find its central meaning.

IV. KINDS OF QUESTIONS

1. Multiple-choice Questions

Most popular of the short-answer questions is the "multiple choice" or "best answer" question. It can be used, for example, to test for factual knowledge, ability to solve problems or judgment in meeting situations found at work.

A multiple-choice question is normally one of three types:
- It can begin with an incomplete statement followed by several possible endings. You are to find the one ending which best completes the statement, although some of the others may not be entirely wrong.
- It can also be a complete statement in the form of a question which is answered by choosing one of the statements listed.
- It can be in the form of a problem – again you select the best answer.

Here is an example of a multiple-choice question with a discussion which should give you some clues as to the method for choosing the right answer:

When an employee has a complaint about his assignment, the action which will best help him overcome his difficulty is to
- A. discuss his difficulty with his coworkers
- B. take the problem to the head of the organization
- C. take the problem to the person who gave him the assignment
- D. say nothing to anyone about his complaint

In answering this question, you should study each of the choices to find which is best. Consider choice "A" – Certainly an employee may discuss his complaint with fellow employees, but no change or improvement can result, and the complaint remains unresolved. Choice "B" is a poor choice since the head of the organization probably does not know what assignment you have been given, and taking your problem to him is known as "going over the head" of the supervisor. The supervisor, or person who made the assignment, is the person who can clarify it or correct any injustice. Choice "C" is, therefore, correct. To say nothing, as in choice "D," is unwise. Supervisors have and interest in knowing the problems employees are facing, and the employee is seeking a solution to his problem.

2. True/False

3. Matching Questions

Matching an answer from a column of choices within another column.

V. RECORDING YOUR ANSWERS

Computer terminals are used more and more today for many different kinds of exams.

For an examination with very few applicants, you may be told to record your answers in the test booklet itself. Separate answer sheets are much more common. If this separate answer sheet is to be scored by machine – and this is often the case – it is highly important that you mark your answers correctly in order to get credit.

VI. BEFORE THE TEST

YOUR PHYSICAL CONDITION IS IMPORTANT

If you are not well, you can't do your best work on tests. If you are half asleep, you can't do your best either. Here are some tips:

1) Get about the same amount of sleep you usually get. Don't stay up all night before the test, either partying or worrying—DON'T DO IT!
2) If you wear glasses, be sure to wear them when you go to take the test. This goes for hearing aids, too.
3) If you have any physical problems that may keep you from doing your best, be sure to tell the person giving the test. If you are sick or in poor health, you relay cannot do your best on any test. You can always come back and take the test some other time.

Common sense will help you find procedures to follow to get ready for an examination. Too many of us, however, overlook these sensible measures. Indeed, nervousness and fatigue have been found to be the most serious reasons why applicants fail to do their best on civil service tests. Here is a list of reminders:

- Begin your preparation early – Don't wait until the last minute to go scurrying around for books and materials or to find out what the position is all about.
- Prepare continuously – An hour a night for a week is better than an all-night cram session. This has been definitely established. What is more, a night a week for a month will return better dividends than crowding your study into a shorter period of time.
- Locate the place of the exam – You have been sent a notice telling you when and where to report for the examination. If the location is in a different town or otherwise unfamiliar to you, it would be well to inquire the best route and learn something about the building.
- Relax the night before the test – Allow your mind to rest. Do not study at all that night. Plan some mild recreation or diversion; then go to bed early and get a good night's sleep.
- Get up early enough to make a leisurely trip to the place for the test – This way unforeseen events, traffic snarls, unfamiliar buildings, etc. will not upset you.
- Dress comfortably – A written test is not a fashion show. You will be known by number and not by name, so wear something comfortable.
- Leave excess paraphernalia at home – Shopping bags and odd bundles will get in your way. You need bring only the items mentioned in the official notice you received; usually everything you need is provided. Do not bring reference books to the exam. They will only confuse those last minutes and be taken away from you when in the test room.

- Arrive somewhat ahead of time – If because of transportation schedules you must get there very early, bring a newspaper or magazine to take your mind off yourself while waiting.
- Locate the examination room – When you have found the proper room, you will be directed to the seat or part of the room where you will sit. Sometimes you are given a sheet of instructions to read while you are waiting. Do not fill out any forms until you are told to do so; just read them and be prepared.
- Relax and prepare to listen to the instructions
- If you have any physical problem that may keep you from doing your best, be sure to tell the test administrator. If you are sick or in poor health, you really cannot do your best on the exam. You can come back and take the test some other time.

VII. AT THE TEST

The day of the test is here and you have the test booklet in your hand. The temptation to get going is very strong. Caution! There is more to success than knowing the right answers. You must know how to identify your papers and understand variations in the type of short-answer question used in this particular examination. Follow these suggestions for maximum results from your efforts:

1) Cooperate with the monitor

The test administrator has a duty to create a situation in which you can be as much at ease as possible. He will give instructions, tell you when to begin, check to see that you are marking your answer sheet correctly, and so on. He is not there to guard you, although he will see that your competitors do not take unfair advantage. He wants to help you do your best.

2) Listen to all instructions

Don't jump the gun! Wait until you understand all directions. In most civil service tests you get more time than you need to answer the questions. So don't be in a hurry. Read each word of instructions until you clearly understand the meaning. Study the examples, listen to all announcements and follow directions. Ask questions if you do not understand what to do.

3) Identify your papers

Civil service exams are usually identified by number only. You will be assigned a number; you must not put your name on your test papers. Be sure to copy your number correctly. Since more than one exam may be given, copy your exact examination title.

4) Plan your time

Unless you are told that a test is a "speed" or "rate of work" test, speed itself is usually not important. Time enough to answer all the questions will be provided, but this does not mean that you have all day. An overall time limit has been set. Divide the total time (in minutes) by the number of questions to determine the approximate time you have for each question.

5) Do not linger over difficult questions

If you come across a difficult question, mark it with a paper clip (useful to have along) and come back to it when you have been through the booklet. One caution if you do this – be sure to skip a number on your answer sheet as well. Check often to be sure that you have not lost your place and that you are marking in the row numbered the same as the question you are answering.

6) Read the questions

Be sure you know what the question asks! Many capable people are unsuccessful because they failed to read the questions correctly.

7) Answer all questions

Unless you have been instructed that a penalty will be deducted for incorrect answers, it is better to guess than to omit a question.

8) Speed tests

It is often better NOT to guess on speed tests. It has been found that on timed tests people are tempted to spend the last few seconds before time is called in marking answers at random – without even reading them – in the hope of picking up a few extra points. To discourage this practice, the instructions may warn you that your score will be "corrected" for guessing. That is, a penalty will be applied. The incorrect answers will be deducted from the correct ones, or some other penalty formula will be used.

9) Review your answers

If you finish before time is called, go back to the questions you guessed or omitted to give them further thought. Review other answers if you have time.

10) Return your test materials

If you are ready to leave before others have finished or time is called, take ALL your materials to the monitor and leave quietly. Never take any test material with you. The monitor can discover whose papers are not complete, and taking a test booklet may be grounds for disqualification.

VIII. EXAMINATION TECHNIQUES

1) Read the general instructions carefully. These are usually printed on the first page of the exam booklet. As a rule, these instructions refer to the timing of the examination; the fact that you should not start work until the signal and must stop work at a signal, etc. If there are any special instructions, such as a choice of questions to be answered, make sure that you note this instruction carefully.

2) When you are ready to start work on the examination, that is as soon as the signal has been given, read the instructions to each question booklet, underline any key words or phrases, such as least, best, outline, describe and the like. In this way you will tend to answer as requested rather than discover on reviewing your paper that you listed without describing, that you selected the worst choice rather than the best choice, etc.

3) If the examination is of the objective or multiple-choice type – that is, each question will also give a series of possible answers: A, B, C or D, and you are called upon to select the best answer and write the letter next to that answer on your answer paper – it is advisable to start answering each question in turn. There may be anywhere from 50 to 100 such questions in the three or four hours allotted and you can see how much time would be taken if you read through all the questions before beginning to answer any. Furthermore, if you

come across a question or group of questions which you know would be difficult to answer, it would undoubtedly affect your handling of all the other questions.

4) If the examination is of the essay type and contains but a few questions, it is a moot point as to whether you should read all the questions before starting to answer any one. Of course, if you are given a choice – say five out of seven and the like – then it is essential to read all the questions so you can eliminate the two that are most difficult. If, however, you are asked to answer all the questions, there may be danger in trying to answer the easiest one first because you may find that you will spend too much time on it. The best technique is to answer the first question, then proceed to the second, etc.

5) Time your answers. Before the exam begins, write down the time it started, then add the time allowed for the examination and write down the time it must be completed, then divide the time available somewhat as follows:
   - If 3-1/2 hours are allowed, that would be 210 minutes. If you have 80 objective-type questions, that would be an average of 2-1/2 minutes per question. Allow yourself no more than 2 minutes per question, or a total of 160 minutes, which will permit about 50 minutes to review.
   - If for the time allotment of 210 minutes there are 7 essay questions to answer, that would average about 30 minutes a question. Give yourself only 25 minutes per question so that you have about 35 minutes to review.

6) The most important instruction is to read each question and make sure you know what is wanted. The second most important instruction is to time yourself properly so that you answer every question. The third most important instruction is to answer every question. Guess if you have to but include something for each question. Remember that you will receive no credit for a blank and will probably receive some credit if you write something in answer to an essay question. If you guess a letter – say "B" for a multiple-choice question – you may have guessed right. If you leave a blank as an answer to a multiple-choice question, the examiners may respect your feelings but it will not add a point to your score. Some exams may penalize you for wrong answers, so in such cases only, you may not want to guess unless you have some basis for your answer.

7) Suggestions
   a. Objective-type questions
      1. Examine the question booklet for proper sequence of pages and questions
      2. Read all instructions carefully
      3. Skip any question which seems too difficult; return to it after all other questions have been answered
      4. Apportion your time properly; do not spend too much time on any single question or group of questions
      5. Note and underline key words – all, most, fewest, least, best, worst, same, opposite, etc.
      6. Pay particular attention to negatives
      7. Note unusual option, e.g., unduly long, short, complex, different or similar in content to the body of the question
      8. Observe the use of "hedging" words – probably, may, most likely, etc.

9. Make sure that your answer is put next to the same number as the question
10. Do not second-guess unless you have good reason to believe the second answer is definitely more correct
11. Cross out original answer if you decide another answer is more accurate; do not erase until you are ready to hand your paper in
12. Answer all questions; guess unless instructed otherwise
13. Leave time for review

b. Essay questions
1. Read each question carefully
2. Determine exactly what is wanted. Underline key words or phrases.
3. Decide on outline or paragraph answer
4. Include many different points and elements unless asked to develop any one or two points or elements
5. Show impartiality by giving pros and cons unless directed to select one side only
6. Make and write down any assumptions you find necessary to answer the questions
7. Watch your English, grammar, punctuation and choice of words
8. Time your answers; don't crowd material

8) Answering the essay question

Most essay questions can be answered by framing the specific response around several key words or ideas. Here are a few such key words or ideas:

M's: manpower, materials, methods, money, management
P's: purpose, program, policy, plan, procedure, practice, problems, pitfalls, personnel, public relations

a. Six basic steps in handling problems:
1. Preliminary plan and background development
2. Collect information, data and facts
3. Analyze and interpret information, data and facts
4. Analyze and develop solutions as well as make recommendations
5. Prepare report and sell recommendations
6. Install recommendations and follow up effectiveness

b. Pitfalls to avoid
1. Taking things for granted – A statement of the situation does not necessarily imply that each of the elements is necessarily true; for example, a complaint may be invalid and biased so that all that can be taken for granted is that a complaint has been registered
2. Considering only one side of a situation – Wherever possible, indicate several alternatives and then point out the reasons you selected the best one
3. Failing to indicate follow up – Whenever your answer indicates action on your part, make certain that you will take proper follow-up action to see how successful your recommendations, procedures or actions turn out to be
4. Taking too long in answering any single question – Remember to time your answers properly

EXAMINATION SECTION

EXAMINATION SECTION
TEST 1

DIRECTIONS: Each question or incomplete statement is followed by several suggested answers or completions. Select the one that BEST answers the question or completes the statement. *PRINT THE LETTER OF THE CORRECT ANSWER IN THE SPACE AT THE RIGHT.*

1. The method most often used to assess academic progress in U.S. schools is _____ testing. 1.____

   A. minimum competency B. IQ
   C. criterion-referenced D. standardized

2. In the landmark case *Wisconsin v. Yoder* (1972), the U.S. Supreme Court ruled that 2.____

   A. religious education that took place in public school classrooms during the school day was unconstitutional
   B. public school teachers could tutor private school students in their private schools, even if the schools were primarily religious in nature
   C. a school district violated the rights of students by forcing them to salute the American flag
   D. the state's compulsory education law violated Amish parents' right to the free exercise of their religion

3. In the United States, a school or district generally has the authority to establish several terms or conditions of employment before hiring a teacher. These include the condition that the candidate 3.____

       I. be of a certain age
      II. be a U.S. citizen
     III. pass a minimum competency test
     IV. pledge not to join a specific political organization

   A. I and III
   B. I, II and III
   C. III only
   D. I, II, III and IV

4. Mortimer Adler's Great Books program was an element of the educational _____ movement that was a reaction against Dewey's progressive educational approaches. 4.____

   A. vocational B. neoclassical C. perennialist D. essentialist

5. Of the following, the two factors that have the strongest correlation to a student's risk of dropping out of school are 5.____

   A. language and literacy
   B. educational and occupational level of parents
   C. race and ethnicity
   D. age and gender

6. An independent public school that is supported by state funds, is exempt from many regulations, and is based on a contract between school organizers and a sponsor is a(n) _____ school.

    A. parochial
    B. charter
    C. academy
    D. magnet

7. According to the Family Educational Rights and Privacy Act of 1974, schools that receive federal funding must make student records available for viewing by parents and legal guardians, and by the students themselves, providing the student in each case is

    A. capable of proving that he or she understands the implications and intended use of the records
    B. no longer enrolled at the institution from which the records are requested
    C. 18 years of age or older
    D. not intending to use the records as the basis for a legal action against the institution from which the records are requested

8. Which of the following is associated with the development of behaviorism in American education?

    A. Edward L. Thorndike
    B. Jerome Bruner
    C. Horace Mann
    D. Lev Vygotsky

9. The critical perspective on curriculum planning asserts that

    A. the most important aim of curriculum planning to compel student to think critically
    B. education is an attempt to challenge the existing power and social structure
    C. curriculum planning should be left to individual teachers
    D. curriculum planning is not an objective process, but is ideological and political

10. The historical trend in the United States has been toward school districts that are

    A. greater in number and increasingly specialized
    B. stable in number, with greater interdistrict collaboration
    C. larger in size and fewer in number
    D. greater in number, with greater interdistrict collaboration

11. The efforts by the National Education Association (NEA) and other groups to establish state standards boards are aimed at

    A. protecting teachers from unwarranted disciplinary actions
    B. decreasing class sizes
    C. expanding the state's ability to regulate educational practices
    D. promoting the concept of professionalism in education

12. Students at a high school are enrolled in a different curriculum according to whether the plan to go to college or enter a trade after graduation. The school most likely practices _____ ability grouping.

    A. age-based
    B. within-class
    C. between-class
    D. criterion-referenced

13. The first state funded school specifically established for the education of teachers opened in Massachusetts in 1839. This was the nation's first _____ school, established by educational reformist _____.

    A. grammar; John Dewey
    B. elementary; James Carter
    C. normal; Horace Mann
    D. parochial; John Calvin

14. Each of the following is a rationale for contracting with for-profit entities to provide support services in schools, EXCEPT that

    A. districts can avoid the burden of benefits for employees
    B. schools may benefit from private management techniques
    C. the quality of service will be tied to the company's "bottom line"
    D. competition is likely to produce a cost savings

15. Which of the following terms is usually identified with the work of Wolfensberger?

    A. Socialization
    B. Normalization
    C. Mainstreaming
    D. Habilitation

16. Each of the following was an opinion included in the Supreme Court's ruling in the *Vernonia School District v. Acton* (1995) case which ruled that random drug testing of high school athletes did not violate the reasonable search and seizure clause of the 4th Amend-

    A. the privacy interests compromised by blood samples are negligible, since the conditions of collection are similar to a blood bank.
    B. the reasonableness of a search is judged by "balancing the intrusion on the individual's Fourth Amendment interests against the promotion of legitimate governmental interests."
    C. the governmental concern over the safety of minors under their supervision overrides the minimal, if any, intrusion in student-athletes' privacy.
    D. high school athletes who are under state supervision during school hours are subject to greater control than over free adults.

17. Curricula that focus on demonstrations of learning are considered

    A. standardized
    B. outcome-based
    C. assessment-based
    D. high-stakes

18. _____, a federally funded education program for at-risk elementary and secondary students that was launched in 1965 as part of President Lyndon Johnson's War on Poverty, required school officials to distribute new federal funds to localities and schools with many low-income students.

    A. Title I
    B. VISTA
    C. Title IX
    D. Head Start

19. The Accelerated Schools Project, launched in the late 1980s by then-Stanford professor Henry Levin, is rooted in the idea that

    A. students with learning deficiencies can succeed if they work with gifted and talented students
    B. gifted students require a richer, more challenging course of instruction than other students
    C. academic content, skills and concepts are traditionally too slowly paced and do not reflect the pace at which students are able and ready to learn them
    D. all students will thrive in an atmosphere of high expectations and engaging curriculum

20. The Individualized Education Plan, or IEP, is a program for students with disabilities that is used to identify current levels of performance, long-and short-term goals, criteria for success, methods of assessing mastery, amount of time to be spent in general education classrooms, and beginning and ending dates for special services. The IEP is mandated by

    A. Title IX of the Education Amendments of 1972
    B. Section 504 of the Rehabilitation Act of 1973
    C. Part B of the Individuals with Disabilities Education Act of 1997 (IDEA)
    D. No Child Left Behind Act of 2001

21. What is the term commonly used to describe the process by which multiculturalism becomes an explicit part of the curriculum throughout all content areas?

    A. Indoctrination
    B. Infusion
    C. Pluralization
    D. Infiltration

22. Teachers are generally allowed to use multiple copies of copyrighted material if their use meets certain tests. Which of the following is NOT one of these tests?

    A. Cumulative effect on the market
    B. Brevity
    C. Fair use
    D. Spontaneity

23. Teachers who following Bloom's taxonomy navigate a hierarchy of simple to complex thought, with the most complex level being

    A. evaluation
    B. application
    C. synthesis
    D. analysis

24. Of the following types of second-language programs, the one LEAST compatible with the concept of assimilation is

    A. ESL
    B. transition
    C. maintenance
    D. immersion

25. Cultural literacy is a concept most closely associated with the educational philosophy known as

    A. perennialism
    B. essentialism
    C. progressivism
    D. social reconstructionism

KEY (CORRECT ANSWERS)

1.	D	11.	D
2.	D	12.	C
3.	B	13.	C
4.	C	14.	C
5.	B	15.	B
6.	B	16.	A
7.	C	17.	B
8.	A	18.	A
9.	D	19.	D
10.	C	20.	C

21. B
22. C
23. A
24. C
25. A

TEST 2

DIRECTIONS: Each question or incomplete statement is followed by several suggested answers or completions. Select the one that BEST answers the question or completes the statement. *PRINT THE LETTER OF THE CORRECT ANSWER IN THE SPACE AT THE RIGHT.*

1. The Chautauqua movement, an eight-week summer program, offering adult courses in the arts, sciences, and humanities, was a significant adult education movement that recalled the principles of the _____ Movement of the late 19th century.

    A. Lyceum
    B. Know-Nothing
    C. Luddite
    D. Freudian

2. Two clauses of the First Amendment concern the relationship of government to religion: the Establishment Clause and the Free Exercise Clause. At an absolute minimum, the Establishment Clause was intended to

    A. prevent the federal government from supporting Christianity in general
    B. prohibit discrimination by state government institutions
    C. prohibit the federal government from declaring and financially supporting a national religion
    D. prohibit the federal government from interfering with or burdening an individual's ability to exercise his or her religious beliefs

3. Generally, the most widely-used form of assessment for determining the need for special education services is

    A. norm-referenced testing
    B. observation
    C. curriculum-based assessment
    D. criterion-referenced testing

4. _____ programs are those that provide students from low-income families with additional educational opportunities beyond those offered in the standard academic program.

    A. complementary education   B. continuous intervention
    C. compensatory education   D. additional schooling

5. The most significant result of the school reform movement of the 1980s was

    A. more stringent graduation requirements
    B. reduced emphasis on standardized testing
    C. more centralized authority in school districts
    D. a more humanistic approach to teaching and learning

6. In *New Jersey v. T.L.O.* (1985), the Supreme Court ruled that school officials, before searching a student suspected of violating school rules or law, must

    A. obtain a legal search warrant
    B. meet the legal standard of "probable cause"
    C. give students 24 hours notice before conducting the search
    D. meet the standard of reasonableness and common sense

7. Typical school district approaches to teacher renewal include each of the following, EXCEPT

    A. advanced-study sabbaticals
    B. changes in assignment
    C. induction programs
    D. visitation programs

8. Much of the multicultural education practiced today relies on James Banks' conception of multicultural curriculum reform, which comprises four levels. The first level, the _____ Approach, focuses on

    A. Additive; important social issues and actions that might help solve them
    B. Transformation; concepts, issues, events, and themes from the perspective of diverse ethnic and cultural groups
    C. Social Action; content, concepts, themes, and perspectives that are added to the curriculum without changing its structure
    D. Contribution; heroes, holidays, and discrete cultural events

9. The regulations issued y the Office of Civil Rights of the U.S. Department of Education are an example of _____ law.

    A. case
    B. constitutional
    C. administrative
    D. common

10. Written behavioral objectives typically include each of the following, EXCEPT

    A. the conditions under which the behavior is to be performed
    B. an action word that connotes an observable student behavior
    C. a statement that specifies how well the student must perform the behavior (criteria for success)
    D. consequences for failure to perform the behavior

11. Which of the following is a term that denotes a trend in education that involves on-line connections, video equipment, and specialized software?

    A. Vocational education
    B. Hypermedia
    C. Distance learning
    D. Web-based teaching

12. The League of Professional Schools, which was formed in the 1980s, involves the critical element of

    A. the didactic mode, or the acquisition of organized knowledge through textbooks, lectures and videos.
    B. action research that provides a systematic way for schools to study the effects of their educational programs on student learning.
    C. peer teaching, active learning strategies, and small group work
    D. a school leadership team composed of the principal, selected school staff, community members, and students

13. The new land-grant institutions established by the Morrill Act of 1862 were colleges that usually emphasized

    A. religious and moral instruction
    B. agriculture and mechanical arts
    C. remedial reading and writing instruction
    D. classic liberal arts

14. Increased parental involvement at the school level tends to have each of the following effects, EXCEPT

    A. a lighter work load for individual teachers
    B. improved student attitudes
    C. higher academic achievement
    D. higher rates of student attendance

15. _____ is an instructional model in which the teacher identifies a goal, gives students information, and guides them to the goal.

    A. Discovery learning
    B. Simulation
    C. Teaching efficacy
    D. Cognitive instruction

16. The individual education program (IEP) mandated for students with disabilities must be reviewed annually, and must include each of the following participants, EXCEPT the

    A. student
    B. parent or guardian
    C. teacher
    D. principal

17. John Dewey's criticism of American public education was grounded in his belief that it

    A. did not adequately prepare students for the vocations they would undertake after leaving school
    B. offered people no realistic preparation for life in a democratic society
    C. too focused on the needs of the student, rather than of the larger society
    D. focused too much on social control and classroom discipline

18. Research indicates that in dealing with low achievers in a classroom, teachers tend to
    I. give too much information in their responses to low achievers' questions
    II. seat low achievers farther away from the teacher
    III. use low achievers' ideas less frequently than those of other students
    IV. demand less from low achievers

    A. I and II
    B. II and III
    C. II, III and IV
    D. I, II, III and IV

19. The term LEA (local education agency) is often used in federal legislation to refer to   19._____

    A. individual schools
    B. school districts
    C. local school boards
    D. all the school administrators in a given geographic area

20. Private schools are NOT typically   20._____

    A. for-profit institutions   B. financed through private funds
    C. tax-exempt   D. governed by boards of trustees

21. If a teacher is involved in a court case that deals with academic freedom, he or she will   21._____
    typically find the strongest legal protection in the fact that

    A. the controversial content does not violate the standards of the school community
    B. the controversial content is related to legitimate educational objectives
    C. students expressed a desire to learn the controversial content
    D. the teacher demonstrates extensive knowledge of the controversial content

22. At the state level, educational practices are regulated and the state government is   22._____
    advised about the conduct of educational business by the

    A. commission on educational business and testing
    B. coalition of essential schools
    C. board of education
    D. teachers' association

23. Which of the following is a multimeasure approach to assessment that emphasizes the   23._____
    functional analysis of student behaviors?

    A. Time sampling   B. Adaptive-process assessment
    C. Psycholinguistic testing   D. Longitudinal study

24. Of the following, the best definition of a school principal is one who   24._____

    A. has the ultimate authority over the hiring and firing of teachers at a given school
    B. has the ultimate responsibility for the operation of individual schools
    C. has administrative duties as well as direct responsibility for student learning in the classrooms
    D. is specifically responsible for maintaining the order and safety of a school

25. As a source of educational funding, the property tax is generally better than sales and   25._____
    income taxes because it

    A. is easier to monitor for compliance
    B. is cheaper to administer and collect
    C. is cheaper to enforce
    D. makes it easier to project revenues

KEY (CORRECT ANSWERS)

1. A
2. C
3. B
4. C
5. A

6. D
7. C
8. D
9. C
10. D

11. C
12. B
13. B
14. A
15. A

16. D
17. B
18. C
19. B
20. A

21. B
22. C
23. B
24. B
25. D

TEST 3

DIRECTIONS: Each question or incomplete statement is followed by several suggested answers or completions. Select the one that BEST answers the question or completes the statement. *PRINT THE LETTER OF THE CORRECT ANSWER IN THE SPACE AT THE RIGHT.*

1. The Civitas curriculum framework, proposed by the Center for Civic Education in Los Angeles, begins with a rationale for the necessity for civic education in a democracy. The rationale states that the first and primary reason for civic education in a constitutional democracy is that

    A. before being able to fully enjoy the promised benefits of democracy, a learner must be able to master certain skills
    B. the health of the body politic requires the widest possible civic participation of its citizens consistent with the common good and the protection of individual rights
    C. the bureaucracy the results as a natural outgrowth of the democratic process presents a litany of problems and obstacles that must be mastered by citizens
    D. citizens who enjoy the rights and protections of democratic government have a responsibility to learn a valuable trade or vocation that will contribute to the wealth and security of the state

2. In Montessori schools, teachers use a curriculum that is

    A. teacher-centered rather than student-centered
    B. based on materials specifically designed to help children discover the physical properties of objects
    C. emphasizes traditional household activities such as cooking, helping with chores, storytelling, rhyming and movement games
    D. rigidly designed to teach children mathematical and scientific principles

3. _____ is a term describing the consistency between teachers' goals, learning activities, student practice, and assessment.

    A. Cognitive instruction   B. Instructional alignment
    C. Pedagogy   D. Teaching efficacy

4. Incentive pay plans for teachers include _____ plans.
    I. competency-based
    II. performance-based
    III. career ladder
    IV. master teacher

    A. I and II   B. I, II and IV   C. II and III   D. I, II, III and IV

5. *Lau v. Nichols,* the major precedent regarding the educational rights of language minorities, is

    A. grounded in the 14th Amendment to the U.S. Constitution
    B. applicable only to the specific case of Spanish-speaking students
    C. grounded in statute rather than in the U.S. Constitution.
    D. grounded in the phrase "pursuit of happiness" in the Declaration of Independence

6. According to Piaget, the first stage of cognitive development is the _____ stage.

    A. preoperational B. formal operations
    C. sensorimotor D. concrete operations

7. A program of federally subsidized preschool programs for 3- and 4-year-old children from low-income families, including health, nutrition, and social sendees, is

    A. Follow Through B. Head Start
    C. Star Search D. Upward Bound

8. Which of the following strategies for lowering the school dropout rate has been most successful?

    A. Ability grouping
    B. Providing a safe and positive school climate
    C. Magnet schools
    D. Remedial education

9. Educational costs are often measured by _____ expenditures, or a division of the funds allocated for services by the number of students to be served.

    A. per-pupil B. student-centered
    C. per capita D. dispersed

10. In _____ programs, states set the same per-pupil expenditure level for all schools and districts.

    A. full-funding B. block grant
    C. shotgun D. integrated funding

11. The Tenth Amendment to the United States Constitution is significant in terms of education because it

    A. guarantees the freedom of religion
    B. grants legal control over education to the states
    C. establishes compulsory education
    D. codifies the separation of church and state

12. Which of the following is LEAST likely to be displayed by a student with a learning disability?

    A. Poor motor coordination
    B. Excessive movement
    C. Highly developed social skills
    D. Impulsive behavior

13. Educators who use _____ approach to multicultural education attempt to teach students directly about oppression and discrimination.

    A. human relations
    B. single-group study
    C. social reconstructionist
    D. teaching the culturally different

14. Each of the following is an "equalization model" for the funding of schools, EXCEPT the

    A. equalized foundation grant
    B. full state funding
    C. flat grant
    D. equalized reward for tax effort

15. Subject-area curriculum design is NOT

    A. a model that emphasizes the student's creative self-expression
    B. the oldest and most widely used curriculum design
    C. viewed as a body of subject matter
    D. developed with an organization and focus that is derived from the content itself

16. In the landmark case *Engel v. Vitale* (1962), the Supreme Court ruled that

    A. New York's practice of beginning school days with a prayer drafted by school officials violated the establishment clause.
    B. extremely sectarian and proselytizing speeches at a graduation ceremony could be prohibited because of the reasonable impression that the religious message was supported by the school.
    C. a New Jersey law providing for reimbursement to parents of parochial school students for transportation costs on public busses is constitutional.
    D. teaching evolution in public school science classes does not infringe upon the rights of any students or parents to the free exercise of their religion, even if they sincerely believe that evolution is contrary to their religious beliefs.

17. Which of the following is NOT a cognitive teaching strategy?

    A. Rehearsal training
    B. Response cost
    C. Attention training
    D. Instrumental enrichment

18. The initial model for the state land grant school, which became officially established in the Northwest Ordinance of 1785, was designed by

    A. Horace Mann
    B. Benjamin Franklin
    C. Thomas Jefferson
    D. Benjamin Disraeli

19. The terms *reward, punishment, conditioning, shaping,* and *extinction* are all associated with

    A. behavioral learning theory
    B. constructivist learning theory
    C. John Dewey
    D. Horace Mann

20. _____ approach to education, pioneered by _____, is a student-centered model that focuses on the use of truth to solve problems and promote change in a global society.

   A. constructivist; Jerome Bruner
   B. behaviorist; B.F. Skinner
   C. progressive; John Dewey
   D. essentialist; Aristotle

21. Research indicates that each of the following is an effective classroom management strategy, EXCEPT

   A. avoiding responses that demean or embarrass students
   B. handling all classroom management tasks personally
   C. making behavioral expectations clear from the very beginning
   D. building responses on what students already know about classroom behavior

22. Which of the following concepts is based on the assumption that virtually all students can learn material if given enough time and taught appropriately?

   A. Mastery learning
   B. Direct instruction
   C. Performance-based education
   D. Constructivist teaching

23. Which of the following is NOT a strategy included in the social family model of teaching?

   A. Individualized instruction
   B. Reciprocal teaching
   C. Cooperative learning
   D. Project-based learning

24. Of the following strategies for helping at-risk children succeed in school, the one that has proven most effective has been

   A. the active involvement of community resources in the redesign of schools
   B. beefed-up security services that make schools safer
   C. zero tolerance programs that address the problems of school crime and violence
   D. rehabilitation programs that stress mental and physical wellness

25. Which of the following is an argument in favor of block scheduling?

   A. It decreases a teacher's planning load.
   B. It creates more opportunities for teachers to become personally acquainted with their students
   C. It minimizes disruptions and provides increased instructional time
   D. It facilitates the integration of curriculum subject areas.

KEY (CORRECT ANSWERS)

1. B
2. B
3. B
4. A
5. C

6. C
7. B
8. B
9. A
10. A

11. B
12. C
13. C
14. C
15. A

16. A
17. B
18. C
19. A
20. C

21. B
22. A
23. A
24. A
25. C

TEST 4

DIRECTIONS: Each question or incomplete statement is followed by several suggested answers or completions. Select the one that BEST answers the question or completes the statement. *PRINT THE LETTER OF THE CORRECT ANSWER IN THE SPACE AT THE RIGHT.*

1. The full-service school movement that gained momentum in the 1990s was driven by the
    I. clear connection between family support and children's capacity to learn
    II. at-risk student's need for more social supports than the traditional school offers.
    III. efficiency and cost-effectiveness of staging collaborative approaches, early interventions, and other integrated sendees at school buildings
    IV. teachers' existing preparedness for dealing with numerous social problems by virtue of their professional training

    A. I and II
    B. I, II and III
    C. II only
    D. I, II, III and IV

    1.___

2. In the United States, the parents of disabled children who first filed suit against their school districts for excluding children with disabilities were inspired by the logic included in the case of

    A. *Brown v. Board of Education* (1954)
    B. *Mills v. Board of Education of the District of Columbia* (1972)
    C. *Board of Education v. Rowley* (1982)
    D. *Stauffer v. William Penn School District* (1993)

    2.___

3. Of the following colleges, which was originally established for the education of Native Americans?

    A. Goddard College
    B. Dartmouth College
    C. Friends University
    D. Grinnell College

    3.___

4. A school district provide additional instructional resources to help preschoolers and kindergartners who are performing below grade level obtain the necessary academic skills to reach grade level performance in the shortest possible time. This is an example of a(n) _____ program.

    A. early intervention
    B. special education
    C. extracurricular
    D. compensatory education

    4.___

5. A primary function of state educational agencies is to

    A. collect information directly from students for statistical reporting purposes
    B. distribute state funds for the operation of local districts
    C. make decisions about whether students should advance to a higher grade
    D. provide funding for the needs of special school populations

    5.___

16

6. To help interpret the establishment clause, the U.S. Supreme Court uses several tests, including the *Lemon* test, which consists of three parts. Of the following, the factor that is NOT a part of the *Lemon* test is the determination of whether the law or government action in question

    A. has the primary effect of advancing or inhibiting religion
    B. has a bona fide secular purpose
    C. excessively entangles religion and government
    D. amounts to an endorsement of religion

7. Poverty in the United States is generally more common
    I. among families headed by single mothers
    II. among minorities
    III. in large urban areas
    IV. among children

    A. I and II   B. I, II and IV
    C. III only   D. I, II, III and IV

8. In gifted and talented education programs across the country, research has consistently demonstrated that _____ students are under-served.

    A. urban
    B. ethnic minority
    C. male
    D. economically disadvantaged

9. Research on the brain has most strongly suggested that girls are more likely to think

    A. inductively
    B. visually
    C. abstractly
    D. deductively

10. In the typical work day, a teacher will spend the LEAST amount of time on

    A. interacting with colleagues
    B. testing and monitoring
    C. desk work
    D. instruction

11. At the end of the fiscal year, a school must justify its entire budget appropriation, rather than justifying only the sums that exceed the previous year's request. This is known as _____ budgeting.

    A. top-down   B. zero-based
    C. indexed   D. capital

12. Brophy's system of classroom management

    A. relies on maximum student engagement
    B. avoids cooperative learning situations because of the likelihood of disruption
    C. stresses individualized instruction
    D. focuses on teachers' reaction to misconduct

13. Which of the following statements about reflective teaching is FALSE?

    A. It applies that same basic instructional approach to all situations.
    B. It emphasizes caring.
    C. It focuses on creative problem-solving
    D. It is a constructivist approach.

14. The Supreme Court's ruling in the 1954 Brown v. Board of Education case reversed the previous ruling in

    A. *Buchanan v. Warley*
    B. *Plessy v. Ferguson*
    C. *State v. Boon*
    D. *Dred Scott v. Sandford*

15. Which of the following terms is different in meaning from the others?

    A. Operant learning
    B. Incidental learning
    C. Inferential learning
    D. Informal learning

16. A typical magnet school DOES NOT

    A. have an enrollment policy that is closed to children outside of a particular region
    B. consist of a student body that is present by choice that meets variable inclusion criteria
    C. concentrate on a particular discipline or area of study
    D. suffer from the perception that it caters to more intellectually adept or "gifted" students

17. The Individuals with Disabilities Education Act (IDEA) defines a "disability" as a(n)

    A. physical or mental impairment
    B. physical or mental impairment that severely limits life activities
    C. physical impairment
    D. difficulty in learning

18. Supporters of integrated curriculum maintain that one of its most important benefits is that

    A. significantly reduces expenditures on extracurricular activities, since much of this activity takes place during the regular school day
    B. students have less work to take home, and can spend more quality time with family members
    C. it uses instructional time more efficiently than the traditional curriculum
    D. it does a better job of preparing students for the non-compartmentalized experiences of life beyond school

19. _____ is a funding plan that allocates funds according to legitimate educational needs, such as low-income students or limited English proficiency (LEP) students.

    A. Site-based budgeting
    B. Discretionary budgeting
    C. Horizontal equity
    D. Vertical equity

20. The most significant criticism of group IQ tests is that they

    A. have a time limit
    B. discount emotional factors
    C. cannot be repeated for a better score
    D. are culturally biased

21. One of the four major learning theory schools, constructivism is the belief that learning is

    A. primarily a social experience
    B. built on prior knowledge and experience
    C. a process in which learners are focused mostly on behaviors modeled by others
    D. the automatic formation of complex ideas, with behavior starting out as being involuntary moving to voluntary as it is learned, and finally automatic

22. In ruling on cases involving professional negligence in the schools, the courts have generally considered each of the following to be important factors, EXCEPT the

    A. experience or conduct of the teacher in previous and similar situations
    B. explicitness of a teacher's warning or caution to students
    C. age and mental abilities of the students
    D. teacher's attempt to anticipate danger

23. A comprehensive assessment is designed to evaluate a student's ability to

    A. reason and solve problems creatively, and express themselves clearly
    B. select the correct answer from a series of possible choices
    C. demonstrate knowledge in each of the five major academic subjects
    D. group ideas thematically in cooperative teams

24. Through _____ programs, a state guarantees a certain amount of money for educational spending and determines the portion of the cost that will be borne by local governments.

    A. land grant   B. ballot measure
    C. foundation   D. divisional

25. In most U.S. public school districts, the primary determinant of teacher salary is the

    A. tax base
    B. pertinent state law
    C. number of students
    D. level of union participation and activity

KEY (CORRECT ANSWERS)

1. B
2. A
3. B
4. A
5. B

6. D
7. B
8. D
9. A
10. B

11. B
12. A
13. A
14. B
15. A

16. A
17. A
18. D
19. D
20. D

21. B
22. A
23. A
24. C
25. A

EXAMINATION SECTION
TEST 1

DIRECTIONS: Each question or incomplete statement is followed by several suggested answers or completions. Select the one that BEST answers the question or completes the statement. *PRINT THE LETTER OF THE CORRECT ANSWER IN THE SPACE AT THE RIGHT.*

1. Curriculum-based assessment is a model that works by means of

    A. observing student performances and behavior in an informal context.
    B. requiring students to demonstrate knowledge and skills in ways other than through the conventional - methods used within a classroom.
    C. directly intervening in the learning environment of the classroom and by measuring the effects of an intervention on a student's performance.
    D. giving paper-pencil tests (multiple-choice, true/false, matching, short answer) that typically must be completed within a specific amount of time.

    1._____

2. Looping is an educational grouping strategy that is designed to

    A. group students together by ability or levels of academic achievement
    B. organize at least part of the daily schedule into longer periods of instructional time
    C. teach disabled students in regular classrooms with other students to the fullest extent possible
    D. keep teachers and students together for more than a single academic year

    2._____

3. A fourth-grade class spends two weeks studying the history and current issues relating to Vietnam's Hmong tribespeople, with a special emphasis on those who have relocated to the United States. This is an example of the _____ approach to multicultural education.

    A. reconstructionist
    B. culturally relevant
    C. human relations
    D. single-group study

    3._____

4. A local school board does NOT typically

    A. inform the community of local educational issues
    B. identify short- and long-term educational needs
    C. establish a budget
    D. employ personnel

    4._____

5. In most cases, a laboratory experiment is an example of the _____ instructional method of teaching.

    A. drill & practice
    B. discussion
    C. demonstration
    D. presentation

    5._____

21

6. The most common means of recertification for experienced teachers is

   A. retaking the required competency examinations
   B. earning continuing education credits
   C. simply reapplying to the state certification agency with documented evidence of one's work history
   D. participating in a certain number and type of state-sponsored professional development activities

7. In ruling on cases involving a teacher's academic freedom, the courts have generally considered each of the following to be important factors, EXCEPT the

   A. age of the students involved
   B. teacher's goal in using the instructional method
   C. relevance of the materials or instruction to the course content
   D. content area in which the instruction has been conducted

8. Which of the following factors is LEAST likely to place a student "at risk" in school?

   A. Family income is at or below the poverty level.
   B. Both parents work outside the home.
   C. The student lives with only one parent.
   D. The student is competent, but not fluent, in English.

9. The most common crime at U.S. schools is

   A. theft
   B. assault
   C. vandalism
   D. sexual assault

10. School-based budgeting occurs when

    A. state departments of education determine how funds are to be distributed among individual schools
    B. the responsibility for allocating school resources is governed at the level of the individual school district
    C. a group of people below the senior administrative level work together in reviewing and recommending major elements of the budget development process
    D. the responsibility for allocating school resources is governed at the level of the individual school building

11. Ensuring that schools operate in accordance with federal and state guidelines is ultimately the responsibility of the

    A. principal
    B. local school board
    C. district superintendent
    D. state superintendent

12. Colonial America's educational efforts were noteworthy for their distinct regional differences. In the Southern colonies, for example, schooling was more likely to be characterized by

A. community schools free of all religious affiliations
B. parochial schools that emphasized religion, mathematics, reading and writing
C. large common schools where different groups were taught together
D. informal family instruction

13. Which of the following programs is based on building a developmental hierarchy of skills in the child, beginning with attendance?   13.____

    A. Instrumental enrichment
    B. Engineered classroom
    C. Kinegenics
    D. Class meeting

14. The most significant influence of state governments on education is through   14.____

    A. writing curriculum and accountability standards
    B. establishing teacher standards
    C. collecting and analyzing educational statistics
    D. taxation and distributing revenues

15. Which of the following is a type of bilingual education program in which as many subjects and possible are taught in two languages while following a regular curriculum?   15.____

    A. Structured immersion
    B. Two-way bilingual immersion
    C. Transitional bilingual
    D. Bilingual maintenance

16. Which of the following is NOT a Supreme Court case that involved the establishment clause of the 1st Amendment?   16.____

    A. *Epperson v. Arkansas* (1968)
    B. *Committee for Public Education v. Nyquist* (1973)
    C. *Goss v. Lopez* (1975)
    D. *Wallace v. Jaffree* (1985)

17. Teachers who prefer to work in private schools rather than public schools generally base this preference on   17.____

    A. smaller class sizes
    B. larger support staff
    C. less parental interference
    D. higher salary

18. In which of the following Supreme Court decisions was it ruled that public facilities for European and African Americans could be "separate but equal?"   18.____

    A. *Plessy v. Ferguson*
    B. *Dred Scott v. Sandford*
    C. *Cooper v. Aaron*
    D. *Brown v. Board of Education*

19. Norms are usually expressed in terms of each of the following, EXCEPT

    A. means
    B. percentiles
    C. instructional objectives
    D. age

20. Multicultural education is an approach that includes each of the following strategies, EXCEPT

    A. equity pedagogy
    B. content integration
    C. attacking stereotypes
    D. immersion programs

21. Cognitivism is an educational philosophy based on the belief that

    A. people actively construct their knowledge of the world through behavioral conditioning
    B. all humans have a drive to learn, which organizations should try to encourage
    C. human forces are determined by forces beyond human control
    D. people learned conditioned responses to various stimuli

22. Summative assessments of student progress are typically performed

    A. while a lesson is in progress
    B. every morning, before instruction begins
    C. after a unit of instruction
    D. at the end of an academic year

23. In the colony of _____ , more so than in other colonies, there was a widespread system of schools established by a variety of religious denominations.

    A. Pennsylvania
    B. Maryland
    C. New York
    D. Rhode Island

24. What is known as the "null" curriculum is
    I. communicated through unofficial routines
    II. implicitly, but not officially, sanctioned by administration
    III. influenced by teaching method
    IV. not taught at all in a classroom

    A. I and II
    B. I, II and III
    C. IV only
    D. I, II, III and IV

25. The School Development Program (SDP) is the organization charged with implementing 25.____
the Comer Process, a school and system-wide intervention formulated by James P.
Comer that aims to combine concepts from the fields of education and

    A. criminal justice
    B. organizational behavior
    C. sociology
    D. child psychiatry

KEY (CORRECT ANSWERS)

1.	C	11.	C
2.	D	12.	D
3.	D	13.	B
4.	D	14.	D
5.	C	15.	B
6.	B	16.	C
7.	D	17.	A
8.	B	18.	A
9.	A	19.	C
10.	D	20.	D

    21. A
    22. C
    23. A
    24. C
    25. D

TEST 2

DIRECTIONS: Each question or incomplete statement is followed by several suggested answers or completions. Select the one that BEST answers the question or completes the statement. *PRINT THE LETTER OF THE CORRECT ANSWER IN THE SPACE AT THE RIGHT.*

1. The Massachusetts Act of 1642 was one of several laws that laid the groundwork for compulsory education in the United States. Passage of the law today signifies that one important factor in the birth of modern education in the United States was the

    A. dawning age of enlightenment in which children were encouraged to contemplate democratic ideals
    B. strict separation of church and state
    C. increased emphasis on practical rather than theoretical learning
    D. pursuit of religious freedom

2. Albert Bandura's model of learning asserts that it

    A. takes place only if the learner perceives that the content to be learned will help fulfill an individual need
    B. takes place through observation and modeling of the behaviors of others
    C. is a process of stimulus, response, and reinforcement
    D. can be organized around an essential core of knowledge

3. At the local level, most of the funding for education is derived from

    A. income taxes
    B. vouchers
    C. "sin" taxes
    D. property taxes

4. The primary strategy of Goodlad's National Network for Educational Renewal is

    A. school/university partnerships where currently enrolled P-12 students and future teachers receive quality educational experiences
    B. an incentive program to convince working teachers to remain in the profession
    C. the launching of multiple renewal efforts at the school level that have a definite beginning and end
    D. state-level Boards of Renewal that set standards for schools to meet as they strive to achieve the results specified in the project's Twenty Postulates

5. Incentive programs for professional teachers include
    I. merit pay
    II. career ladder programs
    III. tenure
    IV. mentoring programs

    A. I and II
    B. I, II and IV
    C. II and III
    D. I, II, III and IV

6. For assessing global ability in school-age children, the most commonly used test is the

    A. Cognitive Abilities Test (CAT)
    B. Otis-Lennon Mental Ability Test (OLMAT)
    C. Kaufman Assessment Battery for Children (K-ABC)
    D. Weschler Intelligence Scale for Children (WISC)

7. In the Middle Atlantic colonies, education was characterized by
    I. schools mostly sponsored by individual colonial governments
    II. some charity schools established to educate girls and minorities
    III. several colleges
    IV. a limited number of secondary schools

    A. I only
    B. I, II and III
    C. II and IV
    D. I, II, III and IV

8. The conflict resolution programs, including peer mediation, which proliferated among schools in the 1990s to stem the trend of student violence, were rooted in concepts associated with

    A. traditional criminal justice
    B. the countercultural movement of the 1960s
    C. restorative justice
    D. labor relations

9. One theory about the relatively low academic achievement of Native American students is that it is a result of the discontinuity between the culture and language of their home and the mainstream culture represented by the school. This is known as _____ theory.

    A. cultural difference
    B. global inequality
    C. artifact-mediated
    D. cultural pluralism

10. School- or site-based management typically involves each of the following benefits, EXCEPT

    A. increased decision-making authority in the central administrative office
    B. greater teacher input in decisions that affect working conditions
    C. greater control of resources at the school site level
    D. bringing power closer to the student

11. In which of the following cases did the Supreme Court rule that direct state financial aid to parochial schools was in violation of the establishment clause?

    A. *McCollum v. Board of Education* (1948)
    B. *Lemon v. Kurtzman* (1971)
    C. *Segraves v. California* (1981)
    D. *Cole v. Oroville Union High School* (1999)

12. The ethnic group that consistently has the lowest high school completion rate is   12.____

    A. African-American
    B. Latino/Hispanic
    C. Euro-American
    D. Asian-American

13. For most American schools, curriculum is defined at the _____ level.   13.____

    A. district
    B. federal
    C. individual school/departmental
    D. state and local

14. Under the provisions of the Family Educational Right to Privacy Act, or Buckley Amendment, parents have the right to examine each of the following, EXCEPT   14.____

    A. their child's standardized test scores
    B. their child's academic record
    C. the record of the dates and types of disclosures a school has made of their child's educational records
    D. the teacher's grade book

15. As amended, the federal Individuals with Disabilities Education Act (IDEA) orders that the state must ensure the provision of a free and appropriate public education to   15.____

    A. all children from birth to 18 years of age
    B. all children from birth to 21 years of age
    C. all children between the ages of 3 and 21
    D. a student of any age who seeks an opportunity for public education

16. Interpersonal intelligence is best described as the ability to   16.____

    A. navigate a complex social setting with success
    B. express one's own ideas and emotions through the use of language and body language
    C. persuade others to share their feelings and emotional state
    D. perceive and make distinctions in the words, feelings, and intentions of others

17. Which of the following federal laws did the most to shift the center of educational policy-making power from states and localities to the federal government?   17.____

    A. Smith-Hughes Act of 1917
    B. National Defense Education Act of 1958
    C. Elementary and Secondary Education Act of 1965
    D. No Child Left Behind Act of 2001

18. Each of the following teacher rights is protected by tenure, EXCEPT the right to   18.____

    A. a continuing contract within a school district
    B. due process
    C. work at the school and grade level of one's choice
    D. be notified of charges for dismissal

19. Horizontal curriculum alignment
    I. is typically centered on a specific grade level
    II. ensures that subjects are connected across grade levels
    III. requires students to experience increasingly complex instruction as they move through grades
    IV. requires examination of curriculum across disciplines

    A. I only
    B. I and IV
    C. II and III
    D. II, III and IV

20. Which of the following is NOT an element of the synectics model of teaching?

    A. Social insight
    B. Hypothesis formation
    C. Problem-solving
    D. Empathy

21. The growing body of research about the brain and learning styles is likely to have the greatest impact on _____ instruction.

    A. discussion
    B. individualized
    C. collaborative
    D. demonstration

22. In the United States today, where would one be most likely to find nongraded classrooms in which students are heterogeneously grouped by ability, and sometimes are of different ages?

    A. Preschools
    B. Primary schools
    C. Middle schools
    D. High schools

23. What is the term for a scoring key created by teachers to help assess how well students have mastered important aspects of learning activities?

    A. Blueprint
    B. Matrix
    C. Norm
    D. Rubric

24. When it comes to dealing with exceptional students, mainstreaming and inclusion are two common strategies. The main difference between them is that

    A. inclusion focuses primarily on classroom adaptations
    B. inclusion is a more detailed and comprehensive approach
    C. mainstreaming is aimed at students with only mild disabilities
    D. mainstreaming focuses on the principle of the least restrictive environment

25. Opponents of the practice of social promotion in education argue that it
    I. leads employers to conclude that diplomas are meaningless
    II. cheats the child of an education
    III. can hide teacher ineptitude
    IV. rewards weak effort and poor performance

    A. I and II
    B. II and IV
    C. II, III and IV
    D. I, II, III and IV

KEY (CORRECT ANSWERS)

1.	D	11.	B
2.	B	12.	B
3.	D	13.	D
4.	A	14.	D
5.	A	15.	C
6.	D	16.	D
7.	C	17.	C
8.	D	18.	C
9.	A	19.	B
10.	A	20.	B

21.	B
22.	B
23.	D
24.	B
25.	D

TEST 3

DIRECTIONS: Each question or incomplete statement is followed by several suggested answers or completions. Select the one that BEST answers the question or completes the statement. *PRINT THE LETTER OF THE CORRECT ANSWER IN THE SPACE AT THE RIGHT.*

1. One of the first types of schools to operate in colonial America was the "Dame School," so named because it

    A. was open only to young women of rank, station, or authority
    B. existed primarily to teach young ladies etiquette
    C. was established by the British Crown to maintain strong ties with the homeland
    D. was set up in the home of the teacher, who was usually a single young woman

2. Which of the following is an information clearinghouse that contains descriptions of exemplary education programs, research results, and other information that can be used by teachers?

    A. NCES
    B. EBSCO
    C. PubEd
    D. ERIC

3. The contrasting views of W.E.B. Dubois and Booker T. Washington about how African Americans ought to be educated in the early 20th century was, on its face, a debate about whether the curriculum should be more scholarly and academic, or practical and vocational in nature. This conflict reflected a tension between

    A. well-schooled Northern and poorly-schooled Southern African-Americans
    B. radical and conservative approaches to achieving racial equality
    C. white Americans and their views about how African-Americans should be integrated into society
    D. empirical scientific reasoning and classic spiritual thought

4. _____ tests assess the lowest level of acceptable student performance in various academic content areas.

    A. outcome-based
    B. standardized
    C. norm-referenced
    D. minimum competency

5. The typical school district spends most of its budget on

    A. student services
    B. administration
    C. operations and maintenance
    D. instructional services

6. Which of the following court cases was related to the timeliness of providing special education placement and services?   6.___

   A. *PASE v. Hannon* (1978)
   B. *Rowley v. Board of Education* (1982)
   C. *Jose P. v. Ambach* (1983)
   D. *Irving Independent School District v. Tatro* (1984)

7. As an indirect scheme of providing funding for schools, state tax credit plans resemble the strategy of   7.___

   A. equalization programs
   B. vouchers
   C. charter schools
   D. site-based management

8. In the United States, teacher shortages have traditionally been more acute in   8.___

   A. suburban areas
   B. Western states
   C. large cities
   D. rural areas

9. When Harvard University was founded in 1636, its purpose was primarily to   9.___

   A. train leaders who would serve the new colonial governments
   B. establish a divinity school to strengthen the ranks of colonial clergy
   C. provide a general classical education to anyone who could afford it
   D. serve as a satellite university for the English academy

10. A curriculum that is perennialistic will place emphasis on   10.___

    A. appreciating diversity
    B. discovering the inner self
    C. intellectual growth in the arts and sciences
    D. global social changes

11. Traditionally, a student who is considered "gifted" or "exceptional" in most schools has   11.___

    A. demonstrated high achievement in the visual or performing arts
    B. scored above a certain level on an IQ or other standardized test
    C. been recognized for outstanding achievement in any of several extracurricular activities, including sports, journalism, the arts, or business
    D. demonstrated remarkable leadership ability

12. Purposes of bilingual education include each of the following, EXCEPT to   12.___

    A. help students maintain an ethnic identity
    B. encourage assimilation into the school culture
    C. gradually phase out the use of the home language
    D. integrate the home language and culture into the mainstream

13. In *Tinker v. Des Moines Independent Community School District* (1969), the Supreme Court ruled that   13.___

A. public authorities did not have the right to apprehend students who were staging a disorderly demonstration against the Vietnam War
   B. public authorities did not have the right to silence students' political or ideological statements because they disagree with them
   C. schools could not sponsor student publications unless the publications were considered part of the curriculum
   D. student journalists had the right to control the editorial content of student publications

14. Critics of teacher reliance on behavioral objectives in schools argue that if they are overused, they can produce   14.____

   A. a lack of student motivation
   B. mechanized and oversimplified teaching
   C. repetitive instructional practices
   D. an emphasis on obedience over learning

15. The revised federal Individuals with Disabilities Education Act (IDEA) states that the services provided to a child with a disability must based on   15.____

   A. the child's specific educational needs
   B. the child's disability category
   C. the parents' or guardians' specific wishes
   D. the resources available at the particular educational institution

16. Across the United States, the leaders of state departments of elementary and secondary education are united informally through an organization known as the   16.____

   A. Committee on Educational Reform
   B. Council of Chief State School Officers
   C. Association of State Superintendents
   D. Coalition of Essential Schools

17. Jerome Bruner's model of learning asserts that it   17.____

   A. takes place through observation and modeling of the behaviors of others
   B. is achieved through operant conditioning and schedules of reinforcement
   C. is an active process in which students construct new ideas or concepts based on their current knowledge.
   D. is simply a reconstruction of experiences

18. The most common explanation of why males and females achieve differently in school is that they   18.____

   A. differ in their rates of stress and depression
   B. have different levels of self-esteem
   C. have brain structures and physiologies that are subtly different from each other
   D. are undergoing the process of sex-role socialization

19. In the case of _____ , the U.S. Supreme Court ultimately ruled that parents could not interfere with reasonable methods chosen by public school officials for maintaining discipline.   19.____

A. *McNeese v. Board of Education* (1962)
B. *Baker v. Owen* (1975)
C. *Maine v. Thiboutot* (1980)
D. *Webb v. Board of Education* (1985)

20. Which of the following is NOT considered to be a key dimension of professionalism in teaching?

    A. Lifelong learning and development
    B. Involvement in peer societies and improvement activities
    C. Compliance with bureaucratic authorities
    D. Codified standards of behavior

21. Research in school effectiveness has suggested that each of the following is a factor that consistently contributes to instructional effectiveness, EXCEPT

    A. maintaining high expectations of what can be achieved
    B. substantial staff development time
    C. grouping students in homogeneous arrangements
    D. maintaining a safe and pleasant learning environment

22. In the Information Age, public schools have generally been slower to achieve technological change than other sectors of society. The most likely reason for this is the

    A. rapid rate of change in school organization
    B. lack of available funds
    C. lack of a focused and organized effort to bring technology into the schools
    D. decentralized configuration of the public school system

23. The social reconstructionists of the 1920s and 1930s differed from the progressives and pragmatists, such as Dewey, in that they

    A. aligned themselves with an approach that was more cognitive than behavioral
    B. were more provocative in advocating systemic change
    C. focused on the promotion of cultural literacy
    D. de-emphasized learning for learning's sake

24. Title IX of the Educational Amendment Act specifically forbids discrimination in the schools that is based on

    A. gender
    B. religion
    C. race
    D. disability

25. One of the arguments in favor of a student-centered curriculum is that it

    A. specifies the scope and sequence of learning experiences
    B. provides for systematic testing of student progress
    C. promotes a teacher's own judgement in selecting content appropriate for a given group of learners
    D. clearly delineates a teacher's responsibilities for developing given skills and knowledge

KEY (CORRECT ANSWERS)

1. D
2. D
3. B
4. D
5. C

6. C
7. B
8. C
9. A
10. C

11. B
12. C
13. B
14. B
15. A

16. B
17. C
18. D
19. B
20. C

21. C
22. D
23. B
24. A
25. C

TEST 4

DIRECTIONS: Each question or incomplete statement is followed by several suggested answers or completions. Select the one that BEST answers the question or completes the statement. *PRINT THE LETTER OF THE CORRECT ANSWER IN THE SPACE AT THE RIGHT.*

1. The Coalition of Essential Schools (CES) is a national network of high schools guided in their restructuring efforts by a set of common principles. Which of the following is NOT one of these principles?

    A. Teaching and learning should be personalized to the maximum feasible extent.
    B. Teachers should introduce a broad, comprehensive range of content, rather than exploring a few subjects in depth.
    C. Teachers should perceive themselves as generalists first (teachers and scholars in general education) and specialists second (experts in but one particular discipline).
    D. The governing practical metaphor of the school should be student-as-worker.

2. Although the educational philosophies of perennialism and essential-ism may seem similar, there are significant differences. Which of the following best explains this difference?

    A. Perennialism focuses first on personal development, while essentialism focuses first on essential skills.
    B. Essentialism insists on consequences, utility and practicality as vital components of truth, while perennialism that human concepts and intellect represent reality.
    C. Essentialist curricula thus tend to be much more liberal and principle-based, and far less vocational and fact-based.
    D. Perennialism focuses on human solutions to human issues through rational thought, more than on sacred texts, traditions or religious creeds.

3. Most school-related court cases involve the

    A. establishment clause of the 1st Amendment
    B. 4th Amendment protections against unreasonable search and seizure
    C. 10th Amendment provision for limited federal government
    D. equal protection clause of the 14th Amendment

4. In _____ assessment, teachers gather or receive data for making decisions about how they can improve their teaching techniques.

    A. contextual
    B. summative
    C. real-time
    D. formative

5. Membership in the National Education Association (NEA) is open to
    I. guidance counselors
    II. school support staff
    III. administrators
    IV. school board members

A. I only
B. I, II and III
C. I, III and IV
D. None of the above

6. One way in which schools attempt to deal with their changing student populations is to encourage minority students to _____ , or become more like the majority student population.

   A. desegregate
   B. pluralize
   C. assimilate
   D. differentiate

7. Colonial secondary grammar schools tended to emphasize

   A. math and science
   B. the practical arts
   C. a classical curriculum
   D. reading and writing

8. The "concept formation" method of instruction usually aims for students to construct knowledge about a specific idea through

   A. analyzing and synthesizing data
   B. reading and committing information to memory
   C. evaluating and applying data
   D. observing and identifying things in their immediate environment

9. Federal copyright law was amended in 1980 to state that teachers could

   A. not lawfully make any copies of a software program
   B. make multiple copies of a software program after at least one copy was purchased
   C. make multiple copies of a software program but must restrict their use to the classroom
   D. make a single backup copy of a software program

10. Under federal law, school districts are responsible for evaluating at public expense all students suspected of having disabilities from birth through _____ years of age.

    A. 16
    B. 18
    C. 21
    D. 25

11. Under the principle of "academic freedom," American teachers have the right to

    A. make the ultimate decision about which texts will be used in the classroom
    B. determine the most appropriate teaching strategy without any unwarranted restrictions
    C. make the ultimate decision on course content
    D. teach the curriculum in any way they choose

12. In the provisions of the Child Abuse Prevention and Treatment Act (CAPTA) of 1974, it is noted that

    A. a teacher's failure to report suspected child abuse constitutes a breach of contract
    B. a teacher should report child abuse only after certain signs occur repeatedly or in combination
    C. child abuse can occur at any socioeconomic level, to both males and females
    D. a teacher should report cases of abuse or neglect resulting in physical injury to a child only if the child corroborates that the abuse has occurred

13. Research on school redesign, conducted in the late 20th and early 21st centuries, documented several characteristics that were consistently associated with successful schools. Which of the following was NOT one of them?

    A. A substantial tax base
    B. Instruction and assessment rooted in a primary concern for high standards of intellectual quality
    C. Increased levels of external support
    D. Focus on student learning

14. Research into the relative success of Asian and Asian-American students in the United States indicates that the most significant factor in this success is

    A. their relative disinterest in extracurricular activities
    B. their status as a "model minority"
    C. the high expectations of their parents and teachers
    D. a relatively high socioeconomic status

15. Which of the following is NOT a principle associated with the concept of authentic assessment?

    A. Eliciting higher order thinking in addition to basic skills
    B. Allowing for the possibility of multiple human judgments
    C. Comparison of results to norm-referenced standards
    D. Direct evaluation of holistic projects

16. The Massachusetts Act of 1647-known also as the Old Deluder Satan Act-was the first law in America requiring that

    A. schools could not restrict a student's religious expression
    B. children could be removed from homes in which parents were failing to educate them properly
    C. every town must have a school
    D. students were compelled to participate in religious activities at school

17. Each of the following has been a major source of state funding for schools, EXCEPT

    A. real estate property taxes
    B. income tax
    C. "sin" taxes
    D. sales tax

18. Which of the following is a classroom observational system in which the verbal interactions between a teacher and the entire class are coded and analyzed?

    A. Sizer
    B. Flesch
    C. Randers
    D. Montessori

19. In the early twenty-first century, for-profit firms seeking contracts to administer schools have generally done one or more of the following, EXCEPT

    A. provide specific support services
    B. focus on specific activities
    C. specialize in underperforming schools
    D. provide a pool of teaching talent

20. Intermediate Educational Units (IEUs) are organizations that operate in states when

    A. the state is large and has a population divided into largely urban and rural subsets, without a significant suburban element
    B. a significant number of high school graduates require remedial instruction to prepare them for college coursework
    C. school districts pool their resources to provide resources and services for costly educational programs
    D. laws governing education have been passed by the legislature, but the districts lack adequate funds to implement them

21. One argument in favor of subject-centered curriculum is that it

    A. allows a wider range of activities that can be creatively planned by the teacher
    B. accommodates individual developmental and behavioral differences
    C. relieves the teacher from having to follow a prescribed sequence and range
    D. reduces overlap and redundancies between grade levels or different sections of the same class

22. John Dewey's explanation for why some students do not like the subject of history would be that

    A. they simply do not yet have enough personal experiences to apply towards history
    B. most are still at the preconventional stage of moral reasoning and cannot judge events in their proper moral context
    C. the teacher has not constructed adequate "scaffolding" to generate interest
    D. they have a poorly defined superego

23. Which of the following statements about tracking or ability grouping is FALSE?

    A. It is prevalent because it is easier on teachers.
    B. It tends to hinder the achievement of low-ability students.
    C. Lower groups tend to be overstocked with cultural minority groups.
    D. It tends to reduce the self-esteem and motivation of low-ability students.

24. Funding for educational programs that are designed for specific groups and purposes, such as bilingual education, are typically funded through federal _____ grants.

    A. Clark
    B. categorical
    C. blanket
    D. block

25. The direction of American education in the early 19th century was influenced by the methods of Prussian schools, as developed by Johann Heinrich Pestalozzi. Pestalozzi described the process of teaching as

    A. molding the child into a productive member of society
    B. leading the child to his or her proper place in the social network
    C. imparting the knowledge necessary for the child to make decisions about how he should be governed
    D. directing the child in the unfolding of his latent powers

KEY (CORRECT ANSWERS)

1.	B	11.	B
2.	A	12.	C
3.	D	13.	A
4.	D	14.	C
5.	B	15.	C
6.	C	16.	C
7.	B	17.	A
8.	A	18.	C
9.	D	19.	D
10.	C	20.	C

21. D
22. A
23. A
24. B
25. D

PROFESSIONAL EDUCATION

EXAMINATION SECTION
TEST 1

DIRECTIONS: Each question or incomplete statement is followed by several suggested answers or completions. Select the one that BEST answers the question or completes the statement. *PRINT THE LETTER OF THE CORRECT ANSWER IN THE SPACE AT THE RIGHT.*

1. Locke's great influence was not exerted *until* 1._____

    A. Comenius made his ideas practical
    B. Rousseau set forth is views
    C. Ratke popularized his views in METHODUS NOVA
    D. Bacon issued his ADVANCEMENT OF LEARNING

2. In the NOVUM ORGANUM, there was formulated 2._____

    A. the catechetical method
    B. the method of inductive reasoning
    C. the reorganization of the sciences
    D. a system of encyclopaedic education

3. The theory of formal discipline was championed CHIEFLY by the 3._____

    A. Humanists   B. Sophists   C. Realists   D. Behaviorists

4. In the ORGANON, Aristotle formulated a(n) 4._____

    A. code of moral conduct
    B. method of scientific politics
    C. method of deductive reasoning
    D. ideal system of State education

5. The teaching of history and literature was emphasized by Herbart chiefly for their 5._____

    A. patriotic value   B. practical value
    C. social value   D. content value

6. Horace Mann is BEST known for 6._____

    A. bringing Pestalozzian methods to America
    B. establishing free, nonsectarian education
    C. establishing high schools
    D. establishing State boards of education

7. The "Indus" was the elementary school of the 7._____

    A. Athenians   B. Romans
    C. early Christians   D. monks of the Middle Ages

41

8. The RATIO STUDIORUM encouraged

   A. pupil participation in the recitations
   B. initiative of the teachers
   C. differentiation of subject matter to meet the needs of the pupils
   D. free discipline

9. The OUTSTANDING characteristic of the content of Chinese education was its emphasis upon

   A. human relationships
   B. material prosperity
   C. property rights
   D. intellectual progress

10. The type of education during the Renaissance movement known as "Ciceronianism" stressed

    A. breadth of learning
    B. social reform
    C. grace of style
    D. intellectual freedom

11. "Negative education," according to Rousseau, meant

    A. compelling a pupil arbitrarily to learn something
    B. using artificial incentive to stimulate the pupil to study
    C. permitting the pupil to learn what he feels the need of knowing
    D. instructing the child in the duties that belong to a man

12. Which one of the following ideas may NOT be ascribed to Comenius?

    A. A graded system of schools for both boys and girls beginning in infancy and continuing through the university
    B. An improved method of teaching languages
    C. The use of objective methods
    D. A complete separation in aims and objectives of the church and the school

13. Which of the following statements is NOT true? Froebel

    A. accepted Rousseau's emphasis upon the rights of childhood
    B. agreed with Pestalozzi that education is the harmonious development of all the powers of the individual
    C. has greatly influenced our present educational system
    D. accepted Rousseau's belief that the child should have little or no social training

14. The educational tendency with which the name of John Locke is associated is

    A. humanistic
    B. disciplinary
    C. naturalistic
    D. psychological

15. A name *largely* identified with investigation in the field of reading is

    A. Ayres   B. Stanford   C. Yerkes   D. Gray

16. Colonial America was MOST interested in

    A. primary education
    B. advanced education
    C. agricultural education
    D. commercial education

17. The Puritans in New England, in respect to elementary education, believed in   17._____
    A. compulsory maintenance   B. pauper school maintenance
    C. church maintenance   D. voluntary maintenance

18. The FIRST city public school system to introduce kindergartens was   18._____
    A. Boston   B. Oswego   C. St. Louis   D. Philadelphia

19. The name of the learning theory associated with Skinner is the   19._____
    A. Reinforcement Theory
    B. Trial and Error Learning Theory
    C. Sign Learning Theory
    D. Conditioned Response Theory

20. Of the following concepts, the one LEAST consonant with John Dewey's philosophy of   20._____
    education is
    A. learning through experience
    B. extrinsic motivation
    C. emphasis on the learner rather than on the subject
    D. democracy and pragmatism

21. Dr. James Bryant Conant wrote all of the following EXCEPT   21._____
    A. THE SCHOOLS
    B. SLUMS AND SUBURBS
    C. MODERN SCIENCE AND MODERN MAN
    D. EDUCATION IN A DIVIDED WORLD

22. Which one of the following educators is NOT noted for his work in the field of intelligence 22._____
    testing?
    A. Louis Terman   B. Rudolph Pintner
    C. David Wechsler   D. Robert Hutchins

23. Spearman is known for his concept of intelligence as consisting of   23._____
    A. the interaction of numerous specific and general factors
    B. a single general factor
    C. a general factor and many specific factors
    D. a limited number of specific factors

24. The concept of the IQ was introduced by   24._____
    A. Binet   B. Goddard   C. Stern   D. Witmer

25. Which one of the following statements is TRUE with regard to the "activity program?" 25._____
    A. The child is displaced as the center of the educative process.
    B. Maximum preparation for effective group living is considered essential.
    C. The learning of a definite body of factual material is stressed.
    D. Distinct effort is made to keep children "up to standard" in drill subjects.

KEY (CORRECT ANSWERS)

1. B
2. B
3. C
4. C
5. C

6. A
7. B
8. B
9. A
10. C

11. C
12. D
13. D
14. B
15. D

16. A
17. B
18. C
19. A
20. B

21. A
22. D
23. C
24. C
25. B

TEST 2

DIRECTIONS: Each question or incomplete statement is followed by several suggested answers or completions. Select the one that BEST answers the question or completes the statement. *PRINT THE LETTER OF THE CORRECT ANSWER IN THE SPACE AT THE RIGHT.*

1. In planning a trip to a market in connection with a core on food,   1.____

    A. the teacher should ask all the children to observe carefully and to report on as many different things as they see
    B. a committee composed of a few children should be held responsible for formulating a report on the trip
    C. definite questions should be formulated before the trip is taken for the purpose of finding answers to them
    D. questions need not be provided, since follow-up activities should be left to the initiative of the pupils

2. In order to secure good group play activities in her class, the teacher of a class should plan   2.____

    A. classroom procedures with a view to minimizing individual play activities on the part of her children
    B. for personal participation in every group play activity which is organized
    C. to play with small groups several times before the children play without her
    D. to set aside one day a week for independent group play activity

3. The instrument MOST useful for determining interpersonal relationships in the classroom is the   3.____

    A. Vineland Social Maturity Scale
    B. Kuder Preference Record
    C. sociogram
    D. California Test of Personality

4. The IQ of a pupil is determined by the following formula: 4.____

    A. MA/CA   B. CA/MA   C. CA/SM   D. MA/SM

5. John and Paul have mental ages of 9-4 on the Stanford-Binet, Form L. From these results, it can be inferred that *each*   5.____

    A. will achieve at about the same level
    B. has an equivalent vocabulary
    C. may be quite different in intellectual functioning
    D. has the same level of aspiration

6. Mary and Helen each have an IQ of 67 on the Stanford-Binet, Form M. Mary has a reading grade of 3.4 and Helen a reading grade of 3.2. These data *suggest* that   6.____

    A. the reading level is in terms of the IQ for both
    B. Mary's IQ must be higher because her reading grade is higher
    C. Helen's progress in general will be slower
    D. general school achievement cannot be predicted from the above results

45

7. Basal age on the Stanford-Binet means

   A. one year below the actual mental age
   B. the year level up through which all the test items are passed
   C. one year above the actual chronological age
   D. the lowest year level at which all the test times are failed

8. A notation on a psychologist's report reads as follows: "Lucy is at the 30th percentile on this test when compared with the norms for her age group." This means that Lucy

   A. exceeded 30% of her age group
   B. had answered 30% of the questions correctly
   C. had failed 30% of the questions
   D. was exceeded by 30% of her age group

9. Which *one* of the following names is identified with school achievement testing?

   A. Goodenough   B. Henmon-Nelson
   C. Metropolitan   D. Kuhlmann-Anderson

10. A child in your class scores 2.7 in an arithmetic test. His IQ is 69. Which of the following is the MOST important in determining whether or not he is working at capacity?

    A. Mean and standard deviation for the class
    B. Range of scores for the class
    C. Chronological age
    D. Social intelligence

11. Andrew uses a large wheel on his desk to steer an imaginary car. He is frequently heard to say, "Make that light," "Turn this way," "Slow down," etc.
    His behavior is an example of

    A. sublimation   B. fantasy   C. retrogression   D. introjection

12. Ronald, a severely retarded boy in your class, tells the other children that he will join the air force and become a famous pilot. He is using the adjustive mechanism of

    A. abreaction   B. conversion
    C. compensation   D. reaction-formation

13. A motor disturbance that lacks any appearance of purpose beyond the action itself is called a(n)

    A. phobia   B. tic   C. compulsion   D. obsession

14. The child reacts to the classroom situation in terms of his

    A. intelligence   B. home background
    C. social development   D. past experience

15. Several children have complained that the other children in the school "push them around" in the school cafeteria. You *should*

    A. arrange for the children to eat earlier or later than the other children
    B. discipline the children who were accused
    C. indicate that if the pupils were better behaved, they would not be "pushed around"
    D. treat it as a problem usual among all children

16. The day before the Easter Vacation the mother of one of your boys tells you that she   16._____
    plans a trip to Washington, D.C., for the school holiday period and that she hesitates to
    take the boy with her because he may be tbo dull to benefit by the trip. You *should suggest*

    A. leaving him with his grandmother
    B. that she board him out for the period involved
    C. an early appointment with the school social worker
    D. that she take the child with her

17. The principal asks the teachers in a junior high school how they feel regarding their   17._____
    classes' participation in the school's safety patrol unit. As the teacher of a class in this
    school, your reply should be that the children of your class

    A. are likely to be injured in this kind of activity
    B. will not be obeyed by the other children in the school
    C. would not like this kind of assignment
    D. would be glad to participate

18. A widely used sight vocabulary list of 220 words *other than* nouns has been prepared by   18._____

    A. Gray   B. Dolch   C. Gates   D. Thorndike

19. The teacher of a class of adolescent students feels the need for a test of oral reading   19._____
    performance in order to obtain a more comprehensive picture of the reading skills of her
    group. A test MOST suitable for this purpose was devised by

    A. Thorndike   B. Harris   C. Gray   D. Kirk

20. The MOST important reason why basal readers are usually inadequate for the slow   20._____
    learner is the

    A. over-abundance of illustrations
    B. insufficient repetition accorded new words
    C. heavy vocabulary load
    D. discrepancy between pupil interests and content

21. In developing functional reading materials on a third-grade level for one of the reading   21._____
    groups in a class of retarded students, the teacher should

    A. refer to the Thorndike lists for the vocabulary to be used and integrate the material
       with the core being taught
    B. extract interesting material from basal readers employing a vocabulary they can
       read with ease
    C. integrate the material with the core being taught employing a functional vocabulary
       not exceeding the third year level
    D. integrate the material with the core being taught, employing the functional vocabulary necessary even if it exceeds the third year level

22. In teaching spelling, the BEST procedure is   22._____

    A. an incidental method best suited to each individual
    B. the application of a minimum number of basic rules for spelling
    C. to permit the student to use his own methods
    D. a systematic method with the entire group

23. The spelling words to be taught to children should be

   A. those functional words which are most often mispelled in children's writings
   B. Board of Education spelling lists for the grade levels involved
   C. those functional words which center about the core
   D. those words which they will write in their everyday living

24. A teacher must recognize that specific skills

   A. must be taught apart from other learnings in order to be most effective
   B. can rarely be integrated with the curricular core
   C. are to be tied into the core experience
   D. are to be taught on occasion as the situation calls for them

25. John, a withdrawn child, often brings curious objects to class, such as dead frogs, a broken clock, and pictures from old magazines. The teacher *should*

   A. ignore his bizarre behavior as much as possible
   B. speak to him privately about leaving such objects at home
   C. hold the objects for him until the end of the day
   D. organize class discussions around the objects

KEY (CORRECT ANSWERS)

1.	C	11.	B
2.	B	12.	C
3.	C	13.	B
4.	A	14.	D
5.	C	15.	D
6.	D	16.	D
7.	B	17.	D
8.	A	18.	B
9.	C	19.	B
10.	C	20.	D

21. D
22. D
23. D
24. C
25. D

TEST 3

DIRECTIONS: Each question or incomplete statement is followed by several suggested answers or completions. Select the one that BEST answers the question or completes the statement. *PRINT THE LETTER OF THE CORRECT ANSWER IN THE SPACE AT THE RIGHT.*

1. Of the following techniques, the one that is of MOST value to the junior high school teacher in curricular planning is

    A. sociograms
    B. projective tests
    C. problem checklists
    D. anecdotal records

2. In order to use standardized test results as a basis for a remedial program for a class, a teacher *should*

    A. use the average grade score made by the class to determine the level at which to begin instruction
    B. begin instruction at the level attained by the poorest pupil
    C. use the items failed by pupils making the highest scores to determine the topics which need emphasis
    D. analyze the items most frequently failed to develop an inventory of common errors

3. In general, the MOST powerful predictors of subsequent vocational successes have been

    A. personality tests
    B. interest tests
    C. clinical interviews
    D. school records

4. The distinction between aptitude tests and achievement tests is CHIEFLY one of

    A. type of content
    B. predictive power
    C. purpose for which used
    D. breadth of content

5. The FUNDAMENTAL characteristic which Binet and Simon believed their early intelligence tests tapped was the

    A. ability to make sound judgments
    B. speed of reaction to oral stimuli
    C. understanding of oral directions
    D. ability to develop vocabulary

6. Of the following terms, the *one* that applies to the development of wholesome mental and emotional reactions and habits is called

    A. psychoanalysis
    B. psychotherapy
    C. mental hygiene
    D. clinical psychology

7. The term *ambivalent* is used to describe a child who

    A. is given to creating dissension among the others
    B. makes a statement and later amplifies it with conscious intent
    C. seems to be day dreaming while actually alert
    D. is aggressive at times and friendly at other times

8. The symbol "AQ" is used to denote the *result* of

   A. iq/ma   B. MA/EA   C. EA/AA   D. AA/MA

9. The term *commonly* used in statistics to refer to the average of a group of scores is the

   A. mean   B. mode   C. central tendency   D. median

10. The BASIC function of the educational and vocational counselor in a coordinated junior high school guidance program is

    A. maintaining adequate guidance records
    B. assembling and disseminating vocational information
    C. work with individual children
    D. coordinating the resources of community agencies

11. When an instrument used as a counseling tool measures what it *purports* to measure, it

    A. has validity   B. has reliability
    C. is standardized   D. is objective

12. A *case study* is a

    A. rating of a pupil's development used in guiding his educational and vocational choices and in correcting personality faults
    B. developmental record of facts and insights about an individual
    C. story of the pupil's life written by the pupil himself
    D. narrative of events in which the pupil reveals something which may be significant about his personality

13. The formula, EA/MA,

    A. gives an index showing whether a personal knowledge and understanding of a group of school subjects are commensurate with his life age
    B. yields a quotient which shows whether or not the individual is working up to capacity
    C. yields a ratio of one's mental age to one's life age
    D. indicates each pupil's position in the hierarchy of intelligence

14. Sociometric testing provides a technique for

    A. analyzing each person's position and status within the group with respect to a particular criterion
    B. revealing the prejudices of each individual
    C. obtaining a picture of boy-girl relationships
    D. analyzing the pupil's understanding of the problems faced by society and encouraging efforts to solve them

15. In the field of psychological testing, the term *norm* may be used to designate

    A. the relationship between the score of the individual and the average of the group
    B. a central tendency of the scores of a specific group
    C. the stages in the intellectucal development of individuals
    D. the relationship between intellectual maturity and the psychological maturity of the group

16. To be of value, anecdotal records of a pupil *should*

    A. describe the teacher's reactions as well as the behavior of the child
    B. objectively describe the child's behavior
    C. be shown to the pupil regularly so that he can see himself as others see him
    D. be periodically circulated among the pupil's teachers so that they may have a better knowledge of what to expect of this pupil

17. A psychological report indicates that a student has been given a Rorschach test. This was used to

    A. test mental ability
    B. discover interests
    C. determine artistic talent
    D. evaluate personality adjustment

18. Three personality inventories or rating scales suitable for use with junior high school pupils are:

    A. Bell Adjustment Inventory, Bernreuter Personality Inventory, Allport A-S Reaction Study
    B. Minnesota Personality Scale, California Test of Mental Maturity, Allport-Vernon Study of Values
    C. California Test of Personality, Haggerty-Olson-Wick-man Behavior Rating Schedules, Washburne Social Adjustment Inventory
    D. Minnesota Multiphasic Personality Inventory, Hurm-Wadsworth Temperament Scale, Dearborn Group Tests

19. THE SCIENCE OF THE EARTH IN RELATION TO NATURE AND THE HISTORY OF MAN was written by

    A. Humboldt   B. Guyot   C. Ritter   D. Froebel

20. Concerning "formal discipline," Spencer held that

    A. it was untenable
    B. only the classics could effect it
    C. scientific studies could effect it
    D. scientific studies could not effect it

21. The methods used in the schools of Lancaster and Bell were

    A. mechanical, inelastic and without psychological foundation
    B. unorganized, wasteful and unproductive
    C. individual, expensive and grossly inefficient
    D. suited as far as possible to the individual needs of the pupils

22. "I wish to psychologize education" is a well-known statement by

    A. Herbart   B. Froebel   C. James   D. Pestalozzi

23. The Public School Society was associated with

    A. New York   B. Philadelphia   C. Boston   D. Charleston

24. First in order of time, in the history of American education, came the

    A. high school
    B. Latin grammar school
    C. academy
    D. normal school

25. The *chief* argument for unification of the first grade and kindergarten is found MAINLY in the fact that

    A. there is no historical justification for the separation
    B. correlation may be secured
    C. there is a large overlapping of mental ages in the two grades
    D. additional drill in the tool subjects may be given to all

KEY (CORRECT ANSWERS)

1.	C	11.	A
2.	D	12.	B
3.	D	13.	B
4.	C	14.	A
5.	A	15.	B
6.	C	16.	B
7.	D	17.	D
8.	D	18.	C
9.	A	19.	C
10.	C	20.	C
21.	A		
22.	D		
23.	A		
24.	B		
25.	C		

TEST 4

DIRECTIONS: Each question or incomplete statement is followed by several suggested answers or completions. Select the one that BEST answers the question or completes the statement. *PRINT THE LETTER OF THE CORRECT ANSWER IN THE SPACE AT THE RIGHT.*

1. *Good* teacher-pupil planning in a class entails   1.____

    A. acceptance of all pupil suggestions
    B. strict adherence to the plan
    C. the teacher's playing a minor role in the planning session
    D. teacher and class evaluation of their success in achieving the plan

2. The MOST important reason why the teacher of a class should group for instruction is to   2.____

    A. make her job easier
    B. meet individual needs and differences realistically
    C. give the children a feeling of working together
    D. avoid conducting the class solely on an individual basis

3. Of the following objectives, the one of LEAST importance in the teaching of art in the elementary grades is to   3.____

    A. provide an outlet of expression for children
    B. produce finished, artistic pieces of work
    C. promote artistic growth in children
    D. increase sensitivity to fine art forms

4. Of the following charges against the modern school, the MOST valid is that it has   4.____

    A. to a large degree neglected the teaching of the basic skills
    B. to a large degree emphasized and condoned "loose" or "free" discipline
    C. to a large degree ignored moral and spiritual values
    D. resulted in interpreting "continuous progress" to mean "100% promotion"

5. Of the following, the BEST reason for emphasis on science in the elementary school is to enable the elementary school curriculum to   5.____

    A. play its proper role in a program of improvement of education
    B. be based on the need for America to live in a "climate of science"
    C. play the major role in coping with the problems of the gifted child
    D. answer the scientific advances made through the Russian schools

6. Given only the information that most "juvenile delinquents" come from low socio-economic neighborhoods, the conclusion that such neighborhoods cause the delinquency is *logically* based on all of the following assumptions EXCEPT   6.____

    A. no other more basic factors cause both the juvenile delinquency and the poor neighborhoods
    B. the higher incidence of such delinquency in low socio-economic areas is not due to chance

53

C. juvenile delinquency is more serious when it occurs in poor neighborhoods
D. the same definition of delinquent behavior has been applied to all socio-economic levels of juveniles

7. To have all children in a given grade in a certain city reading at or above "grade norm" for that grade in that city is

   A. *desirable* since the "norm" represents a minimum for the grade
   B. *immaterial* since the "norm" is merely an arbitrary number set up by "experts" in reading
   C. *difficult* because the "norm" represents a maximum goal intended as a motivating device
   D. *impossible* without changing the "norm" because the "norm" represents the average for the grade

8. Of the following choices for the basis of the goals of education, the one which is BEST is

   A. the needs of the child
   B. the goals of our democratic society
   C. a combination of A and B
   D. the expressed values and wishes of the parents

9. Of the following, the one which is the LEAST valuable reason for considering art an essential area of school experience for elementary school children is that it

   A. provides all children with a means of self-realization
   B. affords excellent opportunities for children to become aware of the values of orderliness, planning and care of materials
   C. provides a way of utilizing, developing and integrating the whole child, nor merely his mental and verbal capacities
   D. allows the gifted child to find himself

10. Of the following purported characteristics of slow learners, the one which is *usually* TRUE is that they are

    A. as much interested in gaining recognition and success in school as faster learners are
    B. very good in manual work
    C. usually motivated by tasks that require constant repetition and little understanding
    D. usually superior to their chronological peers in physical development

11. Of the following possible first steps for helping an awkward child overcome his fear of playground activities, the one which is *usually* BEST is to

    A. give him some easy task connected with the game–"keeping score," for example
    B. send him to another classroom during the game period
    C. insist that he get into the game and play immediately
    D. allow him to work or do something else, alone

12. The last name of the Secretary of the U.S. Department of Health and Human Services from 2005 to 2009 was

    A. Weinberger   B. Thompson   C. Harris   D. Leavitt

13. Of the following statements about unusually bright or gifted young children, the one   13.____
which is INCORRECT is that they are

   A. generally superior in size, muscular control and general health to others of the same age
   B. usually one-sided in their emotional development
   C. usually not eccentric, not queer, and no more unstable than children of "average" mental ability
   D. often difficult to identify at an early age

14. Of the following choices, the one which is MOST effective for a teacher to use in trying to   14.____
learn as much as possible about her children is

   A. standardized tests
   B. informal methods, such as folders of actual work or conferences with the child and his parents
   C. observation of the child's behavior and performance
   D. a combination of all of the above

15. Of the following, the one which is LEAST useful as a practical guide for drill is   15.____

   A. it is better to have a little practice on many skills than much practice on a few skills
   B. a drill exercise should be specific
   C. understanding must precede drill
   D. it is good to have a scoring technique for drill which allows a pupil to watch his daily and weekly progress

16. A VERY important part of "good discipline" in elementary schools involves   16.____

   A. teaching children what is acceptable as well as what is not acceptable behavior in specific circumstances
   B. allowing the children to make nearly all of their own decisions
   C. expecting the children to act like "little ladies and gentlemen" most of the time
   D. adjusting pupil behavior to suit the occasion by allowing complete permissiveness when there are no visitors and requiring absolute quiet when adult company comes

17. In connection with the study of the International Geophysical Year, the one of the follow-   17.____
ing TV programs BEST for elementary school children was

   A. Mr. Wizard   B. Science Fiction Theatre
   C. "See It Now"   D. "80,000 Leagues Under the Sea"

18. An unusually worthwhile TV program called "Sunrise Semester" which featured the study   18.____
of great classics in literature was conducted by

   A. Clifton Fadiman   B. Bergen Evans
   C. Hal March   D. Floyd Zulli, Jr.

19. Teaching of all subjects in the elementary school should be   19.____

   A. on an individual basis
   B. varied to meet the needs of individuals, of groups, and of the whole class
   C. geared to the normal youngsters who make up the majority of the class
   D. always by the unit approach

20. The school should begin the study of science when the

   A. child enters the fifth grade
   B. child enters school
   C. average child enters the junior high school
   D. child has begun to study geography

21. In discussing discipline at an individual parent-teacher meeting, the teacher should try to get the parent to understand the meaning of discipline as

   A. immediate punishment for an infraction of a rule
   B. complete permissiveness so as not to develop any sense of frustration or failure
   C. self-control developed over a long period through understanding, kindness, firmness, and consistency
   D. immediate and unquestioning obedience at all times to adults in authority

22. The IQ is PRIMARILY a measure of

   A. scholastic aptitude
   B. interest in verbal activities
   C. achievements in the 3 R's
   D. ability to adjust to school

23. Of the following statements regarding juvenile delinquency, the one that is *most nearly* true is they

   A. almost invariably come from families of low economic level
   B. are almost invariably of a low intellectual level
   C. are usually more mature socially and physically than other children
   D. often suffer from a combination of emotional illness and lack of conscience

24. The term which *most clearly* expresses the psychological basis of modern educational practice is

   A. atomistic   B. organismic
   C. analytic   D. behavioristic

25. In developing good character traits in young children, the BEST of the following techniques is *probably*

   A. short dramatic discussions on good behavior
   B. TV programs which have good behavior as "the moral"
   C. administration of a personality test and follow-up discussion of the results
   D. the desired type of behavior on the part of the adults with whom the children come into contact regularly

KEY (CORRECT ANSWERS)

1. D
2. B
3. B
4. D
5. A

6. C
7. D
8. C
9. D
10. A

11. A
12. D
13. B
14. D
15. A

16. A
17. A
18. D
19. B
20. B

21. C
22. A
23. D
24. B
25. D

TEST 5

DIRECTIONS: In each of the following questions there is a pair of numbered sentences. Each pair is followed by four lettered choices. Select the choice which indicates your judgment concerning the accuracy of the information contained in *each* of the pairs. *PRINT THE LETTER OF THE CORRECT ANSWER IN THE SPACE AT THE RIGHT.*

1. I. WINDOWS FROM THE CROWN PRINCE is a book dealing with the experiences of a teacher in the Far East.
    II. Two plays dealing with the experiences of teachers are "The King and I" and "Bells are Ringing."

    A. Both I and II are correct
    B. Both I and II are incorrect
    C. I is correct; II is incorrect
    D. I is incorrect; II is correct

    1.____

2. I. Jean Jacques Rousseau based his philosophy of education on his theory of man's natural perfection or perfectibility.
    II. William James was an exponent of pragmatism.

    A. Both I and II are correct
    B. Both I and II are incorrect
    C. I is correct; II is incorrect
    D. I is incorrect; II is correct

    2.____

3. I. The Constitution of the United States clearly provides for equal educational opportunities for all.
    II. The administrative emphasis in the American public school system is upon decentralization and local control.

    A. Both I and II are correct
    B. Both I and II are incorrect
    C. I is correct; II is incorrect
    D. I is incorrect; II is correct

    3.____

4. I. Deprivation of privileges as a means of discipline is most effective if it is logically related to the child's misbehavior.
    II. Deprivation of privileges as a means of discipline is most effective if it is not delayed but immediately follows the misbehavior.

    A. Both I and II are correct
    B. Both I and II are incorrect
    C. I is correct; II is incorrect
    D. I is incorrect; II is correct

    4.____

5. I. The resource unit is designed to provide a guide for the teacher, prescribing exact content and procedures.
    II. Resource units are likely to be most effective when they are used by the group that had no hand in their preparation.

    5.____

A. Both I and II are correct
B. Both I and II are incorrect
C. I is correct; II is incorrect
D. I is incorrect; II is correct

6. I. To discover how much her children are benefiting from classroom instruction, a teacher should use the Stan-ford-Binet Scale or the Wechsler Intelligence Scale.
   II. Standardized tests are of significant value in the guidance of children.

   A. Both I and II are correct
   B. Both I and II are incorrect
   C. I is correct; II is incorrect
   D. I is incorrect; II is correct

6.____

7. I. In parent-teacher conferences, it is easier to build a cooperative relationship if the teacher is not seated behind her desk.
   II. In parent-teacher conferences, the teacher should bear in mind the fact that most parents cannot be objective about their own children.

   A. Both I and II are correct
   B. Both I and II are incorrect
   C. I is correct; II is incorrect
   D. I is incorrect; II is correct

7.____

8. I. Kindergarten children who do not skip should be taught to do so.
   II. Children should not be permitted to read in the kindergarten.

   A. Both I and II are correct
   B. Both I and II are incorrect
   C. I is correct; II is incorrect
   D. I is incorrect; II is correct

8.____

9. I. Kindergarten training in the U.S.S.R. is on a very formal basis and does not include most of the activities carried on in the American kindergarten.
   II. A primary objective in the kindergarten is to increase children's facility in the use of oral language.

   A. Both I and II are correct
   B. Both I and II are incorrect
   C. I is correct; II is incorrect
   D. I is incorrect; II is correct

9.____

10. I. Parents of kindergarten children should never be permitted to stay in the classroom with their children.
    II. Kindergarten children who cry on entering school and refuse to leave their parents should be referred to a psychologist.

    A. Both I and II are correct
    B. Both I and II are incorrect
    C. I is correct; II is incorrect
    D. I is incorrect; II is correct

10.____

11. I. In the elementary school, guidance and teaching are inseparable.
    II. Guidance is concerned primarily with causes, rather than with symptoms.

    A. Both I and II are correct
    B. Both I and II are incorrect
    C. I is correct; II is incorrect
    D. I is incorrect; II is correct

12. I. Science experiments have no place in the kindergarten.
    II. "Just listening" to music has a place in the kindergarten.

    A. Both I and II are correct
    B. Both I and II are incorrect
    C. I is correct; II is incorrect
    D. I is incorrect; II is correct

13. I. The "Corsi Bill" permitting corporal punishment in schools was passed by the New York State Legislature and was vetoed by the Governor.
    II. Homogeneous grouping on the basis of IQ assures classes of similar abilities in reading and mathematics.

    A. Both I and II are correct
    B. Both I and II are incorrect
    C. I is correct; II is incorrect
    D. I is incorrect; II is correct

14. I. There is a high correlation between success in reading and achievement in other fields.
    II. There is a high correlation between success in mathematics and IQ.

    A. Both I and II are correct
    B. Both I and II are incorrect
    C. I is correct; II is incorrect
    D. I is incorrect; II is correct

15. I. Following the Supreme Court decision banning segregated schools, all states have undertaken at least token integration of the races in their schools.
    II. Congress recently passed a bill making direct grants to the various states for the purpose of increasing teachers' salaries.

    A. Both I and II are correct
    B. Both I and II are incorrect
    C. I is correct; II is incorrect
    D. I is incorrect; I is correct

16. I. The five-year-old cannot work for prolonged periods of time, and is not capable of completing a project.
    II. Differences are great even among "typical" children.

    A. Both I and II are correct
    B. Both I and II are incorrect
    C. I is correct; II is incorrect
    D. I is incorrect; II is correct

17. I. Lack of language facility is a significant factor in the negativism and resistance to authority which are normal for five-year-olds.
    II. At times a kindergarten teacher is justified in arbitrarily assigning children to groups or tasks without regard for their preferences.

    A. Both I and II are correct
    B. Both I and II are incorrect
    C. I is correct; II is incorrect
    D. I is incorrect; II is correct

18. I. UNESCO, an agency of the United Nations, has as its principal objective, the promotion of a world government.
    II. The National Education Association is an agency of the Federal Government.

    A. Both I and II are correct
    B. Both I and II are incorrect
    C. I is correct; II is incorrect
    D. I is incorrect; II is correct

19. I. A. T. Jersild is a writer in the field of child psychology.
    II. James L. Hymes has written extensively on the teaching of reading.

    A. Both I and II are correct
    B. Both I and II are incorrect
    C. I is correct; II is incorrect
    D. I is incorrect; II is correct

20. I. Comenius based his philosophy of education on his theory of man's perfection or perfectibility.
    II. Maria Montessori emphasized the necessity of play in the education of the young child.

    A. Both I and II are correct
    B. Both I and II are incorrect
    C. I is correct; II is incorrect
    D. I is incorrect; II is correct

KEY (CORRECT ANSWERS)

1.	C	11.	C
2.	A	12.	D
3.	D	13.	C
4.	A	14.	A
5.	B	15.	B
6.	D	16.	D
7.	A	17.	A
8.	C	18.	B
9.	D	19.	C
10.	B	20.	B

EXAMINATION SECTION
TEST 1

DIRECTIONS: Each question or incomplete statement is followed by several suggested answers or completions. Select the one that BEST answers the question or completes the statement. *PRINT THE LETTER OF THE CORRECT ANSWER IN THE SPACE AT THE RIGHT.*

1. The statement among the following which is NOT appropriately applied to the modern concept of individualized education is: 1.____

    A. Growth and learning are almost synonymous.
    B. Readiness for learning is determined by the individual's intellectual acumen.
    C. Standardized teaching methods may run counter to the individual's optimum learning methods.
    D. The good life is not fully realized unless maximum individual and social growth is taking place.

2. The description among the following which is NOT properly associated with core curriculum is: 2.____

    A. Units which cut across subject fields and which may be taught by one or more teachers are used.
    B. Learning is centered on large topics around which activities are organized.
    C. Pupils play a major part in planning, launching, and developing the work of the group.
    D. Activities, excursions, and community resources are utilized instead of textbooks and research.

3. In which one of the following areas does conditioning play a major role? 3.____

    A. Development of motor skills
    B. Acquisition of facts
    C. Development of attitudes
    D. Formation of concepts

4. Most present-day psychologists accept the principle that drill should be used in the modern classroom only when 4.____

    A. reviewing material that has already been covered
    B. it is necessary to clarify pupil understanding of a concept
    C. test results reveal poor mastery of factual material
    D. an automatic response is considered desirable

5. Of the following, which would ordinarily be the LEAST effective means of modifying an attitude? 5.____

    A. Listening to a lecture
    B. Role playing
    C. A panel discussion following a film
    D. Group discussion

6. In the guidance of pupil learning, research has indicated that

    A. emphasis on correct responses is more effective than emphasis on errors
    B. demonstration is more effective than practice
    C. massed practice is more effective than distributed practice
    D. verbal guidance is more effective than demonstration

7. In grades kindergarten through 2, mathematics is taught by the teacher

    A. in a definite sequence, beginning in first grade
    B. in a definite sequence, beginning in the kindergarten
    C. in a definite sequence, beginning in the second grade
    D. as the topics arise naturally from projects in other areas or from real experiences

8. Which one of the following procedures is of MOST value in developing problem-solving ability in grades 1-4?

    A. Children should be encouraged to solve problems in a variety of ways.
    B. Children should represent problems symbolically before attempting to solve them.
    C. Most problems should be presented to children in written form.
    D. Problems presented in written form should be discussed before children attempt to solve them.

9. Which one of the following incentives should be stressed by the teacher in promoting learning of a given skill by her pupils?

    A. Need to use the skill
    B. Desire to please the teacher
    C. Fear of low grades or failure
    D. Desire for good grades

10. The rate of forgetting of information acquired by rote memorization is

    A. gradually accelerating
    B. gradually decelerating
    C. slow at first, and then more rapid
    D. rapid at first, and then slower

11. Questioning is one of the most valuable devices of the teacher. Of the following, which statement is the LEAST valid?

    A. A good question provides for reflective or critical thinking.
    B. Teachers' questions can directly affect the development of children's thinking skills.
    C. Questions are useful in diagnosing an individual child's progress.
    D. Effective questions result from the innate talents of teachers.

12. Each of the following principles is valid in daily planning EXCEPT that it

    A. includes specific time allotments to the topics to be taught
    B. reflects the needs, interests, and abilities of the children
    C. provides sufficient time for all subject areas
    D. is flexible to allow for unexpected occurrences

13. Of the following classroom practices, the one which is generally UNDESIRABLE is: 13.____

    A. Whenever possible, classroom bulletin boards and charts should be placed at children's eye level.
    B. Windows in the classroom should be covered with crepe paper to make the room attractive
    C. Classroom "centers of interest" should vary from grade to grade in accordance with children's learning needs
    D. A room indicator card should be used to indicate the whereabouts of the class when it is not in the classroom

14. The MOST effective method of helping children to develop the concept of cooperation is to provide 14.____

    A. opportunities for listening to stories about children cooperating with each other
    B. speakers to tell about how they cooperated with people of various ethnic groups
    C. audio-visual materials which illustrate the concept of cooperation among ethnic groups
    D. many experiences that will involve them in cooperating with children of different ethnic groups

15. The LEAST effective strategy in stimulating children to express themselves orally in social studies lessons would be for the teacher to 15.____

    A. direct questions to specific children and get a response
    B. encourage children to talk with classmates and to give guidance when needed
    C. accept contributions from all the children
    D. help shy children express their ideas

16. Of the following statements regarding pupil discussion, the LEAST valid is: 16.____

    A. Use of the amenities helps to move a discussion forward
    B. Discussion of a topic or problem leads to a solution or an agreement
    C. A discussion period allows for an honest interchange of comments among pupils
    D. Discussion by pupils is more or less organized talking directed to a matter of common concern

17. Of the following, the MOST valid reason for using mimeographed sheets for homework assignments for pupils is that 17.____

    A. the chance of pupil error in copying the assignment from the blackboard is reduced
    B. they make possible more interesting, varied assignments
    C. if a pupil is absent, there is no problem about getting the assignment
    D. it saves the teacher a good deal of time

18. The FIRST and MOST important step in planning a test is to 18.____

    A. decide what kinds of questions are to be used
    B. define the objectives of instruction
    C. determine how much time is to be allocated for testing
    D. determine the ability levels of the students

19. If, as the lesson progresses, the teacher feels that he will NOT be able to cover all of the content included in his lesson plan, he should

   A. eliminate a final summary
   B. halt discussion and write the important notes on the blackboard
   C. conclude the lesson on the following day
   D. discontinue questioning and complete the lesson by lecturing

19.____

20. The MAJOR difference between the developmental lesson and the unit organization is that the unit plan

   A. usually lasts from one week to two months
   B. falls entirely within one subject field
   C. is motivated by some item of current events and is introduced by the teacher
   D. is logically organized around a small subdivision of subject matter

20.____

21. During a lesson, a student who is not paying attention does not hear the teacher's question. The BEST procedure for the teacher to follow is to

   A. repeat the question for the student
   B. have another student repeat the question
   C. elicit the answer from another student
   D. reprimand the student and repeat the question

21.____

22. Good class discussion is LEAST encouraged if

   A. it is guided by questions presented by the teacher
   B. a give-and-take procedure is employed in evaluating the points introduced by the pupils
   C. the slower as well as the better student presents his idea even if it may be of little value
   D. the teacher at the start of the discussion presents his point of view

22.____

23. If a student's answer to a question is so important that it calls for further stress, it is POOR teaching for the teacher to

   A. ask various members in the class to comment on the answer
   B. repeat it for its proper emphasis
   C. follow it with subsidiary queries
   D. use this answer as the basis for his next question

23.____

24. The MOST worthwhile technique for the teacher to check on whether and how well homework assignments are being done is to

   A. collect the assignments daily and return them the next day
   B. walk around the room and examine each student's homework
   C. have appropriate answers read aloud
   D. have the first student in each row examine the assignments

24.____

25. The BEST procedure is to have the aim of a lesson

   A. stated clearly by the teacher at the outset of the lesson
   B. contain more than is achievable during the lesson

25.____

C. erased from the board after it has been accepted and understood by the class
D. grow out of the motivation

26. Of the following, the MOST appropriate summary for a lesson is the one in which the

    A. teacher briefly reviews the highlights of the lesson
    B. students briefly review the highlights of the lesson
    C. students apply to a situation the information learned in the lesson
    D. teacher quizzes the students at the end of the lesson on the information taught in the lesson

27. For an effective final summary, the teacher should

    A. have the pupils repeat the facts learned during the lesson
    B. point out the significant facts himself
    C. determine a summary question as the lesson progresses, rather than in advance of the lesson
    D. seek a recapitulation of the material presented during the lesson

28. In teaching, rapid questioning BEST serves the purpose of

    A. recalling essential facts learned earlier
    B. developing judgment
    C. evaluating viewpoints
    D. recalling concrete experiences

29. An organized discussion of a definite problem by a selected group of pupils in a class is called a

    A. forum   B. symposium
    C. sociodrama   D. debate

30. The BEST method of evaluating the affective outcomes of education is to utilize

    A. anecdotal records kept by pupils
    B. frequent short unannounced quizzes
    C. reports to the class by pupils
    D. standardized tests with national norms

31. The BEST approach for the teacher to use in an effort to enhance pupil participation and the quality of discussion is to

    A. allow volunteers to carry the discussion
    B. restrict the slow or shy pupil who may stall the discussion
    C. discourage the evaluation of student responses
    D. provide an answer himself rather than continually rephrase a question

32. All of the following are examples of behavioral objectives EXCEPT:

    A. "The student can list six links of the infectious disease process."
    B. "Under supervision, the student can safely apply a triangular bandage."
    C. "The student chooses food in the cafeteria that comprises a well-balanced diet."
    D. "The student knows that communicable diseases are caused by microorganisms."

33. An auto-instructional approach to teaching relying on the psychological principles of reinforcement and associative learning is called

    A. programmed instruction
    B. problem solving
    C. socio-dramatization
    D. role playing

34. If a student's answer to a key question posed by the teacher is correct but ungrammatically expressed, of the following, it is WISEST for the teacher to

    A. interrupt the pupil's answer in order to correct the error
    B. ignore the error since the content of the answer is more important
    C. accept it and have the answer rephrased by another student
    D. ask the class what was wrong with the answer

35. In the use of a blackboard, all of the following are desirable practices EXCEPT the one in which the teacher

    A. provides sketches large enough so that they are visible to all pupils in the room
    B. places complex drawings on the blackboard in advance of the lesson to aid in pupils' understanding
    C. keeps all information on the blackboard to assist in the final summarization of the lesson
    D. stands to one side as he sketches a diagram or writes information

36. Of the following, the MOST desirable use of questioning during a lesson is the one which

    A. provides discovery of pupils' inadequate preparation of homework
    B. allows for the learning of the answers the teacher considers important enough to be remembered
    C. checks on pupil inattention during the development of the lesson
    D. focuses pupil attention on important aspects of the topic

37. During a lesson, it is LEAST advisable to use audio-visual material

    A. when a new unit of work is being introduced
    B. during the body of the lesson in which these materials are the basis for the lesson
    C. as a means of summarizing the lesson
    D. as the means of encouraging spontaneous oral student reactions

38. In the planning of developmental lessons, there should be great *similarity* of the

    A. aim and motivation
    B. motivation and medial summary
    C. aim and summary
    D. pivotal questions and summary

39. Note-taking by pupils should be

    A. eliminated since it detracts from the pupils' ability to listen attentively
    B. limited to the recording of the essentials presented during the lesson
    C. used by the teacher as a means of measuring the extent to which a pupil uses his notebook
    D. concerned with the copying of all notes from the blackboard which were presented during the lesson

40. In order to determine if a test question has the ability to discriminate between better and poorer students, the teacher should

   A. compare the results of the better students
   B. compare the results of the poorer students
   C. perform an item analysis
   D. perform a validity and reliability analysis

41. The BEST method of appraising the understandings of students with language difficulties is the use of _____ tests.

   A. essay
   B. oral
   C. objective
   D. standardized achievement

42. If a teacher wanted to elicit from students spontaneous responses regarding any topic, the method she would have the MOST success with is called

   A. role playing
   B. problem solving
   C. brainstorming
   D. self-appraisal

43. The MAIN purpose of a pivotal question is to

   A. direct thought from one aspect of a topic to another aspect of the same topic
   B. have students recall facts related to the topic being discussed
   C. drill students in specific knowledge previously learned
   D. encourage students to come up with a variety of answers

44. In providing for individual differences, of the following, the one that represents the MOST advisable plan for the teacher to adopt is to

   A. allow each child in the class complete freedom of choice in pursuing his projects
   B. have each student apprised of his specific weakness and to work toward correcting it
   C. arrange the students into small groups and plan his work so that the needs of each group are provided for
   D. provide short, frequent tests to determine variations in individual differences and to provide drill to reduce the variations

45. In dealing with slow learners in a heterogeneous class, the teacher should

   A. exempt them from any special reports
   B. spread them throughout the classroom
   C. call upon them only if they volunteer
   D. require them to do the exact same homework assignments as others in the class

46. Of the following, the one which is a disadvantage of grouping bright students together is that

   A. the standard high school curriculum will be covered too quickly
   B. in being with other bright students, these talented pupils become too humble
   C. the teachers with special talents have to be assigned to the bright group at the expense of the rest of the students
   D. it tends to deprive them of leadership opportunities

47. If a class as a whole does very poorly on a full-period unit test, the MOST effective of the following procedures is to

   A. return the papers and warn the pupils they must improve
   B. give another test on the same unit after clarifying the main concepts with which the students had had difficulty and providing remedial instruction
   C. go over the test and then have each pupil bring in two copies of the correct solution of every problem he failed to work correctly
   D. discard the test papers and proceed to the next topic, resolving to deal with it more effectively

47.____

48. Of the following, the one which is usually the LEAST important purpose for giving a quiz is that it

   A. is often part of the learning process
   B. often provides a basis for remedial work
   C. gives an opportunity for additional review and drill
   D. provides objective evidence on which to base marks

48.____

49. Which one of the following principles of learning is the LEAST acceptable?

   A. Concepts and processes should be developed from concrete and familiar situations in the life of the pupil.
   B. The pupils should always understand the reason for a process.
   C. Drill may occasionally be conducted effectively in preparation for understanding.
   D. When a rule is developed, it should be, as far as possible, the pupil's own generalization on the way he solves a problem.

49.____

50. Of the following, the LEAST desirable function of a school club is to

   A. promote interest in a subject and develop a broader understanding of its nature
   B. select bright pupils for a subject team, thus providing opportunities to coach them
   C. discuss with interested students the many applications of the subject
   D. foster special interests and talents along subject lines

50.____

KEY (CORRECT ANSWERS)

1. B	11. D	21. A	31. A	41. B
2. D	12. C	22. D	32. D	42. C
3. C	13. B	23. A	33. A	43. A
4. D	14. D	24. A	34. B	44. A
5. A	15. A	25. A	35. D	45. C
6. A	16. B	26. C	36. D	46. D
7. A	17. A	27. C	37. D	47. B
8. A	18. D	28. A	38. C	48. D
9. A	19. C	29. A	39. B	49. C
10. D	20. D	30. C	40. D	50. B

TEST 2

DIRECTIONS: Each question or incomplete statement is followed by several suggested answers or completions. Select the one that BEST answers the question or completes the statement. *PRINT THE LETTER OF THE CORRECT ANSWER IN THE SPACE AT THE RIGHT.*

1. Which one of the following questions asked by a teacher is MOST acceptable?

   A. "The answer to question 5 is what?"
   B. "Mary, is her answer to question 5 right?"
   C. "What is your answer to question 5, George?"
   D. "Class, tell George the answer to question 5!"

2. The technique of using a team teaching design which includes a master teacher, regular teachers and teacher-aides is based MOST directly upon which one of the following concepts?

   A. Teachers who have served faithfully deserve master teacher status.
   B. Teaching is a complex art requiring different levels of competence and training.
   C. The conservation of public funds is a moral obligation.
   D. Teacher-aides are often more knowledgeable and skillful than teachers.

3. In conducting a developmental lesson, the usually MOST desirable way, among the following, of responding to a student's correct answer to your question is to

   A. enter a grade in your record book
   B. call on another pupil to answer the same question
   C. follow up with another question
   D. elaborate on the pupil's answer

4. Which one of the following procedures is MOST acceptable to use in class when several pupils make flagrant errors in grammar and usage?

   A. Correct the students unobtrusively and proceed with your lesson.
   B. Take a few minutes to explain since every teacher is a teacher of English.
   C. Ignore the errors since such deviations are time-consuming.
   D. Write a note to each pupil's English teacher to inform him of the errors.

5. A technique which permits students to talk about their own impressions, opinions, and feelings is called

   A. a learning activities packet
   B. values clarification
   C. team teaching
   D. individualized instruction

6. Good questioning technique involves all of the following objectives EXCEPT the one in which questions

   A. are multiple in type in order to satisfy the varying abilities of the pupils in the class
   B. are limited to one or two points in the chain of reasoning

C. follow a predetermined order which develops the train of thought in logical sequence
D. place the burden of thinking upon the student

7. The MOST desirable type of classroom discipline is BEST attained through which one of the following practices?

   A. encouraging traits of self-discipline
   B. including class behavior in the final rating
   C. establishing the idea that rules and regulations will be strictly enforced
   D. anticipating difficulty and sending the first few minor cases of breach of discipline to the chairman or dean

7.____

8. If you find a student in one of your classes doing very poorly despite an obviously high potential, the MOST desirable procedure among the following to take is to

   A. refer the student to the guidance counselor
   B. ask the student to bring his parents to school to see you
   C. write a letter to his parents asking them to come to school to see you
   D. interview the student yourself before making any referrals or calling his parents

8.____

9. The procedure of requiring students to stand and face the class, when responding, is

   A. advisable because it discourages calling out of answers
   B. inadvisable because it creates an ordeal for the shy student
   C. advisable because it increases audibility of answers
   D. inadvisable because a recalcitrant student would dispute the rule

9.____

10. Of the following, the BEST procedure for obtaining the aim of a specific lesson is

    A. for the teacher to state the aim of the lesson and write it on the blackboard so that all will be sure to have it
    B. to elicit the aim from the class and have it written on the board
    C. for the teacher to dictate the aim of the lesson so that all students can get it in their notebooks
    D. to give the aim the previous day so that the students can prepare for the lesson

10.____

11. To obtain better results, when a problem has arisen, a teacher should

    A. ignore the problem and not become picayune over every little detail
    B. reprimand the group, knowing that their pride will cause them to work harder
    C. reprimand specific students who have caused the problem in class
    D. learn the positive effects of praise and optimism on his students

11.____

12. One method of creating an atmosphere for successful learning is to

    A. compare students with one another
    B. indiscriminately criticize students' abilities
    C. treat students with respect
    D. single out students who are not performing up to standards set by class

12.____

13. The prescribed procedure for recording the attendance in the official class is that it   13._____

    A. may be recorded in the roll book by a reliable pupil, with the clear understanding that the teacher assume full responsibility for the accuracy of the report
    B. may be recorded in the roll book by a pupil, provided the teacher checks daily
    C. must be recorded in the roll book by the teacher daily, since it is a legal document, the accuracy of which is imperative
    D. may be kept on a card and, in a day or so, be recorded in the roll book after errors have been corrected, excuse passes obtained, etc., to avoid having corrections frequently made in the roll book itself

14. Which one of the following would be the LEAST effective procedure for insuring a prompt start of a lesson?   14._____

    A. Give a quiz as the initial step in the lesson.
    B. Assign pupils to blackboard work while others copy the next assignment.
    C. Take attendance and call for attention.
    D. Have pupils copy the new assignment and start on a "warm-up" exercise.

15. During a supervised study period on an assignment, the teacher should NOT   15._____

    A. grade test papers and prepare reports
    B. confer quietly with individual pupils about proper study habits
    C. note the common errors made and the difficulties encountered by several pupils and conduct a quiet discussion with these pupils
    D. note the general quality and quantity of the pupils' work and modify plans for subsequent lessons, if necessary

16. A curriculum guide *usually* contains   16._____

    A. specific techniques which the teacher must follow
    B. a file of tests that the teacher can duplicate
    C. a list of cultural and linguistic items which should be covered
    D. the daily lesson plans for the topics to be taught at each level

17. A student should be removed from class   17._____

    A. if he habitually fails to hand in completed assignments
    B. when the positive benefits to the student are outweighed by his negative influence on the group
    C. if he continually falls asleep in class
    D. if he comes late constantly and wears his hat during class

18. A KEY element in developing classroom discipline is   18._____

    A. the socio-economic background of the students
    B. behavior modification
    C. a big, husky male teacher
    D. a strong administration

19. Teachers who assign reference tasks must be sure that children are capable of performing them. Of the following, the task that is LEAST significant is

   A. the assignment should consist of finding answers to fairly specific questions
   B. children should know how to locate printed information in reference books
   C. children are to know that they are to copy word-for-word from the reference book
   D. the information should be available and locatable in the classroom or the school library

20. All of the following are criteria for worth-while homework assignments EXCEPT:

   A. All homework assignments should be written assignments
   B. Homework assignments should serve a valid educational purpose
   C. They should extend the pupil's fund of information or give practice that he needs
   D. Homework assignments should be specific and completely understood

21. The LEAST effective method for dealing with discipline problems in the classroom is to

   A. keep students busy with appropriate assignments
   B. single out difficult children for reprimand before the whole class
   C. make sure children understand what is expected of them
   D. keep expectations within the ability level of children

22. Which one of the following types of learning is stressed in the gestalt psychologists' explanation of how the individual learns?

   A. Classical conditioning
   B. Instrumental learning
   C. Perceptual learning
   D. Programmed learning

23. The concept that one can train school children to be neat in their appearance and in the care of their belongings by teaching them to be neat in their arithmetic and spelling papers

   A. is a characteristic tenet of the advocates of behavioristic psychology
   B. has been proved by recent experimental studies
   C. has been virtually abandoned by educators today
   D. is of central importance in the development of programs of "life adjustment education"

24. Of the following, the MOST important purpose served by teaching machines is

   A. updating curriculum material presented to the children
   B. eliminating the need for drill work
   C. providing the learner with continuous knowledge of results
   D. teaching the learner systematic study technique

25. Of the following, which one constitutes the GREATEST stumbling block faced by the teacher in helping a pupil learn how to study effectively?

   A. Identifying good methods of study
   B. Teaching pupils how to organize a study routine
   C. Developing motivation to study
   D. Teaching pupils how to pace themselves

26. If the goal of a composition is self-expression, the teacher should base the grade *primarily* on

   A. content and secondarily on form
   B. content and secondarily on appearance
   C. form and secondarily on content
   D. appearance and secondarily on content

27. A printed statement which describes a desired performance by a student is called a

   A. student program
   B. lesson contract
   C. study module
   D. behavioral objective

28. One of the teacher's MOST important tasks is to

   A. provide a variety of purposeful listening activities
   B. repeat students' questions and answers
   C. remain totally silent to students' utterances
   D. give detailed instructions

29. Maximizing class time and maintaining discipline are two categories of

   A. lesson planning
   B. reading exercises
   C. classroom management
   D. group work

30. The BEST way to make classroom dialogue more meaningful to the student is to

   A. personalize questions
   B. use the same techniques consistently
   C. call on students who know the answers
   D. let the student read out of the book

31. Of the following, the LEAST effective method for obtaining pupil participation is to

   A. give a warm-up drill to the entire class
   B. group the class and give different assignments to each group
   C. have pupils answer in concert
   D. use experiences of pupils in the lesson development

32. A test which is too difficult will USUALLY yield scores that fall into a

   A. bell-shaped distribution
   B. negatively skewed distribution
   C. positively skewed distribution
   D. bimodal distribution

33. The MOST desirable routine procedure for going over homework is to

   A. compare answers orally with the class
   B. have students put their work on the board and explain it to the rest of the class
   C. have the teacher do each example together with the class
   D. collect it and mark it outside of class, returning it within a week

34. Of the following characteristics of a good lesson plan, the one which applies LEAST is that it

   A. forms part of a larger unit
   B. helps give direction to the lesson
   C. be adhered to even if vital side issues appear
   D. focuses on a meaningful problem

35. Which one of the following statements concerning the aim of a lesson is MOST valid?

   A. The teacher should write the aim on the blackboard at the beginning of each lesson.
   B. The aim should be an outgrowth of and developed from the motivation.
   C. Each child should write the aim of each lesson in his notebook each day.
   D. The teacher should announce the aim of the lesson to the class at the beginning of each period.

36. If a class you inherit from another teacher is poorly motivated and many of the students talk to one another during lessons, you should NOT

   A. teach carefully planned lessons daily for those who listen and try to ignore the others
   B. look up records of each member of the class and consult the guidance counselor where appropriate
   C. plan lessons in which students change activity every 15 minutes from written work to oral work to reading, etc.
   D. rearrange the seating so that groups who talk to one another are separated as far as possible

37. Among the following, the MOST obvious fact that faces the teacher of a ninth grade class is that

   A. the future doctors, chemists, engineers, and nurses can be accurately identified
   B. the boys are generally more talented in science and math than are the girls
   C. the girls are generally more mature than the boys
   D. the girls prefer the biological aspects of science, while the boys prefer the physical aspects of science and mathematics

38. Which one of the following methods for getting a lesson started promptly is LEAST sound pedagogically?

   A. Have a challenging motivating question on the blackboard at the beginning of the period.
   B. Stand near the door with the marking book and give a demerit to any student who does not sit down and take out his work at once.
   C. Give a quiz on the previous lesson at the beginning of the period.
   D. Stand quietly in front of the room and wait for attention.

39. Of the following, experience with various kinds of tests and measurements utilized for predicting academic success of pupils in advanced high school courses and honor classes in a given subject has shown that

   A. an aptitude test is the most satisfactory single instrument
   B. previous achievement represented by pupil's grades in that subject is best

C. all other factors should be subordinated to the I.Q.
D. the child's motivation is the paramount factor

40. It has been found that "learning by wholes," i.e., being challenged by a total situation, is usually BEST achieved by which one of the following groups? 40.____

   A. Dull-normal pupils
   B. Girls
   C. Pupils whose attention span is small
   D. The brighter pupils

41. MOST psychologists would agree that knowledge of results facilitates learning because it 41.____

   A. makes the learner more cautious
   B. leads to correction of erroneous responses
   C. stresses competition within a peer group
   D. provides the learner with social recognition when results are good

42. Of the following, the factor that has the GREATEST effect in contributing to the quality of pupil learning in the classroom is the 42.____

   A. personality of the teacher
   B. structure of the group
   C. characteristics of the learner
   D. physical aspects of the setting in which learning takes place

43. Of the following, research in the field of learning has MOST closely established the efficacy of 43.____

   A. whole rather than part learning
   B. reward rather than punishment as a stimulus for learning
   C. distributed rather than massed practice
   D. the Law of Exercised advanced by Thorndike

44. Of the following, it is MOST essential that an anecdotal record include 44.____

   A. verbatim quotations by witnesses
   B. a thoughtful interpretation of the child's behavior
   C. an objective description of what the child said and did
   D. a daily log of the problems the child presents

45. Which one of the following is the MOST desirable way of economizing on time during a subject-class period? 45.____

   A. Review the homework only occasionally.
   B. Establish definite routines for the pupils.
   C. Use the blackboard sparingly.
   D. Discourage the asking of questions by students.

46. If, soon after the start of a new term, a pupil in one of your academic classes should refuse to do the class work, which one of the following procedures would, as a general rule, be the BEST one to follow in such a case?

    A. Send the pupil to your chairman immediately.
    B. Assert your authority at once and let him know who is "boss".
    C. Speak to him after class to ascertain the cause of his behavior.
    D. Ignore the pupil but give him a failing mark at the end of the term.

47. Of the following possible criteria for evaluating the success of the teaching of reluctant learners in "second track" courses, the LEAST significant is

    A. achievement on standardized tests
    B. improvement in social behavior
    C. improvement in work habits
    D. improvement over past performance

48. Which one of the following statements about lesson plans is pedagogically sound?

    A. They should be made up at least a month in advance and adhered to strictly so that nothing is neglected.
    B. They are not needed by the experienced teacher.
    C. They should be made up week by week, according to the special needs of each class, and be used flexibly.
    D. They need not include pivotal questions.

49. The PRIMARY aim of assigning homework should generally be to

    A. review for class and term tests
    B. drill
    C. develop habits of working hard
    D. instill concepts

50. The daily homework assignment should USUALLY

    A. not include exercises on the new work if the class understands it
    B. have part devoted to review and part based on the new lesson
    C. consist, at least in part, of reading ahead in the new work to be taught
    D. be patterned after Regents-type questions

KEY (CORRECT ANSWERS)

1. C	11. C	21. B	31. C	41. B
2. B	12. C	22. C	32. C	42. C
3. C	13. C	23. C	33. B	43. C
4. A	14. C	24. C	34. C	44. C
5. B	15. A	25. C	35. B	45. B
6. A	16. C	26. A	36. A	46. C
7. A	17. B	27. D	37. C	47. A
8. D	18. A	28. A	38. B	48. C
9. C	19. C	29. C	39. B	49. D
10. B	20. A	30. A	40. D	50. B

EXAMINATION SECTION
TEST 1

DIRECTIONS: Each question or incomplete statement is followed by several suggested answers or completions. Select the one that BEST answers the question or completes the statement. *PRINT THE LETTER OF THE CORRECT ANSWER IN THE SPACE AT THE RIGHT.*

1. Which of the following court cases was directed PRIMARILY at the due process rights of students?   1._____

    A. Goss v. Lopez
    B. Pierce v. Society of Sisters
    C. West Virginia State Board of Education v. Barnette
    D. Tinker v. Des Moines Independent School District
    E. San Antonio Independent School District v. Rodriguez

2. The social development of adolescents tends to be MOST strongly influenced by the attitudes and behaviors of which of the following groups?   2._____

    A. Parents
    B. Teachers
    C. Peers
    D. Siblings
    E. Counselors

3. Of the following, most educators would agree that the key person or persons in curriculum improvement in a school is the   3._____

    A. school board
    B. school psychologist
    C. school principal
    D. school superintendent
    E. guidance counselor

4. The means and standard deviations of the scores for 900 pupils who were administered the reading and arithmetic sections of a standardized test are reported as follows: 4._____

	Mean	S.D.
Reading	54	12
Arithmetic	50	10

    On the basis of the data above, what score on the arithmetic test has the same relative value as a score of 48 on the reading test?

    A. 44   B. 45   C. 48   D. 49.5   E. 50

5. The phrase *in loco parentis* refers to   5._____

    A. a situation in which a school-age child lives with both of her or his natural parents
    B. a situation in which a child attends a neighborhood school close to her or his home
    C. those actions that the school carries out in place of a child's parents
    D. the teacher's responsibility to refrain from interfering with parental authority
    E. the parent's input into the decisions of the school administration

6. The relationship of measured intelligence to measured creativity is BEST reflected in which of the following statements?

   A. Recognized creativity is confined almost entirely to the upper 10% of the intelligence distribution.
   B. People with very high intelligence are less likely to be judged creative than people with average intelligence.
   C. People with slightly below average intelligence are the ones most likely to be judged creative.
   D. Intelligence tends to be negatively related to performance on creativity tests.
   E. There is a small positive relationship between intelligence and creativity.

7. What is the mean of the following set of numbers: 6, 5, 4, 5, 2, 3, 3?
   A. 3.0   B. 3.5   C. 4.0   D. 4.5   E. 5.0

8. A plateau in student learning of a physical skill is MOST likely to result when the student has

   A. reached her or his ultimate capacity in the development of the skill
   B. been taught through the use of ineffective instructional methods
   C. not received sufficient extrinsic motivation toward further development
   D. not yet integrated the various facets of learning involved
   E. shifted her or his interests elsewhere and temporarily stopped learning

9. Maria took the same standardized intelligence test in the fourth grade and the sixth grade and obtained scores of 102 and 107, respectively.
   It is reasonable to attribute most of the difference in her scores to which of the following?

   A. Increased experience with taking tests
   B. Improvement of the home environment
   C. Increased intellectual growth
   D. The recall of test questions
   E. Errors of measurement

10. Belief in the critical importance of educational experience during the preschool years has been strengthened by

    A. publicity attendant to the achievement of child prodigies
    B. evidence of the high proportion of mental development completed before the age of 6
    C. the successes of child-rearing communes
    D. popular accounts of psychoanalytic studies of young children
    E. generalizations derived from studies of the maturation processes of institutionalized children

11. From the perspective of the Constitution, public education in the United States is a legal responsibility of the

    A. federal government   B. respective states
    C. counties or townships   D. school districts
    E. local communities

12. Research evidence on learning and retention supports the generalization that

    A. rapid learning results in rapid forgetting
    B. meaningful material is rapidly learned but is more quickly forgotten than less meaningful material
    C. meaningful material is more readily learned and remembered longer than less meaningful material
    D. material that is overlearned is more quickly forgotten than is material that is not overlearned
    E. spaced learning results in increased forgetting

13. If the academic learning potential of a child with reading difficulties is to be measured, the MOST appropriate test to use would be a(n)

    A. reading diagnostic test
    B. reading comprehension test
    C. group intelligence test
    D. independent reading inventory
    E. individual intelligence test

14. The democratic administration of the school is MOST compatible with which of the following?

    A. A distribution of power that reduces arbitrary actions
    B. A system that allows for the development of collective negotiations
    C. The development of community-school councils
    D. The elimination of the board of education
    E. The election of principals by the faculty

15. Which of the following functions of schooling in the United States would MOST likely be common to schooling in all other countries?

    A. Transmitting the cultural heritage
    B. Providing universal education
    C. Developing every individual's potential
    D. Developing decision-making abilities
    E. Improving social interaction

16. Plato proposed the following paradox:
    Inquiry is impossible since either we know that which we seek to discover or we do not. If we do know, we cannot inquire, for we cannot inquire about what we already know. If we do not know, we cannot inquire, for we would be ignorant of the subject of investigation and unable to recognize the truth if we found it. Which of the following solutions to this paradox is Plato's?

    A. Knowledge must be revealed by God.
    B. Inquiry is impossible. We must always be skeptical.
    C. The mind must be able to abstract ideas directly from experience.
    D. If we are to inquire, we must know the criteria which govern inquiry.
    E. Inquiry, like remembering, is a process of making explicit something we already know.

17. A necessary assumption of a salary schedule based on merit raises is that

    A. poor teachers eventually will be eliminated
    B. cumulative teaching experience is unimportant
    C. degrees of teaching effectiveness can be reliably identified
    D. competition among teachers is healthy
    E. administrators will not misuse their power

18. A teacher consistently follows all efforts on the part of students with a *You did well, but...* type of remark. This teaching procedure will tend to

    A. keep students highly motivated
    B. reduce fear of failure in the classroom
    C. keep the level of student aspirations high
    D. increase tension and reduce learning effectiveness
    E. minimize the emotional thwarting of students in the classroom

19. A child reacts unfavorably to a new teacher who resembles in appearance a former teacher whom the child disliked. What learning concept helps to explain the child's reaction?

    A. Extinction   B. Discrimination
    C. Unconditioned response   D. Instrumental conditioning
    E. Stimulus generalization

20. The question, *Should classroom achievement be measured by teacher-made tests or by standardized tests,* is a controversial one.
    Which of the following statements BEST justifies the position that teacher-made tests should be used?

    A. The teacher knows what has been taught in the class.
    B. The students know what the teacher expects.
    C. The teacher can direct teaching toward the tests.
    D. Tests prepared externally are unfair to students.
    E. The teacher is the one who must assign the class grades.

21. Of the following, the GREATEST barrier to the provision of equal educational opportunities for all school children in the United States lies in the fact that communities tend to

    A. realize that they are unable to affect their educational facilities
    B. differ greatly in their ability to support educational facilities
    C. differ greatly in their need for trained personnel
    D. dislike having their schools compared with those of other communities
    E. differ greatly in the efficiency of their local governments

22. The basic principles of the progressive education movement that influenced American education in the first half of the twentieth century are BEST described by which of the following?

    A. Child-centered, learning by doing
    B. Teacher-centered, structured learning
    C. Focus on basic subjects, discovery learning
    D. Teacher-student interaction, personal learning
    E. Focus on formal disciplines, learning by recitation

23. The BEST way to tell whether giving a child a gold star is a reinforcement or not is to

    A. note whether the child prizes the gold star by carefully keeping it and showing it to others
    B. find out by observation and informal conversation whether the child really likes the gold star
    C. discover whether the gold star was, in the child's eyes, relevant to the task for which it was given
    D. see if the behavior just preceding the giving of the star is more likely to reoccur
    E. find out how much the child is willing to pay, out of her or his own money, for the gold star

24. Which of the following is the MOST probable basis for the mandate that handicapped children be placed in the least restrictive educational environment?

    A. The regular classroom usually affords a broader range of learning opportunities for the handicapped than do special classes.
    B. The potential for motor development is considerably better in regular classrooms than in special education classes or special facilities.
    C. Special education classes typically place too much emphasis on the remedial aspects of the education of the handicapped.
    D. Special education classes for the handicapped are too expensive
    E. It is difficult to recruit and train teachers of special education classes

25. Which of the following questions raised by a teacher is MOST likely to encourage divergent thinking on the part of a student?

    A. Which of these three marbles is the largest?
    B. What ocean lies to the east of Central America?
    C. Is it correct to say that all school children are mannerly?
    D. Which of these three equations is most efficient in solving for W?
    E. Other than searching all passengers, what else could be done to deter skyjacking?

26. Which of the following persons was very instrumental in the early study of individual differences among human capabilities, particularly as these differences related to creativity, giftedness, and genius?

    A. Spearman   B. Thorndike   C. Galton
    D. A. Anastasi   E. T. Hunt

27. A research article concludes that the correlation between junior high school students' self-concepts and their scholastic achievement is .40, significant at the .05 level. This finding means that

    A. 40% of the students' achievement may be attributed to their self-concepts
    B. the way the students see themselves determines how well they will do in school
    C. the way the students achieve in school modifies how good they think they are
    D. the relationship between self-concept and school achievement is too low to be concerned about
    E. there is a positive relationship between how the students see themselves and how they achieve in school

28. According to the TAXONOMY OF EDUCATIONAL OBJECTIVES: THE COGNITIVE DOMAIN, the MOST complex of the following cognitive operations is

    A. synthesis
    B. extrapolation
    C. knowledge of facts
    D. knowledge of processes
    E. application of principles

29. In an effort to reduce the number of temper tantrums by a child, the teacher has instituted a program of ignoring the child when such behavior is exhibited and giving the child extra attention when more appropriate behavior is exhibited.
    Which of the following techniques is the teacher using?

    A. Proactive inhibition
    B. Role playing
    C. Modeling
    D. Behavior modification
    E. Programming

30. The decentralization of authority in school systems usually results in all of the following EXCEPT

    A. greater uniformity of programs and practices within a school system
    B. greater autonomy for the staffs of the individual school buildings
    C. a decrease in bureaucratic procedures
    D. greater importance for the role of the school principal
    E. placing decision making closer to the source of effective action

---

KEY (CORRECT ANSWERS)

1.	A	16.	E
2.	C	17.	C
3.	C	18.	D
4.	B	19.	E
5.	C	20.	A
6.	E	21.	B
7.	C	22.	A
8.	D	23.	D
9.	E	24.	A
10.	B	25.	E
11.	B	26.	C
12.	C	27.	E
13.	E	28.	A
14.	A	29.	D
15.	A	30.	A

EXAMINATION SECTION
TEST 1

DIRECTIONS: Each question or incomplete statement is followed by several suggested answers or completions. Select the one that *BEST* answers the question or completes the statement. *PRINT THE LETTER OF THE CORRECT ANSWER IN THE SPACE AT THE RIGHT.*

1. The Coleman Report, EQUALITY OF EDUCATIONAL OPPORTUNITY devoted a major section to achievement in the public schools.
   Which of the following was NOT among the findings of the report?

   A. With some exceptions, average minority pupil scores were distinctly lower than average white pupil scores.
   B. The schools provide little opportunity for minority groups to overcome their initial deficiency.
   C. Black students in the South score below black students in the North.
   D. There was no notable difference between scores of various ethnic groups.

   1.____

2. Which of the following did the Coleman Report, EQUALITY OF EDUCATIONAL OPPORTUNITY, find to be MOST significantly related to pupil achievement?

   A. Degree of parent participation
   B. Socio-economic background of the students
   C. Quality of the curriculum
   D. Class size

   2.____

3. The one of the following that is the CHIEF obstacle to establishing a system of measuring teacher competence is that

   A. tenure provisions make it difficult to get rid of incompetent teachers
   B. methods of training teachers vary widely
   C. the ability of pupils varies widely from district to district
   D. there is neither a common definition of competence nor a substantial empirical base for building one

   3.____

4. Benjamin S. Bloom is credited with having influenced attitudes toward day care and planning of day care programs. In his writing, as exemplified by his book STABILITY AND CHANGE IN HUMAN CHARACTERISTICS, he has

   A. stressed the need to make day care an integral part of the school program
   B. recommended a structureed approach for preschool children
   C. pointed to the family as the major influence and the preschool years as the crucial ones for mental development
   D. stressed the need for thorough evaluation of all day care centers

   4.____

5. The one of the following which has been LEAST emphasized by the *alternative school movement* in recent years has been the need to

   A. provide special education for the handicapped
   B. be more responsive to change
   C. be more responsive to communities
   D. be more humane to students and teachers

   5.____

6. Efforts to improve inner city school districts are often handicapped by the absence of adequate housing, health care, recreation facilities and other social services in the area. Of the following, the federal program aimed at coordinating and supporting the broad spectrum of urban services in a given area is

    A. Housing and Redevelopment
    B. Title III of the Elementary and Secondary Education Act
    C. Urban Renewal
    D. Model Cities

7. The term *pupil mobility factor* refers to the

    A. problems encountered in zoning pupils into other than neighborhood schools
    B. pupils who leave their schools to go to other schools
    C. unwillingness of parents to move once their children have started school
    D. transportation problems related to educational parks

8. Which of the following statements is INCORRECT regarding publication of scores of the city-wide reading tests in the city?

    A. Law mandates that the reading tests be given.
    B. Publication of poor results often raises children's anxiety.
    C. Percentage scores related to national norms are easily understood and interpreted by most parents.
    D. Scores on these reading tests can be used as the basis for planning reading programs.

9. Which of the following statements concerning school boards in the United States is the MOST accurate?

    A. The decisions of school boards are often reached only after bargaining and compromising.
    B. Most school board members today receive salaries for their services.
    C. Most of the activities of school boards are mandatory rather than discretionary.
    D. States are now beginning to set educational qualifications for board membership.

10. Which of the following statements concerning federal aid to education is MOST valid?

    A. Federal aid to education will result in loss of control by the states over their schools.
    B. The tax system of the federal government is generally more efficient and equitable than those of state and local governments.
    C. Aid to nonpublic schools has not been an issue in the debate on federal aid to education.
    D. The strong support given by the states to vocational education has been used as an argument against federal aid.

11. Which of the following is a well-known proponent of the *comprehensive high school concept*?

    A. Jerome Bruner
    B. James B. Conant
    C. Robert J. Havighurst
    D. Hyman Rickover

12. The one of the following which would be LEAST useful in facilitating the learning of educable mentally retarded children is

    A. insuring that the child's successful experiences are balanced with unsuccessful experiences
    B. teaching new concepts with an emphasis on drill rather than on transfer to a new situation
    C. conducting a day-to-day program aimed at the completion of easy short range goals
    D. eliminating school experiences that tend to cause frustration

13. According to research on learning as applied to the education of educable mentally retarded children, which one of the following practices should NOT be used by a teacher of such children?

    A. They should be asked to learn and retain materials in very small units or sequences.
    B. Massed practice, rather than distributed practice should be used to facilitate learning.
    C. Devices should be found to encourage the children to focus on the material to be learned.
    D. They should be taught how to memorize by repeating many times what they are asked to retain.

14. The one of the following whose work has provided the MAJOR theoretical basis for the *open classroom* is

    A. Frederick Froebel
    B. John Holt
    C. Maria Montessori
    D. Jean Piaget

15. In introducing the *open classroom* into a school system, the one of the following which is necessary in order for the *open classroom* to function effectively and become a successful educational experience is that it should

    A. be implemented in larger, rather than smaller schools
    B. use advisors from inside the school rather than from outside the school, working directly with the teachers in implementing the school's goals
    C. redefine slowly, rather than all at once, the roles of the administrator, teachers, and children
    D. involve, from its inception, the whole school and the whole school day

16. The one of the following concepts which is NOT specified in the Bereiter and Englemann approach for preschool education of the disadvantaged is

    A. direct instruction
    B. discovery conditioning
    C. sensory stimulation
    D. verbal processes

17. When a teacher's focus of interest is on the response patterns of the pupil in a given situation, she is, knowingly or unknowingly, using the *concept* of _____ learning.

    A. classical B. operant C. signal D. type-S

18. In his book, BEYOND FREEDOM AND DIGNITY, B. F. Skinner implied that

    A. to control or change human behavior, it is necessary only to control or change the environment
    B. since man is an autonomous agent, prediction and control of his behavior are impossible
    C. man's behavior is controlled by his wishes, perceptions, and ideas
    D. we need less rather than more *intentional* control in order to survive

19. In the Guilford structure-of-intellect model, which one of the following operations is considered to be the MOST closely related to creative thinking in children?

    A. Evaluation B
    B. Cognition
    C. Convergent thinking
    D. Divergent thinking

20. Arthur Jensen has hypothesized two genotypically distinct basic processes of learning. They are associative learning (Level I) and conceptual learning (Level II).
    His theory about the relationship of these two processes of learning to socio-economic status (SES) is that middle SES children are _____ to low SES children in _____ learning.

    A. superior; associative
    B. superior; conceptual
    C. equal; conceptual
    D. inferior; associative

21. Piaget has conceptualized four basic stages of intellectual development. Which of the following reflects the PROPER *order* of these different stages?

    A. Formal Operations, Concrete Operations, Sensorimotor, Preoperational
    B. Concrete Operations, Formal Operations, Sensorimotor, Preoperational
    C. Sensorimotor, Preoperational, Concrete Operations, Formal Operations
    D. Preoperational, Sensorimotor, Concrete Operations, Formal Operations

22. Which one of the following intellectual tasks would be the MOST advanced according to Piaget's theory and observations?

    A. Conserve quantities
    B. Construct and use propositions
    C. Reciprocate logical relations
    D. Understand superordinate-subordinate classes

23. According to Christopher Jencks, evaluation of a school should be based PRIMARILY on whether or not

    A. the students and teachers find it a satisfying place to be
    B. school reform has long-term cognitive effects on the students
    C. school reform has any significant effect on the degree of inequality among the students as adults
    D. the school budget, its policies, and its teachers have any effect on the cognitive inequality among students

24. The one of the following which is the MAJOR aim of computer-managed instruction is 24.____
    A. elimination of grade levels
    B. decrease in expenditure for books and other instructional materials
    C. reduction in number of teachers needed
    D. individualization of instruction

25. Which one of the following statements describes the fundamental difficulty in the 25.____
    evaluation of teacher behavior for certification purposes?
    A. Specific teacher behaviors do not sum to a measure of competent teaching.
    B. The specific behaviors to be measured are too numerous.
    C. Behavioral objectives exist at only one level of specificity.
    D. Behavioral objectives cannot be logically derived from a theory of teaching.

KEY (CORRECT ANSWERS)

1.	D	11.	B
2.	B	12.	A
3.	D	13.	B
4.	C	14.	D
5.	A	15.	C
6.	D	16.	C
7.	B	17.	B
8.	C	18.	A
9.	A	19.	D
10.	B	20.	B

21. C
22. B
23. A
24. D
25. A

TEST 2

DIRECTIONS: Each question or incomplete statement is followed by several suggested answers or completions. Select the one that *BEST* answers the question or completes the statement. *PRINT THE LETTER OF THE CORRECT ANSWER IN THE SPACE AT THE RIGHT.*

1. The MOST important role that evaluation could play in a competency-based teacher education program is that of

    A. assessing teacher education students for the appropriateness of their attitudes about children
    B. examining curriculum, physical facilities, library, personnel, and other resources
    C. conducting follow-up studies of teachers on the job in order to produce desired changes in teacher education programs
    D. developing state-monitored certification agencies

2. Which of the following ways of assessing a teacher trainee's competencies are *likely* to be ACCEPTABLE in a competency-based teacher certification program?

    A. Microteaching and simulation tests *only*
    B. Microteaching and paper-and-pencil tests *only*
    C. Simulation tests and paper-and-pencil tests *only*
    D. Microteaching, simulation tests, and paper-and-pencil tests

3. State education departments are requiring new programs in teacher education to be competency-based in order to gain state approval for certification of graduates of these programs.
   The one of the following which is an ESSENTIAL element for a program to be accredited as competency-based is that the program

    A. include program units developed in module form
    B. be highly individualized
    C. include a teacher center for students' practice teaching
    D. provide for instruments to assess a trainee's performance in the classroom

4. A long-term goal in planning for competency based teacher certification is to certify only teachers who can

    A. demonstrate acceptable professional attitudes in the classroom
    B. present evidence of general background knowledge, subject matter knowledge and teaching skill
    C. produce specified learning gains for pupils they are to teach
    D. demonstrate that they have participated in a field-centered teacher education program

5. A MAJOR trend in teacher certification policy reflected in *most* state plans for competency-based teacher certification is the

    A. elimination of permanent certificates and the substitution of renewable certificates
    B. establishment of uniform statewide standards for permanent certification
    C. emphasis on university-based graduate study for permanent certification
    D. elimination of the baccalaureate requirement for provisional certification

6. Which of the following groups of educational personnel are *likely* to be included under competency-based certification? Teachers, 6.____

   A. *only*
   B. and counselors *only*
   C. and administrators *only*
   D. administrators, and counselors

7. The MAJOR obstacle to implementing competency-based teacher certification is the inability to 7.____

   A. develop competency-based teacher education instructional materials and methods
   B. specify the relationship between teacher competencies and measured pupil performance
   C. develop teacher centers for the distribution of instructional modules
   D. persuade taxpayers and legislators of the essential validity of the process

8. Competency-based certification might not be acceptable under the Guidelines on Employee Selection Procedures of the Equal Employment Opportunity Commission if fewer minority group teachers are certified on this basis than would be certified by use of the National Teachers Examination (NTE). 8.____
   In order to be acceptable under the Guidelines, competency-based certification would have to demonstrate that

   A. the teachers certified under the competency-based certification are more effective than those certified under the NTE
   B. it yields more reliable assessments of teacher competency than the NTE
   C. the costs of administering competency based certification are lower than the costs of administering the NTE
   D. minority group members have no objection to this procedure

9. An important distinction on certification made in most state plans is that 9.____

   A. the employer and NOT the teacher education institution should certify the teacher
   B. the teacher education institution and NOT the employer should certify the teacher
   C. either the teacher education institution or the employer should certify the teacher
   D. neither the teacher education institution nor the employer should certify the teacher

10. Assume that the following measures have been suggested to assess teacher competency. 10.____
    The one which is the MOST objective is a

    A. judgement as to the clarity with which a teacher presents material
    B. record of the frequency with which a teacher asks questions
    C. record of the frequency with which a teacher asks questions which are at the right difficulty for pupils
    D. record of the extent to which a teacher uses student ideas

11. A MAJOR issue in current teacher education programs is the apparent conflict between advocates of 11.____

    A. a systems-analytic approach and advocates of a humanistic approach
    B. a performance-based approach and advocates of a systems-analytic approach

C. a humanistic approach and advocates of a person-centered approach
D. microteaching and advocates of simulation training

12. Which of the following teacher training techniques has been the BEST example of a *systems approach* to teacher education?

    A. Field experience in a community agency
    B. Training student teachers to use audio-visual equipment
    C. Assigning student teachers to two or more schools in a system
    D. Microteaching

13. Which of the following would it be essential to include in a systems approach to teacher training?
    I. Precise specification of the desired teaching behavior and a training program designed to develop this behavior
    II. Measurement of the results of training in terms of behavioral objectives
    III. Feedback to the learner and instructor of measurement results

    The correct combination is:

    A. I *only*   B. I and II
    C. II and III   D. I, II, and III

14. Which of the following combinations of approaches to continuing education for teachers is receiving INCREASED emphasis?

    A. Teacher centers and university graduate courses
    B. Teacher centers and career development centers
    C. Career development centers and university graduate courses
    D. Career development centers, teacher centers, and university graduate courses

15. A recent trend in teacher education is early, direct involvement in the professional roles to be acquired. This trend is BEST demonstrated by the INCREASED emphasis on

    A. minicourses in the culminating student teaching experience
    B. classroom simulation and sensitivity training laboratories
    C. school and community participation in the design of teacher education programs
    D. the master of arts in teaching program

16. A new approach in teacher effectiveness research is the

    A. use of simulation techniques to study teacher behavior
    B. description of classroom observations in everyday language
    C. use of pupil gain as the major criterion
    D. application of personaltiy theory to the descriptions of effective teacher behavior

17. Under the Equal Employment Opportunity Act of 1972, sex should NOT normally be an occupational qualification. However, jobs may be restricted to members of one sex when

    A. prior employment practices can be cited as a precedent
    B. the job involves heavy physical labor (e.g., laborer)
    C. there is a need for authenticity (e.g., female to model women's clothing)
    D. the job requires personal charm (e.g., receptionist)

18. Which of the following is NOT a basic merit system factor in the development of an effective Affirmative Action Plan for women?
    Reviewing

    A. job requirements to assure that unnecessary sex qualifications are eliminated
    B. salary and pay scales to assure that men and women receive equal pay for equal work
    C. selection processes to assure that they are bias-free
    D. job performance standards to assure that they will be met by both men and women

19. Of the following, the FIRST step in establishing an effective program to combat discrimination against women in employment in any organization is to

    A. develop a quota system for future employment
    B. obtain top management support for the program
    C. recognize that there is no difference between men and women
    D. determine those jobs for which women are best suited

20. Discrimination in employment because of age, sex, or physical requirements may be defensible if

    A. there are a large number of highly qualified applicants for a job
    B. the requirements represent a bona-fide qualification necessary to fulfill a job properly
    C. a change in requirements would be detrimental to long-standing employment policies
    D. it can be proved that a change in requirements for employment would so disturb present employees that their performance would be impaired

21. The BASIC purpose in developing an Affirmative Action Plan for equal opportunity in employment is to

    A. create new jobs specifically for members of minority groups
    B. accept responsibility for past discriminatory actions
    C. take positive steps to promote equal opportunity
    D. give preferential treatment to minority groups discriminated against in the past

22. Which one of the following steps is NOT advisable in the development of recruitment and upward mobility practices for an Affirmative Action Plan?

    A. Placing special emphasis on the identification and development of sources of minority group members and women for positions in which they are currently under-represented
    B. Establishing production standards so that those employees who are recruited will be fully productive workers within a minimum time period
    C. Providing for the establishment of training and education programs to give employees maximum opportunity to advance to their highest potential
    D. Planning for participation in community efforts to improve conditions which affect employability and employment opportunities

23. Under Equal Employment Opportunity Commission Guidelines on Employee Selection Procedures, the use of any test which results in a disproportionate number of persons of one race who are appointed or promoted constitutes discrimination unless the test

    A. has been validated and has a reliability of .80 or higher
    B. is reliable and differential validity has been proven
    C. is job-related, has been validated, and alternative selection procedures are unavailable
    D. has been validated, has a high degree of reliability, and has equal cut-off scores for minority and non-minority groups

24. According to Equal Employment Opportunity Commission Guidelines on Employee Selection Procedures, *satisfactory* assessment of the utility of a test is defined as

    A. testimony by at least two competent authorities that the test is job-related
    B. the cost and feasibility of test administration
    C. a statistically significant relationship between the test and at least one relevant criterion
    D. a relationship between test and criterion that is both statistically significant and practically significant

25. The first and most basic step in the development of a job-related test is to

    A. make a job analysis to determine skills, knowledge, and abilities necessary to perform the job
    B. conduct a criterion-validity study to determine how well the test predicts success on the job
    C. prepare an outline for the test plan according to psychological principles
    D. select a sample of subjects for a pilot test representative of the minority population available for the job

KEY (CORRECT ANSWERS)

1. C	11. A
2. D	12. D
3. D	13. D
4. C	14. B
5. A	15. B
6. D	16. C
7. B	17. C
8. A	18. D
9. D	19. B
10. B	20. B

21. C
22. B
23. C
24. D
25. A

EXAMINATION SECTION
TEST 1

DIRECTIONS: Each question or incomplete statement is followed by several suggested answers or completions. Select the one that BEST answers the question or completes the statement. *PRINT THE LETTER OF THE CORRECT ANSWER IN THE SPACE AT THE RIGHT.*

1. Advantages of the American common school as Mann promoted it were that it
    I. avoided the stigma of the English poorhouse
    II. had superior instruction to paupers' schools in Britain
    III. would improve because prominent citizens would send their children
    IV. was cheaper
    V. was more useful in training for practical skills
   The CORRECT answer is:

   A. I, II, III
   B. III, IV, V
   C. II, IV, V
   D. II, V
   E. III only

   1.____

2. One of the MOST significant of Mann's educational achievements was

   A. achieving desegregation
   B. promoting theory and philosophy in school
   C. adding kindergarten to primary schools
   D. setting up teacher institutes
   E. donating a private fortune to education

   2.____

3. The American educator Henry Barnard was
    I. a colleague of Horace Mann's in the common school movement
    II. opposed to Mann's common school movement
    III. primarily an administrator
    IV. opposed to nationalism in education
    V. a believer in non-sectarian education
   The CORRECT answer is:

   A. I, III
   B. I, II
   C. I, IV, V
   D. IV, V
   E. IV only

   3.____

4. Henry Barnard's non-administrative activities included being
    I. Chancellor of the University of Wisconsin
    II. United States Commissioner of Education
    III. editor of the AMERICAN JOURNAL OF EDUCATION
    IV. a journalist
    V. a painter
   The CORRECT answer is:

   A. I, II
   B. III only
   C. III, IV
   D. IV, V
   E. V only

   4.____

5. Barnard's educational philosophy consisted in the beliefs that
    I. Christianity should be included in education
    II. capitalism requires educated masses
    III. education should be used to build individual character
    IV. poverty and child labor are necessary evils
    V. laissez-faire economics should be encouraged

    The CORRECT answer is:

    A. I, II, III
    B. III, IV
    C. III, V
    D. II, IV
    E. all of the above

6. The primary goal(s) of education, for Henry Barnard, is(are) to
    I. prepare the student for college
    II. create Christian citizens
    III. ensure intelligent workers for capitalism production
    IV. ensure secularism in the schools
    V. encourage nationalism and patriotism

    The CORRECT answer is:

    A. II, III
    B. II, III, V
    C. III, IV
    D. IV, V
    E. I, III

7. The primary difference(s) between Mann's and Barnard's educational views is (are) that the
    I. former was more theoretical and the latter practical
    II. latter was more practical and the former theoretical
    III. latter believed that education should be primarily functional
    IV. former believed that education should be primarily functional
    V. latter rejected secularism

    The CORRECT answer is:

    A. I, III, V
    B. II, IV, V
    C. V only
    D. II, IV
    E. I, III

8. The accomplishments of Mann and Barnard include
    I. establishing the American educational ladder
    II. enacting into law taxation to support schools
    III. that private philanthropy was depended upon more and more
    IV. insuring teacher education
    V. expanding American education into secondary schools

    The CORRECT answer is:

    A. I, III
    B. I, II
    C. III only
    D. IV only
    E. I, II, IV

9. The famous "American ladder of education" consists of
    I. open admissions to secondary schools
    II. equality of opportunity
    III. free education from kindergarten through college
    IV. education based on merit
    V. climbing the social ranks to wealth
   The CORRECT answer is:

   A. I, V
   B. V *only*
   C. II *only*
   D. II, III, IV
   E. III *only*

10. Characteristic of the development of American secondary schooling is that it
    I. developed parallel to primary schooling
    II. developed with much more difficulty than primary schooling
    III. lacked the leadership of such educators as Mann and Barnard
    IV. developed with ease and speed
    V. had constant public support
   The CORRECT answer is:

   A. I *only*
   B. II, III
   C. IV, V
   D. IV *only*
   E. V *only*

11. The American educational ladder describes
    I. the various educational institutions of the various states
    II. the single, articulated sequential school system
    III. the school system open to all
    IV. schools available regardless of religious or social class
    V. what Jefferson and Jackson had in mind as equality of opportunity
   The CORRECT answer is:

   A. I, III
   B. II, III
   C. I, IV, V
   D. II, III, IV, V
   E. all of the above

12. Secondary school development in America occurred
    I. together with the primary school development
    II. many years after primary school development
    III. in three phases
    IV. in at least six phases
    V. over a period of 100 years
   The CORRECT answer is:

   A. I, IV
   B. I *only*
   C. III *only*
   D. II, IV
   E. III, V

13. Secondary schooling in America FIRST developed during
    I. the 16th century
    II. the 17th century
    III. colonial American times
    IV. the times when American education imitated Latin Grammar schools
    V. the times when only upper class Americans were educated
    The CORRECT answer is:

    A. I, V
    B. II, III, IV
    C. III, IV, V
    D. IV, V
    E. III only

14. The Latin Grammar school was found deficient
    I. because it bred church or political leaders
    II. because it became too elite
    III. because it was too narrow in its curriculum
    IV. by Benjamin Franklin, among others
    V. after the American Revolution
    The CORRECT answer is:

    A. I, II
    B. II, III
    C. I, III, IV
    D. III, IV, V
    E. all of the above

15. The 18th and 19th centuries in American education saw the secondary school
    I. in the form of the Academy
    II. develop through a faith in social reform
    III. develop slowly because of opposition from church leaders
    IV. become privately controlled through small entrepreneurs
    V. enroll over a quarter of a million people
    The CORRECT answer is:

    A. I, II
    B. II, III
    C. I, II, IV, V
    D. III, IV, V
    E. IV, V

16. Of DIRECT help to the rise of secondary schooling in America was
    I. female suffrage
    II. frontier individualism
    III. upward mobility
    IV. laissez-faire economics
    V. open enrollment
    The CORRECT answer is:

    A. I, III
    B. II, IV
    C. I, III, IV
    D. I, II, V
    E. all of the above

17. The American Academy of the 19th century
    I. was designed to prepare people to be citizens
    II. helped prepare one for college
    III. trained teachers
    IV. had a narrow curriculum
    V. had a wide and diverse curriculum
    The CORRECT answer is:

    A. I, II, III
    B. I, IV, V
    C. I, II, III, V
    D. III, IV
    E. I, V

18. Of the courses offered in 19th century American Academies, subjects NOT included were
    I. oratory and logic
    II. moral philosophy
    III. algebra and trigonometry
    IV. bookkeeping and accounting
    V. religion
    The CORRECT answer is:

    A. I, II
    B. II, III
    C. III only
    D. IV only
    E. none of the above

19. Problems with American 19th century Academies included
    I. lack of a common standard
    II. imposition of too strict a standard of conformity
    III. lack of a system of accreditation for teachers
    IV. lack of a system of accreditation for schools
    V. too many workers entering the system
    The CORRECT answer is:

    A. I, III, IV
    B. II, IV, V
    C. V only
    D. III only
    E. III, IV

20. Of the interesting characteristics of the American Academy are
    I. its religious affiliations
    II. its sponsorship by religious organizations
    III. that they eventually gave rise to some denominational colleges of today
    IV. that they were publicly funded
    V. that they were secular
    The CORRECT answer is:

    A. I, II
    B. V only
    C. III only
    D. I, II, III
    E. all of the above

21. The transition from the Academy to the public high school was
    I. due largely to the rise of urban society
    II. due largely to the rise of the agricultural population
    III. partly because of the large tax base of cities
    IV. helped by the rise of corporations
    V. hurt by the rise of corporations
    The CORRECT answer is:

    A. I, III, IV
    B. I, III, V
    C. II, III, IV
    D. IV, V
    E. III only

22. In the beginning, the American high school
    I. began in Boston in 1821
    II. became popular only after 1870
    III. grew upon the acceptability of elementary schools
    IV. benefitted from child labor laws
    V. benefitted from urban tax bases
    The CORRECT answer is:

    A. I, II
    B. III, IV
    C. I, III, V
    D. III, IV, V
    E. all of the above

23. The current form of the American high school
    I. developed during the 1870's
    II. developed between 1880 to 1920
    III. developed after 1920
    IV. began very undifferentiated from each other
    V. began standardized
    The CORRECT answer is:

    A. I, V
    B. I, IV
    C. III only
    D. II, IV
    E. II, V

24. The Committee of Ten, formed in 1892, was
    I. created by the National Education Association
    II. designed to standardize high schools
    III. designed to diversify high schools
    IV. oriented toward college preparation
    V. oriented toward vocational training
    The CORRECT answer is:

    A. I, III, V
    B. I, II, IV
    C. III, IV
    D. V only
    E. I, II

25. The Chairman of the Committee of Ten was
    I. William T. Harris
    II. Charles W. Eliot
    III. an advocate of differentiated education for terminal and college preparatory students
    IV. an advocate of identical education for terminal and college preparatory students
    V. an advocate of early introduction of basics during elementary school
    The CORRECT answer is:

    A. I, III
    B. II, IV, V
    C. I, III, IV
    D. IV, V
    E. I, V

26. The Committee of Ten experience showed that
    I. higher education dominates lower education
    II. lower education dominates higher education
    III. interest in historical studies was low
    IV. interest in historical studies was high
    V. mental discipline was the primary goal of high school
    The CORRECT answer is:

    A. I, V
    B. I, II
    C. II, III
    D. I, IV, V
    E. II, III, V

27. The early forms of high school accreditation
    I. were highly regionalized
    II. concentrated on a "core" curriculum
    III. were nationally decided
    IV. allowed diversified electives
    V. included college entrance exams
    The CORRECT answer is:

    A. I, II, V
    B. I, II
    C. II, III
    D. III, IV
    E. V only

28. The 1918 NEA Commission on the Reorganization of Secondary Education was
    I. supposed to re-examine whether or not America should have high schools
    II. supposed to re-examine the scope and function of theigh school
    III. to cut down the social involvement of high schools
    IV. to determine proper objectives for secondary education
    V. to undermine the legislative process on educational matters
    The CORRECT answer is:

    A. I, II
    B. II, III
    C. II, IV
    D. I, III, V
    E. all of the above

29. The results of the Commission on the Reorganization of Secondary Education in 1918 included
    I. three primary aims
    II. general axioms of learning
    III. seven principles for secondary schools to follow
    IV. advice against sloth
    V. recommendations for legal bans on questionable reading material
   The CORRECT answer is:

   A. I, III
   B. II *only*
   C. III *only*
   D. IV, V
   E. I, II, III

30. Objectives of secondary education during the early 20th century in America included
    I. health and family responsibility
    II. citizenship
    III. vocation
    IV. ethical character
    V. worthy use of leisure
   The CORRECT answer is:

   A. I, II
   B. II, III
   C. I, III, V
   D. II, IV, V
   E. all of the above

31. The overall function of high school, during the first two decades of 20th century American education, was to

   A. prepare functional workers in industrial capitalism
   B. form honorable character
   C. accomplish social integration of ethnic groups
   D. make gentlemen out of proletarians
   E. encourage theoretical scholarship

32. The "Cardinal Principles" of the Commission of 1918 met with criticism
    I. from George Counts
    II. because they did not deal with industrialization
    III. because they embodied a social theory
    IV. because they lacked a social theory
    V. from Horace Mann
   The CORRECT answer is:

   A. I, II
   B. II, III
   C. II, IV, V
   D. I, II, IV
   E. I, III

33. During the period from 1880 to 1920, the American high school was
    I. *decreasing* in enrollment
    II. *increasing* in enrollment
    III. *primarily* college preparatory
    IV. *primarily* vocationally oriented
    V. *gradually* discredited
   The CORRECT answer is:

A. I, V   B. II, III
C. IV *only*   D. V *only*
E. II, IV, V

34. The American high school of the turn of the 20th century was *criticized*
    I.   by G. Stanley Hall
    II. because colleges dominated high school curricula
    III. because the adolescent was being neglected
    IV. because the adolescent was the focal point of its curriculum
    V.   by very few people
    The CORRECT answer is:

    A. I, II   B. I, II, III
    C. IV *only*   D. II *only*
    E. V *only*

35. The "social efficiency movement" in American education consisted of
    I.   claims made by David Snedden
    II. reaction against college oriented high school curricula
    III. reaction against vocationally oriented high school curricula
    IV. a utilitarian criterion of social reform
    V.   an egoist criterion of economic development
    The CORRECT answer is:

    A. I, III, V   B. I, IV
    C. I, II, IV   D. I, III, IV
    E. II, IV, V

36. Between 1880 and 1920, the American high school population

    A. gradually *decreased* because of urbanization
    B. gradually *decreased* because of increasing ruralization
    C. *increased* by more than 200%
    D. *increased* by about 50%
    E. remained about the same

37. Critics of the American secondary school at the turn of the century
    I.   focused on its selectivity
    II. pointed to the close correlation between parental occupation and high school attendance
    III. were mostly socialists and anarchists
    IV. included George S. Counts
    V.   pointed to the relative lack of immigrant children in the system
    The CORRECT answer is:

    A. I, V   B. I, II, III
    C. III *only*   D. I, II, IV, V
    E. all of the above

38. The American educator William French claimed that
    I. deficiencies in the high school system had an explanation
    II. there were no deficiencies in high school education
    III. immigrants lacked a secondary education tradition
    IV. rural districts lacked the tax base to support secondary education
    V. hidden costs kept many from attending secondary schools

    The CORRECT answer is:

    A. I, II
    B. II, IV
    C. I, III, IV, V
    D. III, IV, V
    E. IV, V

39. By 1930, the American high school
    I. became very unpopular
    II. had an attendance of approximately 9 million
    III. had an attendance of approximately 4 million
    IV. became established as an institution for adolescents
    V. became established as an institution for vagrants

    The CORRECT answer is:

    A. I, V
    B. II only
    C. III, IV
    D. III, IV, V
    E. III, V

40. World War I affected the American high school in that
    I. very few people attended because they were at war
    II. German was not included in the curriculum
    III. physical education was added to the curriculum
    IV. physical disabilities of war veterans had to be handled
    V. military strategy was a mandatory subject

    The CORRECT answer is:

    A. II, V
    B. I only
    C. III only
    D. III, IV
    E. III, V

41. The Smith-Hughes Vocational Education Act was
    I. enacted in 1917
    II. designed to increase college enrollment
    III. designed to increase vocational studies
    IV. sponsored by the federal government
    V. sponsored by individual states

    The CORRECT answer is:

    A. I, II, IV
    B. I, II, V
    C. III, IV
    D. I, IV, V
    E. II, III

42. One of the MOST influential educators of the 1950's was

    A. William French
    B. G. Stanley Hall
    C. David Snedden
    D. George Counts
    E. James B. Conant

43. James B. Conant was an American educator who
    I. was President of Harvard University
    II. authored THE AMERICAN HIGH SCHOOL TODAY
    III. was active in the 1950's
    IV. used objective documented evidence in his analysis
    V. distinguished between comprehensive and specialized high schools
    The CORRECT answer is:

    A. I, II
    B. II, III
    C. I, III, V
    D. IV, V
    E. all of the above

44. Conant's account of the comprehensive high school
    I. condemned it entirely
    II. condemned it in part
    III. neither condemned nor recommended it
    IV. used constructive suggestions to improve it
    V. was never very influential
    The CORRECT answer is:

    A. I, V
    B. I *only*
    C. II *only*
    D. III, IV
    E. V *only*

45. Conant's recommendations included
    I. twenty-one recommendations
    II. advocating a counseling program
    III. encouraging corporal punishment
    IV. individual instruction
    V. a core curriculum
    The CORRECT answer is:

    A. I, II
    B. I, III
    C. III, V
    D. I, II, IV, V
    E. II, IV, V

46. Included in Conant's core curriculum were
    I. foreign languages
    II. English
    III. social studies
    IV. mathematics and science
    V. political science
    The CORRECT answer is:

    A. I, V
    B. II, III, IV
    C. I, III, V
    D. I, II, V
    E. III, V

47. Conant's innovative ideas concerning secondary education included
    I. electives accounting for half the student's program
    II. elimination of electives
    III. encouraging the development of marketable skills
    IV. discouraging the development of marketable skills
    V. creating programs for gifted students
    The CORRECT answer is:

    A. I, III, V
    B. II, IV
    C. IV *only*
    D. II *only*
    E. V *only*

48. James Conant is *largely* recognized for
    I. authoring SLUMS AND SUBURBS
    II. distinguishing between comprehensive and specialized high schools
    III. pointing out the class background between school curricula
    IV. emphasizing the bifurcation of high schools
    V. constructive reform of high schools
    The CORRECT answer is:

    A. I, II
    B. II, IV
    C. III *only*
    D. IV *only*
    E. all of the above

49. One of the MAIN consequences of Conant's research is

    A. the reluctance of the public to change the educational system
    B. the development of vocational schools
    C. the preponderance of college-oriented high schools
    D. revealing the educational ladder system to be endangered
    E. that it discouraged further research

50. A dual track secondary school education, in Conant's view, would be
    I. socially progressive
    II. socially regressive
    III. class biased
    IV. representative of class structure and so legitimate
    V. abandoning the principles of American education
    The CORRECT answer is:

    A. I, IV
    B. II, III
    C. II, III, V
    D. IV *only*
    E. II *only*

KEY (CORRECT ANSWERS)

1. A	11. D	21. A	31. C	41. A
2. D	12. E	22. E	32. D	42. E
3. A	13. C	23. D	33. B	43. E
4. C	14. E	24. B	34. B	44. D
5. E	15. C	25. B	35. C	45. D
6. B	16. E	26. D	36. C	46. B
7. A	17. C	27. A	37. D	47. A
8. E	18. E	28. C	38. C	48. E
9. E	19. A	29. C	39. E	49. D
10. B	20. D	30. E	40. D	50. C

110

EXAMINATION SECTION
TEST 1

DIRECTIONS: Each question or incomplete statement is followed by several suggested answers or completions. Select the one that BEST answers the question or completes the statement. *PRINT THE LETTER OF THE CORRECT ANSWER IN THE SPACE AT THE RIGHT.*

1. Issues popular among members of the student movement in the 1960's include
    I. university involvement in private corporations
    II. the presence of ROTC offices on college campuses
    III. the immorality of the War in Vietnam
    IV. the lack of federal funding for universities
    V. the lack of a broad curriculum to encourage creativity
   The CORRECT answer is:

   A. I, V
   B. I, II
   C. I, II, III
   D. III, IV, V
   E. I, III, V

2. Problems of universities attacked by student activists include
    I. lack of personal contact between students and faculty
    II. an excessive concern among faculty members for liberal arts
    III. personal alienation in large universities
    IV. class size of over 300
    V. political rights of free speech on campus property
   The CORRECT answer is:

   A. I, II
   B. II, III
   C. I, III, IV, V
   D. III, IV, V
   E. all of the above

3. Educational reforms inspired by student unrest in the 1960's include
    I. more specialized faculty members
    II. seminars and tutorials
    III. student involvement in administration
    IV. more introductory survey courses
    V. more emphasis upon teaching rather than research for faculty members
   The CORRECT answer is:

   A. I, V
   B. II, III, V
   C. I, III, IV
   D. II, III, IV
   E. I, IV, V

4. MAJOR factors causing the student unrest of the 60's were
    I. rapidly increasing student population
    II. rapidly decreasing faculty supply
    III. rapidly decreasing student population
    IV. insufficient facilities
    V. communist infiltration of college campuses
   The CORRECT answer is:

A. I, V   B. II, IV, V
C. II, IV   D. I, II, IV
E. I, II, IV

5. Racial integration in education faced many difficulties because
   I. of the more than 4 million freed slaves after the Civil War
   II. of prejudices
   III. Southern states had separate but equal traditions
   IV. of lack of legislation
   V. of lack of concern in American society for equal opportunity
   The CORRECT answer is:

   A. I, III   B. I, III, IV
   C. I, II, III, IV D. II, III
   E. all of the above

6. The MAJOR breakthrough for racial integration in education was

   A. the Brown v. the Board of Education of Topeka case
   B. World War II
   C. an increase in the black student population
   D. student activism in the 1960's concerning civil rights
   E. President Kennedy's active involvement in education

7. Included among the factors *delaying* racial integration in education are
   I. the Plessy v. Ferguson decision
   II. a court case of 1896
   III. the United States Supreme Court upholding separate education in the 19th century
   IV. the United States Supreme Court being influenced by Presidents
   V. northern activism
   The CORRECT answer is:

   A. II, V   B. I, II, III
   C. IV, V   D. II, V
   E. II, III, IV

8. Southern reaction to the Brown v. Board of Education case
   I. was varied
   II. was mild and receptive
   III. was defiant and obstinate
   IV. argued for "states' rights" against integration
   V. appealed to the President for intervention
   The CORRECT answer is:

   A. I, V   B. II only
   C. III, IV   D. III, V
   E. I, III, V

9. When Governor Faubus of Arkansas tried to block integration in Little Rock schools,
    I. the federal government did nothing
    II. President Eisenhower authorized using federal troops to enforce the law
    III. the populace in Little Rock supported him
    IV. the populace in Little Rock rebelled against him
    V. he succeeded with little effort
   The CORRECT answer is:

   A. I, V
   B. II only
   C. I, III
   D. I, IV
   E. III, V

10. When James Meredith, a Negro, attempted to enroll in the University of Mississippi in 1962,
    I. the legal system had removed previous obstacles against him
    II. he encountered opposition
    III. the Governor of Mississippi tried to stop his enrollment
    IV. President Kennedy ordered federal troops into Mississippi
    V. racists used the "order and safety" clause of the Tenth Amendment to stop him
   The CORRECT answer is:

   A. I, II
   B. II, III
   C. III, IV, V
   D. II, III, IV, V
   E. all of the above

11. Southern opposition to integrated education
    I. stems from slaveowners refusing to allow slaves to read
    II. is sometimes justified by the Bible
    III. is defended on the rationale of Social Darwinism
    IV. is largely comprised of hostility of poor whites
    V. can be attributed to attitudes of white supremacy
   The CORRECT answer is:

   A. I, III
   B. II only
   C. III, IV
   D. I, III, V
   E. all of the above

12. Educational segregation of the races
    I. exists in the South *only*
    II. exists in the North *only*
    III. is de jure in the South and de facto in the North
    IV. is de facto in the South and de jure in the North
    V. is not good pedagogical practice
   The CORRECT answer is:

   A. I, V
   B. II, V
   C. II, IV, V
   D. II, III, V
   E. V *only*

13. School integration is supported by the
    I. Ku Klux Klan
    II. Black Nationalists
    III. National Association for the Advancement of Colored People
    IV. Urban League
    V. White Citizens' Council
    The CORRECT answer is:

    A. III, IV
    B. II, V
    C. II, III, IV
    D. III only
    E. IV only

14. The Progressive Movement in American education
    I. originated in the pedagogical theories of Rousseau and Pestalozzi
    II. was heavily influenced by Froebel
    III. is almost identical to the experimental movement in education
    IV. began in the late 19th century
    V. began in the early 20th century
    The CORRECT answer is:

    A. I, V
    B. III only
    C. I, II, IV
    D. I, II, V
    E. III, IV, V

15. The *primary* difference(s) between progressive and experimental education is(are) that
    I. the former is systematic and scientific
    II. the latter is systematic and scientific
    III. the former became very popular
    IV. the latter became very popular
    V. only the former was optimistic about educational improvement
    The CORRECT answer is:

    A. I, III
    B. II, IV
    C. V only
    D. II only
    E. IV only

16. Progressivism in education was
    I. not influenced by political pressures
    II. paralleled in politics
    III. encouraged by such leaders as LaFollette and Roosevelt
    IV. influenced by Jane Adams' pioneering efforts in social work
    V. based on traditional approaches
    The CORRECT answer is:

    A. I, V
    B. II, III, IV
    C. III, IV, V
    D. I, IV
    E. II, V

17. Fundamental tenets of progressivism in American educational pedagogy include
    I. that human beings are perfectable
    II. faith in natural abilities of children
    III. that discipline is an essential part of education
    IV. that mastery of subject matter is crucial to a good education
    V. that the student's needs, abilities and interests should guide education
    The CORRECT answer is:

    A. I, II
    B. II, III
    C. I, II, V
    D. III, IV, V
    E. all of the above

18. Educational reforms recommended by progressivists include
    I. increasing the role of teachers
    II. increasing the freedom of students
    III. the developmental approach
    IV. the content approach
    V. teachers as guides, not taskmasters
    The CORRECT answer is:

    A. I, V
    B. II, III, V
    C. II, IV
    D. I, IV, V
    E. I, III, IV, V

19. William Heard Kilpatrick was an educator who
    I. advocated Dewey's experimentalism
    II. advocated Skinner's behaviorism
    III. strongly emphasized tradition
    IV. strongly objected to educational tradition
    V. taught at Columbia University's Teachers College
    The CORRECT answer is:

    A. I, IV, V
    B. II, III
    C. II, IV
    D. I, II, V
    E. I, III, IV

20. The types of projects Kilpatrick recommended in education were
    I. rote learning and memorization
    II. problem solving and drill project
    III. tutored lessons and seminars
    IV. creative and appreciative projects
    V. physical and mental
    The CORRECT answer is:

    A. I, V
    B. II, III
    C. I, III
    D. II, IV
    E. none of the above

21. Pestalozzi was an educator noted for
    I. innovative ideas about how children learn
    II. having been very sheltered as a child
    III. modeling his pedagogy on his own innovative childhood
    IV. relating language to observation
    V. basing all learning on sensation and development
    The CORRECT answer is:

    A. I, II, III
    B. I, II, IV, V
    C. III, IV
    D. IV, V
    E. IV only

22. An approach suggested by Pestalozzi that has been incorporated into American education is

    A. student respect for teachers
    B. beginning with simple elements and progressing to abstract
    C. beginning with abstract principle and progressing to concrete tests
    D. group-centered learning
    E. operant conditioning

23. Pestalozzi's pedagogy influenced
    I. John Dewey
    II. progressivists opposed to abstract learning
    III. the American philanthropist William Maclure
    IV. Joseph Neef, whose progressive school was founded in Philadelphia
    V. the English Utopian socialist Robert Owen
    The CORRECT answer is:

    A. I, III
    B. I, IV, V
    C. II, IV
    D. I, III, V
    E. all of the above

24. Pestalozzi's influence was
    I. confined to the first half of the 19th century
    II. considerable throughout the 19th century
    III. popularized by Edward Sheldon in New York
    IV. revolutionary for his time
    V. minor during his own time
    The CORRECT answer is:

    A. I, V
    B. II, III
    C. II, III, IV
    D. II, IV
    E. III, V

25. Rousseau's influence on American education was
    I. confined onto to naturalists
    II. primarily confined to behaviorists
    III. largely due to his novel EMILE
    IV. based on the inherent goodness of human nature
    V. supported by Calvinist and Puritan beliefs
    The CORRECT answer is:

A. I only B. II, III
C. III only D. IV only
E. III, IV

26. Important elements in Rousseau's pedagogy are
    I. a belief in structuring educational programs around children
    II. the belief that people develop through three stages
    III. the belief that people develop through five stages
    IV. avoiding excessive verbalism
    V. embracing social institutions and their assets
    The CORRECT answer is:

    A. I, V B. I, II
    C. I, III, V D. I, III, IV
    E. I, III, IV, V

27. Friedrich Froebel influenced 19th century American education in that he
    I. encouraged the use of toys in the learning process
    II. followed Pestalozzi's approach
    III. originated the kindergarten
    IV. rejected Protestant notions that man is born into sin
    V. accepted child weakness and deficiencies
    The CORRECT answer is:

    A. I, II B. II, III
    C. II, III, IV, V D. II, III, IV
    E. I, III, V

28. Lingering effects of Froebel's innovative experiments in American education are
    I. the popularity of the kindergarten
    II. the belief in the child as a spiritually precious creature
    III. the belief in the child as a latent adult
    IV. structured lessons in logically ordered steps
    V. current concentration on child development
    The CORRECT answer is:

    A. I, IV B. II only
    C. III, IV D. II, IV, V
    E. I, II, V

29. Johann Friedrich Herbart was a German educator who
    I. studied philosophy
    II. studied psychology
    III. was influenced by Pestalozzi
    IV. encouraged development and creativity in lessons
    V. encouraged frequency and association in lessons
    The CORRECT answer is:

    A. I, V B. I, II, III, V
    C. II, IV, V D. III, IV, V
    E. I, IV, V

30. Herbart's widely popular teaching methodology consisted of
    I. letting children progress at their own rate
    II. one system designed for all students
    III. four steps in clearly defined phases
    IV. gradual phases in creatively determined steps
    V. intense teacher involvement
    The CORRECT answer is:

    A. II, III, V
    B. I, IV
    C. II, III
    D. I, III
    E. III, V

31. The elements included in Herbart's methodology include
    I. preparation and presentation
    II. association and generalization
    III. memorization and stimulation
    IV. sensitization and emotionalism
    V. vitalism and intellectualism
    The CORRECT answer is:

    A. I, II
    B. III, IV
    C. I, IV
    D. II, V
    E. II, III

32. Critics of Herbart's method claimed that it
    I. was practically unusable
    II. was sloppy and unprecise
    III. emphasized history and literature too much
    IV. was too rigid for student creativity
    V. created passivity in the student
    The CORRECT answer is:

    A. I, III
    B. II, III
    C. IV, V
    D. I, III, V
    E. all of the above

33. John Dewey was an American educator who
    I. was also a philosopher
    II. was influenced by German idealism
    III. followed Hegel's philosophy
    IV. encouraged educational reform
    V. created pedagogical theory but did not test it
    The CORRECT answer is:

    A. I, II
    B. I, II, III
    C. I, III, V
    D. I, II, III, IV
    E. IV, V

34. John Dewey authored
    I. THE SCHOOL AND SOCIETY
    II. HOW WE THINK
    III. INTEREST AND EFFORT IN EDUCATION
    IV. INDIVIDUALISM OLD AND NEW
    V. DEMOCRACY AND EDUCATION
    The CORRECT answer is:

    A. II, IV
    B. I, III, IV
    C. I, III, V
    D. I, II, III
    E. all of the above

35. Dewey's educational philosophy
    I. is clearly defined and precise
    II. is eclectic and difficult to summarize
    III. emphasized the organism and its environment
    IV. was influenced heavily by Darwinism
    V. concentrated on classroom learning
    The CORRECT answer is:

    A. I, V
    B. II, III, IV
    C. I, III, V
    D. I, IV, V
    E. III, IV

36. According to Dewey, the human mind
    I. is largely determined by genetics
    II. begins as a clean slate
    III. is naturally adapted toward problem solving
    IV. is created only through experience
    V. is highly resistant to change
    The CORRECT answer is:

    A. I, II
    B. III, IV
    C. I only
    D. IV only
    E. II, IV

37. The school's function, in Dewey's opinion, is to
    I. teach, reform and conform
    II. discipline, train and build character
    III. simplify, purify and balance culture
    IV. represent the political and economic system
    V. encourage, stimulate and inspire
    The CORRECT answer is:

    A. I, V
    B. II, IV
    C. III, IV
    D. III only
    E. IV only

38. Samuel Hall was an American educator who
    I. was the first to contribute to the literature on teacher education
    II. was a Congregational minister
    III. conducted a private academy to prepare teachers
    IV. taught at Phillips Andover Academy
    V. wrote LECTURES TO SCHOOL MASTERS ON TEACHING in 1833
    The CORRECT answer is:

    A. I, II
    B. II, III, IV
    C. III, IV, V
    D. I, III, V
    E. all of the above

39. According to Hall, teachers should
    I. have common sense and judgment to realistically appraise conditions
    II. be fair and morally sound
    III. have literary qualifications, including geography and American history
    IV. have affection for their students
    V. not be indecisive
    The CORRECT answer is:

    A. I, IV
    B. III, IV, V
    C. I, II
    D. II, III, IV
    E. all of the above

40. The normal school was
    I. established in the tradition of the common school
    II. established in opposition to the common school
    III. created by James Carter, a Massachusetts politician
    IV. designed to train teachers
    V. designed to house model schools
    The CORRECT answer is:

    A. I, III, V
    B. I, III, IV, V
    C. III, V
    D. I, V
    E. all of the above

41. Horace Mann and James Carter were associated in that
    I. the latter sponsored bills for legislation helping Dewey's activities
    II. the former was named by the latter as the first secretary of the first Board of Education
    III. they both saw the normal school as a way to advance humanity
    IV. they entered into frequent public debates
    V. their pedagogical theories were sharply contrasted
    The CORRECT answer is:

    A. I, II, III
    B. II, IV
    C. V only
    D. I, III, V
    E. I, IV, V

42. Teacher education changed from
    I. two year normal schools to four year degree granting colleges
    II. being attached to other disciplines to being independent
    III. being independent to being attached to other disciplines
    IV. being challenged by traditionalists to being supported by them
    V. being supported by traditionalists to being challenged by them
    The CORRECT answer is:

    A. I, II, IV
    B. I, III, V
    C. I, III, IV
    D. I, II, V
    E. none of the above

43. Andrew Draper, the 19th century educator, was
    I. dedicated to improving teachers' professional status
    II. influential in discouraging separate schools for teachers
    III. an advocate of educational psychology
    IV. an advocate of philosophy of education
    V. concerned over curricula that were too broad
    The CORRECT answer is:

    A. I, V
    B. II, V
    C. I, III
    D. I, III, IV
    E. I, III, IV, V

44. American educators who *closely* followed Herbartian pedagogy include
    I. Frank and Charles McMurry
    II. C. C. Van Liew
    III. Elmer Brown
    IV. Charles De Garmo
    V. E. L. Thorndike
    The CORRECT answer is:

    A. I, IV
    B. I, II, III, IV
    C. II, III, IV
    D. I, III, V
    E. all of the above

45. The National Herbartian Society of 1892
    I. promoted the study of education as a discipline
    II. sought to simplify the curriculum of the elementary school
    III. sought to broaden the curriculum of the elementary school
    IV. sought to include literature and nature in elementary studies
    V. sought to systematize and categorize education
    The CORRECT answer is:

    A. I, II, V
    B. I, III, IV
    C. II, IV, V
    D. I, III, V
    E. I, II

46. L. Thorndike was an American educator who
    I. is best known for using statistical methods in education
    II. developed testing of educational services
    III. developed tests for spelling achievement
    IV. wrote AN INTRODUCTION TO THE THEORY OF MENTAL AND SOCIAL MEASUREMENTS
    V. was active at the turn of the century
    The CORRECT answer is:

    A. I, II, IV, V
    B. III only
    C. I, III, V
    D. II, IV, V
    E. IV, V

47. The educational innovations of the 1950's and 1960's
    I. lead to the "new" mathematics and physics
    II. were encouraged by the Ford Foundation
    III. were encouraged by Carnegie philanthropy
    IV. were heavily influenced by B. F. Skinner's psychology
    V. were dropped as quickly as they were adopted
    The CORRECT answer is:

    A. I, II
    B. I, II, III
    C. I, IV, V
    D. I, II, III, IV
    E. all of the above

48. The *primary* influence(s) B. F. Skinner had on American education is(are)
    I. the development of programmed learning
    II. teaching by using elemental steps in a process
    III. encouraging team teaching
    IV. the emphasis on discovery and structure
    V. his full professorship at Harvard
    The CORRECT answer is:

    A. I, V
    B. I only
    C. II only
    D. I, II
    E. III, IV

49. The American kindergarten
    I. was modeled after the German version
    II. came to the U.S. through German refugees
    III. was introduced by William Torrey Harris
    IV. has steadily decreased in enrollment
    V. has steadily increased in enrollment
    The CORRECT answer is:

    A. I, V
    B. I, II, III
    C. I, III, IV
    D. I, II, V
    E. I, II, III, V

50. John Dewey's philosophy and pedagogy can BEST be described as

    A. idealism
    B. humanism
    C. pragmatism
    D. scholasticism
    E. behaviorism

KEY (CORRECT ANSWERS)

1. C	11. E	21. B	31. A	41. A
2. C	12. D	22. B	32. C	42. A
3. B	13. A	23. E	33. D	43. D
4. D	14. C	24. C	34. E	44. B
5. C	15. D	25. E	35. B	45. B
6. A	16. B	26. D	36. B	46. A
7. B	17. C	27. D	37. D	47. D
8. C	18. B	28. E	38. E	48. D
9. B	19. A	29. B	39. E	49. E
10. D	20. D	30. A	40. B	50. C

EDUCATIONAL ADMINISTRATION AND SUPERVISION
EXAMINATION SECTION
TEST 1

DIRECTIONS: Each question or incomplete statement is followed by several suggested answers or completions. Select the one that BEST answers the question or completes the statement. *PRINT THE LETTER OF THE CORRECT ANSWER IN THE SPACE AT THE RIGHT.*

1. Although local, regional, and national efforts are in progress to elevate the status of the teacher to that of a fully-recognized profession, membership in the ranks is not being replenished with an adequate number of high caliber, competent recruits to meet the needs.
   Of the following obstacles to effective recruitment, the LEAST likely to be surmounted through the efforts of educators in the immediate future is
   A. ability of youth to select more remunerative careers whose requirements are lower in terms of time and money spent for preparation
   B. inadequate school buildings and equipment
   C. inadequacy and ineffectiveness of counseling and recruiting programs to attract promising young men and women into teacher preparation programs
   D. belief shared by a large proportion of those enrolled in secondary schools and colleges that teaching is unattractive as a career
   E. undemocratic administrative practices and procedures to which some teachers are subjected

1.____

2. The MOST effective of the following suggestions that educators might use for attracting young people to teaching as a career is:
   A. Arrange for a high school senior day on a teachers college campus where the emotional satisfactions to be gained from following teaching as a career are stressed.
   B. Arrange for as many high school students as possible to obtain such teaching experiences as are provided in playground and camp work
   C. Have outstanding professional educators speak on the importance of the educational system at school assemblies
   D. Plan a semi-annual school career day during which special emphasis will be placed on teaching
   E. Sponsor college scholarships for capable young people who have chosen teaching as their lifework

2.____

3. Of the following contributing causes for the inability of school systems to recruit an adequate number of well-qualified teachers, the MAJOR one is:
   A. Antiquated and biased state certification regulations
   B. Ineffective and meager recruitment programs
   C. Little opportunity for promotion and recognition of merit
   D. Low standards of selective admission to teacher education institutions
   E. Poor working conditions

3.____

4. The one of the following groups of factors which should be MOST important in the selection of educational personnel is:
    A. Educational point of view, health, relations with others, understanding of leaders, social viewpoint
    B. Age, health, speech, knowledge of facts in instruction area, appearance
    C. Knowledge of facts used in instruction, knowledge of instructional material, speech, knowledge of human growth and development, health
    D. Age, high school record, college record, teaching experience, intellectual ability
    E. Understanding of learners, background and experience, health, knowledge of instructional material, knowledge of facts in instructional area

5. Of the following, the GREATEST limitation of the interview as a means of selecting educational personnel is that
    A. the interview is time-consuming and costly
    B. adaptation of the interview to allow for differences among candidates is sometimes not possible
    C. the interview has been discredited as a selection method
    D. answers obtained are usually superficial because candidates have not sufficient time to think through the full implication of the questions put to them
    E. the procedures involved are essentially subjective

6. The school administrator has many administrative tools available to solve the problems with which he is faced. One of the most important of these is the conference.
   When compared to other administrative tools, the GREATEST value of the conference is to solve problems which
    A. are familiar and rather simple
    B. are new and difficult
    C. do not require a solution in the foreseeable future
    D. are not amenable to solution
    E. do not involve any research or analysis

7. You have been asked to answer a letter from the dean of a nearby school of education requesting certain information. After giving the request careful consideration, you find that it cannot be granted.
   Of the following ways of beginning your answering letter, the BEST is to begin by
    A. discussing the problem of releasing confidential information
    B. explaining in detail why the request cannot be granted
    C. indicating, if possible, that the information may be available from other sources
    D. quoting the laws which prohibit the dissemination of information of the type requested
    E. saying that you are sorry that the request cannot be granted

3 (#1)

8. The furtherance of mental hygiene in the schools is desirable PRIMARILY because
   A. it keeps the disturbing problems of the pupil-teacher relationship at a minimum
   B. optimum conditions for the personal-social development of individual pupils are thus provided
   C. pupils learn essential subject matter better in a favorable emotional atmosphere
   D. serious future problems of maladjustment can be prevented by dealing with maladjustments in their early stages
   E. children should be as happy as possible while in school

8._____

9. Education for democracy is BEST formulated when it
   A. is based on a uniform interpretation of the term "democracy"
   B. recognizes that democracy calls for cooperation founded on self-sacrifice to make it function
   C. holds that a new social order must be built before current economic and social problems can be solved
   D. is based on the thesis that the state has its origin in a social contract
   E. recognizes that social values are subject to constant change

9._____

10. The present trend is to extend the period of pre-service preparation for teachers at all levels of instruction. Leaders in the field are advocating that the additional time available be employed in
    A. additional training in the subject of specialization
    B. course instruction in materials dealing with the psychological bases of pupil behavior
    C. extending the mastery of general cultural materials
    D. observing the classroom work of skilled teachers and in practice teaching
    E. providing advanced and intensive instruction in professional subjects

10._____

11. Written tests employed for the purpose of selecting educational personnel are NOT completely satisfactory CHIEFLY because, in general, they
    A. do not allow for probing in depth into a candidate's background, emotional problems, etc.
    B. do not allow for a wide enough sampling of a candidate's skills and knowledge
    C. do not attempt to evaluate a candidate's personality
    D. do not measure ability to perform
    E. have been useful only in the evaluation of factual knowledge

11._____

12. The MOST important of the following reasons for reviewing the non-teaching experiences of an applicant for a teaching position is that non-teaching experiences may
    A. indicate the range of experience the applicant has had in dealing with people
    B. provide basic evidence of the patriotic or subversive thinking of the applicant through the groups or organizations with which he has been associated

12._____

C. reveal sources of potential maladjustment which may develop
D. provide evidence concerning the applicant's motivation in choosing teaching as his life work
E. show avocational interests which the examiner should consider in prognosticating the mental health of the candidate as a teacher

13. No educational system can live without teachers who are competent, qualified, and above all, enthusiastic. The public school system is starving because of a lack of this kind of teacher.
    The problem implied in this statement
    A. is likely to confront educational leaders everywhere for a long time
    B. would tend to be solved if higher intellectual standards were set by teacher examining boards
    C. is limited for the most part in its more crucial aspects to the smaller communities and to rural areas
    D. would tend to be solved if there were more teacher education institutions
    E. is probably a temporary, natural aftermath of the war period

13.____

14. Of the following procedures, the one which would probably be MOST effective in reducing teacher criticism of the standards used on examinations for supervisory positions in a school system is to
    A. eliminate all controversial qualifying tests from the examination
    B. hold periodic public hearings for the discussion of standards used on examinations
    C. provide for teacher participation in determining standards
    D. publish a detailed statement of the standards in advance
    E. use a fixed standard for all examinations

14.____

15. Experience requirements for newly-appointed teachers at the elementary and junior high school levels are much less prevalent today than 30 years ago. Of the following, the MAJOR justification for elimination of experience requirements is the
    A. demonstrated low value of teaching experience in predicting efficiency in teaching
    B. difficulty in recruiting young men and women interested in teaching
    C. longer period of professional preparation now required for appointment
    D. prevalence of in-service training opportunities in most urban areas
    E. undesirable competitive situations among school systems which result from experience requirements tied to higher salaries

15.____

16. Buros' MENTAL MEASUREMENTS YEARBOOK is a valuable reference for administrators who want to
    A. identify the causes of failure on teacher-selection examinations
    B. know the group intelligence-test scores for teachers and other professional groups
    C. locate and to evaluate standardized tests and references on testing
    D. know the techniques for administering diagnostic tests
    E. measure the degree of efficiency of instruction among beginning teachers

16.____

17. To the maximum extent possible, each school should be permitted to have the responsibility for planning its own program. Adoption of this policy would MOST likely lead to
    A. *less effective* planning primarily because members of a central planning agency tend to have a more objective viewpoint than teachers in a school
    B. *more effective* planning primarily because plans would be conceived in terms of the actual situation, and the participants would have a greater will to succeed
    C. *less effective* planning primarily because if planning is left to the school, there will be no agency qualified to determine whether the plans are properly executed
    D. *more effective* planning primarily because the men and women in the schools tend to be better qualified technically than the members of a staff agency
    E. *less effective* planning primarily because schools are usually undermanned and, consequently, are in no position to assign staff for planning purposes

17._____

18. Of the following publications, the one which is MOST useful for a comprehensive overview of most of the major research related to the selection of educational personnel is:
    A. McCall's MEASUREMENT OF TEACHER MERIT
    B. Monroe's ENCYCLOPEDIA OF EDUCATIONAL RESEARCH
    C. The latest triennial issue of the REVIEW OF EDUCATIONAL RESEARCH which deals with "Teachers and Non-academic Personnel"
    D. THE IMPROVEMENT OF TEACHING, a monograph published by the National Commission on Teacher Education and Professional Standards
    E. PRINCIPLES AND PROCEDURES OF TEACHER SELECTION, a monograph published by the American Association of Examiners and Administrators of Educational Personnel

18._____

19. Verified evidence of deep emotional disturbances in the records of an applicant for a teaching position should point to a rejection of his application MAINLY because
    A. educational systems should not employ people for teaching positions who have a history of emotional disturbance
    B. every child has the right to be taught by healthy, well-adjusted teachers
    C. it is generally agreed that people once afflicted with mental or emotional disturbances cannot be inspiring teachers
    D. some emotional experiences tend to have lasting deleterious effects upon a person's mental health
    E. teachers having deep emotional disturbances are not capable of teaching logical organized subjects, such as mathematics

19._____

20. The consensus of research findings to date indicates that teacher effectiveness
    A. is negatively related to the amount of professional preparation beyond the bachelor's degree for elementary school teachers, but positively related to such preparation for high school teachers
    B. consists of two primary factors – knowledge of children and knowledge of subject – the latter being closely related to supervisors' efficiency ratings
    C. is not a unitary quality and, as variously defined has shown little or no consistent positive relationship to the amount of professional preparation, length of teaching experience, or supervisors' efficiency ratings
    D. consists of three primary factors – knowledge of children, knowledge of subject, and knowledge of the learning process – and that a substantial positive correlation exists between the first and teacher-pupil relations, the second and teacher-parent relations, and the third and teacher-supervisory relations
    E. is positively correlated with both the amount of teaching experience and supervisors' efficiency ratings, but that there is a slight but consistent negative relationship between these two factors

20.____

21. The one of the following sets of tests which would provide, in general, the MOST practical and useful battery in the selection of elementary school teachers in a large metropolitan school system is:
    A. An analysis of teaching-learning situations observed in films, a personality interview, a speech test, and the National Teacher Examination
    B. A multiple-choice test on child psychology as applied to the school situation and on general education and cultural background, a summary of teaching experience and preparation, and an analysis of the applicant's teaching performance
    C. An autobiography, including a summary of teaching experience and preparation, written response to a cases or situation presented, and a speech test
    D. A multiple-choice test on subject matter and educational methods , a test of personality, a speech test, and an analysis of classroom work observed by the applicant and the administrator
    E. The National Teacher Examination, an objective test of personality, a summary of teaching experience and preparation, and letters of recommendation

21.____

22. Too often the school administrator does not realize that the organization chart is only an idealized picture of his intentions, a reflection of his hopes and aims, rather than a photograph of the operating facts within his organization.
    This statement is BEST supported by the fact that the organization chart
    A. cannot be a photograph of the living organization but must be either a record of past organization or proposed future organization
    B. deals in terms of positions rather than of people
    C. defines too explicitly the jurisdiction assigned to each component unit
    D. does not indicate unresolved internal ambiguities
    E. sometimes contains unresolved internal ambiguities

22.____

23. When interviewing teacher candidates, to which of the following characteristics should GREATEST weight or consideration be accorded?
   A. Fluency of verbal expression
   B. Poise and self-assurance
   C. Interest in teaching
   D. Speech pattern
   E. Tact and courtesy

24. A fifth-grade teacher experimented with a form of experience curriculum which emphasized pupil-teacher planning to meet the psychological needs of pupils. At the end of the year, a comprehensive achievement test revealed that the scores of pupils were a good deal higher than usual for that school in language, art, geography, history, and literature, but lower in arithmetic.
Of the following, the MOST acceptable action to be taken on the basis of these findings is:
   A. Essentially the same plan should be used for another year to determine whether corrective measures need be applied, and where
   B. Less emphasis should be given in the future to language, art, etc. so that more time will be available for arithmetic
   C. No radical change should be made in the experimental program, but the supervisor should help the teacher in the teaching of arithmetic in the experience curriculum
   D. Not enough emphasis was given to arithmetic, so that the future arithmetic skills should be taught separately, not as part of the experience curriculum
   E. The experience curriculum should be abandoned or at least de-emphasized, and greater emphasis should be place don subject-matter teaching

25. Curriculum development has been furthered MOST by research on
   A. the application of more meaningful tests and other instruments for evaluating curriculum effectiveness
   B. the effectiveness of such learning materials as audio-visual aids and their relationship to the curriculum
   C. better construction of courses of study from the viewpoint of the learning process
   D. the effects of remedial programs on pupil achievement in new areas
   E. the influence of the maturation, growth, and development of the child in relation to the scope and sequence of the curriculum

26. The departmental chairman in a high school executes policy formulated at higher levels. He does not make policy. He is the element of the administrative structure closest to the teacher.
Accepting this description of the duties of the departmental chairman, it follows that he BEST carries out his responsibilities when he
   A. assigns teachers to classes on the basis of their abilities and interests
   B. checks on the progress of the teachers in his department in order to make certain that they will complete teaching assignments
   C. disciplines teachers who break rules

D. interprets and executes policies in a manner that respects teacher needs and interests
E. suggests desirable changes in the curriculum on the basis of his department's experience

27. You have been assigned to conduct a classroom teaching test. The one of the following means of preparing for this assignment that would be of LEAST value is to
    A. become acquainted with the teacher's plan for the day
    B. clarify your own thinking regarding effective teaching
    C. review the forms and rating blanks to be used in the appraisal
    D. study records and other data about the learners
    E. visit the classroom for several days prior to the day of appraisal

27._____

28. The mental hygiene concept in modern teacher training requires that the classroom teacher should
    A. be able to cope with all types of emotional problems as they arise in the classroom
    B. prevent pupils from experiencing frustration
    C. be able to discuss behavior problems with parents in simple terms
    D. structure learning situations so that they strengthen pupils' adjustive processes
    E. be a thoroughly well-adjusted individual

28._____

29. An approach to personality that represents a new influence on personality measurement is to be found in
    A. Adorno, THE AUTHORITARIAN PERSONALITY
    B. Bales, INTERACTION PROCESS ANALYSIS
    C. Cronbach, ESSENTGIALS OF PSYCHOLOGICAL TESTING
    D. Symonds, DIAGNOSING PERSONALITY AND CONDUCT
    E. Traxler, TECHNIQUES OF GUIDANCE

29._____

30. The Committee on the Criteria of Teacher Effectiveness of the American Educational Research Association has issued several reports on discussions of the subject that have been held.
    The PRINCIPAL contribution of these reports is the
    A. detailing of a program of cooperative research on the character and causes of good teaching
    B. formulation of a conceptual frame of reference for the study of teacher effectiveness
    C. keen analysis of the characteristics of the democratically oriented teacher
    D. listing of the published and unpublished tests which, in the opinion of the Committee, have been found most valid in measuring teacher characteristics
    E. searching critique of the limitations of the several techniques currently employed in teacher selection and retention

30._____

31. Teacher participation in developing plans which will affect administrative and supervisory personnel as well as teachers will contribute to greater understanding of the entire system. When possible, such teacher participation should be encouraged.
    This policy, in general, is
    A. *good*, primarily because it will enable the teacher to make intelligent suggestions for adjustment of the plans in the future
    B. *bad*, primarily because teachers can be given administrative background instruction more effectively in an in-service training course
    C. *good*, primarily because plans tend to be better when more persons participate in formulating them
    D. *bad*, primarily because teachers should participate only in those activities which affect their own level; otherwise, conflicts in authority may arise
    E. *good*, primarily because teachers will accept administrative decisions more readily if they are aware of the real reasons for making them

31._____

32. Legal proof that an applicant for a position in an educational system has served a sentence in a penal institution, no matter how early in his life, should constitute an automatic rejection of his application.
    This basis for rejection is
    A. *desirable*, primarily because children will not respect teachers who have broken the laws of adult society
    B. *undesirable*, primarily because applications for teaching positions cannot reasonably be expected to have higher standards of conduct that citizens in any other occupation or profession
    C. *desirable*, primarily because educational systems should not employ people for teaching responsibilities who have served a sentence for a lapse in responsibility
    D. *undesirable*, primarily because it indicates little discrimination in terms of type and extent of crime or of subsequent conduct
    E. *desirable*, primarily because payment of the legal price for an unlawful act is no certain guarantee of the exercise of good citizenship thereafter

32._____

33. It is generally considered desirable to attract more men into the teaching profession PRIMARILY because it is believed that
    A. men are generally better at maintaining discipline and coaching teams
    B. children usually respect men more than women, and commonly achieve greater maturity and self-control under the guidance of men teachers
    C. men are needed for eventual promotion into positions of administrative leadership
    D. children should have an opportunity to be associated with men as well as women in school
    E. men are needed to give greater continuity to the school program

33._____

34. The MOST justifiable and, probably, MOST effective of the following proposals for increasing the supply of teachers of trade subjects in the near future is:
    A. Allow increased salary credit for journeyman experience in the trade
    B. Induct the trade unions in each of the several trades to cooperate in a recruitment drive
    C. Reduce initial eligibility requirements to a minimum of education and three years of journeyman experience, and permit appointees to take the required courses in educational subjects after they have begun to serve
    D. Simplify the examination for the regular license so that it will consist only of an interview to evaluate personal qualifications and a trade competence test
    E. Sponsor legislation under which teachers of trade subjects would be paid on a higher salary schedule than that paid to teachers of academic subjects

34.____

35. Improvement of mental hygiene practices in the schools must be CHIEFLY a matter of
    A. carefully selecting mentally healthy teachers in the first place because empathic relations with others depend almost entirely on innate personal qualities
    B. continuous training of the teacher, both pre-service and in-service, in mental hygiene theory and practice
    C. eliminating those candidates who are not aware of the best mental health practices
    D. insisting that training in mental health practices be provided to those teachers already on the job who are in need of it
    E. regular consultation with professional mental health practitioners on pupil personality problems before and after they arise

35.____

36. In a school system where the superintendent of schools habitually decides on all policy changes without staff consultation, the MOST probable staff reaction is to
    A. accept the decisions if they are rational
    B. resent and obstruct all policy changes
    C. appreciate the source of authority in the situation
    D. demand opportunity to participate in future policy changes
    E. feel insecure

36.____

37. Management of educational personnel, when compared with management of personnel in business and industry,
    A. cannot be based on the same principles as essentially different kinds of people are involved
    B has been in the direction of permitting the teacher greater freedom
    C. has, in all ways, been quite similar
    D. has, in all ways, been quite dissimilar
    E. should be based on the same principles without appropriate modification

37.____

38. In general, policies within a school system should evolve from 38.____
    A. analysis by the supervisor and his immediate staff and then be communicated to the rest of the staff
    B. participation of the entire staff
    C. studies made by persons who, because they are not concerned, can be objective
    D. participation of those most concerned
    E. analysis by the supervisor and his immediate staff, and then be voted upon by the entire staff

39. The relationship between mental ability and school achievement is illustrated by the fact that a relatively satisfactory mental ability test for school administrators would be 39.____
    A. a test consisting of achievement items in current events and mechanical comprehension
    B. a test consisting of achievement items in grammatical classification and American history
    C. a test consisting of achievement items in spelling and arithmetic computation
    D. a test consisting of achievement items in word meaning and arithmetic reasoning
    E. impossible to attain through the use of achievement test items

40. The superintendent of schools asks you to prepare a statement dealing with a controversial matter for public distribution. 40.____
    Of the following approaches, the one which would usually be MOST effective is to
    A. buttress the board of education's viewpoint with all the statistical data and research techniques which were used in arriving at it
    B. avoid taking a definite stand if at all possible
    C. develop the board of education's viewpoint from ideas and facts well-known to most readers
    D. avoid taking a definite stand where you know that your views conflict with those of the superintendent
    E. present the board of education's viewpoint as tersely as possible without any reference to any other matters

41. Of the following, the GREATEST danger the average administrator of a school system faces is 41.____
    A. being too personal in his dealings with staff who work directly with him
    B. failure to delegate responsibility effectively
    C. delegating responsibility he should keep
    D. failure to keep channels of communication open
    E. questioning his basic policy of subordinates

42. Plans for the organization of the school of the future must be flexible; the kind of school which will develop depends to a great extent on the quality of teachers we will have.
In general, this statement is
    A. *not correct*, primarily because individual teachers should not be able to change the organization of a school
    B. *correct*, primarily because if we have high quality teachers, the problem of organization tends to solve itself
    C. *not correct*, primarily because it is the function of any good school system to train its teachers rather than let them change it
    D. *correct*, primarily because school organization cannot be considered apart from teacher qualifications
    E. *not correct*, primarily because school organization is only remotely affected by the quality of teachers

43. Teachers can BEST related mental hygiene to discipline in the school by
    A. helping children develop standards of conduct in the classroom which make for the best possible conditions for learning and development
    B. holding children to consistent and thoroughly-understood standards of group behavior at all times
    C. maintaining a highly permissive spirit in the classroom so that misbehavior ceases to have individual meaning
    D. relying on the exercise of self-discipline of group members based on democratic sanctions created by the group itself
    E. using sound and long-understood teaching methods with normally well-behaved children, referring deviates to disciplinary authorities

44. Of the following mental health principles for dealing with the common mental health problems of individual pupils, the MOST important is to
    A. depend almost entirely on recommendations of professional specialists who can make adequate diagnoses
    B. do nothing until a thorough case study can be made
    C. employ common techniques which experience has shown to be effective in most cases
    D. let the problems work themselves out in the give-and-take of wholesome classroom activity
    E. work in terms of the specific causes and effects operating upon the individual child

45. School administrators frequently interview people in order to obtain information. This means of obtaining information has limitations which should not be overlooked.
The MOST important limitation of those listed is that
    A. information, which can be obtained by this method, tends to be necessarily subjective
    B. during an interview, people frequently refuse to give information which they are willing to submit in writing
    C. it is more difficult to conduct an interview than to construct a questionnaire

D. people who are interviewed frequently answer questions with guesses rather than admit their ignorance
E. the interview is usually of value for obtaining specific information only

46. The one of the following which is usually the FIRST step in the development of a test to be used in selecting educational personnel is to
    A. prepare the job description
    B. determine attributes and competencies required for success on the job
    C. review tests previously used for this purpose
    D. determine the types of tests to be used
    E. set up minimum requirements to be met by all applicants

47. Announcements of examinations for teaching positions have been attacked because they do not contain sufficient specific information concerning the scope of the written test for candidates to prepare properly for the test.
    Of the following, the CHIEF limitation on giving information to prospective candidates is that
    A. candidates sometimes interpret the scope, as defined, differently from the examiner, and conflicts arise
    B. some candidates who are not familiar with some of the fields listed will not file for the examination
    C. the board of examiners may not be able to arrive at a decision on what fields should be tested
    D. the examination will not be a proper test of candidates' abilities as they will know in advance the areas to be tested
    E. the examiner assigned to prepare the examination may find himself unduly restricted in test scope

48. It has been recommended that explicit information concerning appeal procedures be made available to all candidates.
    To put this recommendation into effect would be
    A. *desirable*, primarily because candidates will have a better understanding of the procedures of the board of examiners
    B. *undesirable*, primarily because it would encourage more candidates to appeal
    C. *desirable*, primarily because it would encourage greater confidence in the selection procedure
    D. *undesirable*, primarily because there is no point in making information about these procedures public as only appellants are interested
    E. *desirable*, primarily because this would tend to standardize the appeal process, making it more efficient for both the appellants and the board of examiners

49. In reviewing the experience record of a candidate for a supervisory position, an examiner decides that he should give credit for the candidate's contributions to the improvement of educational conditions in the school system.
This decision is MOST justified on the basis that
   A. this practice has been satisfactory in industrial firms, which seek to place a premium on administrative or supervisory ability
   B. such contributions constitute a reliable index of current professional growth and future promise
   C. recognition of successful experience in any teaching, administrative, or supervisory situation is a matter of equity
   D. such contributions were not require in the normal line of duty
   E. this is an important way in which this type of work can be encouraged

49._____

50. In the course of planning for a series of individual interview tests for a given license, it is decided to rate applicants on a number of traits.
The MOST important consideration to be borne in mind in such planning is that the traits selected should
   A. be carefully defined
   B. include those which research has demonstrated to be characteristic of good teachers generally
   C. be objectively measurable
   D. not overlap
   E. be weighted in terms of their relative importance

50._____

KEY (CORRECT ANSWERS)

1. A	11. D	21. B	31. A	41. D
2. B	12. A	22. B	32. D	42. D
3. D	13. A	23. C	33. D	43. A
4. E	14. C	24. C	34. A	44. E
5. E	15. C	25. E	35. B	45. D
6. C	16. C	26. D	36. A	46. A
7. E	17. B	27. E	37. E	47. E
8. B	18. B	28. D	38. D	48. C
9. B	19. B	29. A	39. D	49. B
10. C	20. C	30. B	40. C	50. D

TEST 2

DIRECTIONS: Each question or incomplete statement is followed by several suggested answers or completions. Select the one that BEST answers the question or completes the statement. *PRINT THE LETTER OF THE CORRECT ANSWER IN THE SPACE AT THE RIGHT.*

1. In the administration of a teacher-selection program, the standardization of qualifications is important PRIMARILY because it
    A. eliminates the need for comparing candidates for teaching positions with each other
    B. enables examiners to eliminate subjective judgment as a factor in the selection process
    C. makes the task of comparing candidates easier and more reliable
    D. provides a basis for the development of sound teacher-education programs
    E. tends to dissuade lower-ranking college graduates from applying for available positions

    1.____

2. An examiner has the task of evaluating the teaching experience of candidates who have served only as student-teachers.
    Of the following sources, the one which would be of the MOST value to him in making the evaluations is the
    A. confidential ratings of critic-teachers
    B. candidates' ratings on a written test of teaching methods
    C. course grades they received
    D. candidates' written statements describing their successes and failures as student-teachers
    E. written comments of the principal in the school where their student-teaching was performed

    2.____

3. Two assistant examiners who have been assigned to prepare the outline for the essay section of an examination for principal of a high school disagree over the form of the proposed test. One wants five long essays while the other wants thirty short essays.
    The one of the following considerations which would tend to influence your decision in favor of the FIRST choice is that a principal should have
    A. a fine sense of discrimination   B. considerable organizing ability
    C. a good cultural background   D. the ability to reason logically
    E. a good command of language

    3.____

4. You are preparing a written test for the selection of high school social science teachers. The test is designed to measure their knowledge of a specified area of content.
    Once the items have been completed and edited, you should
    A. administer the test to a group of social science teachers of known capabilities to derive evaluative data
    B. ask a committee of experts in the field to examine the items to determine their validity

    4.____

C. administer the test to the candidates and eliminate those items which are not reliable
D. check the items against texts used in teaching the course to make sure they have valid teaching content
E. administer the test to the candidates and eliminate those items which are not valid

5. In constructing objective-type tests for the purpose of selecting educational personnel, the multiple-choice type item is effective PRIMARILY because it
   A. is familiar to the testee because of widespread usage
   B. is reasonably free from the guessing element
   C. constitutes a superior measure of verbal memory
   D. is simple to construct in such a way that several responses appear plausible
   E. is well adapted to the measurement of understanding and discrimination

6. To give "face-validity" to items of a written test, the examiner should
   A. avoid use of items that attempt to forecast rather than measure acquired knowledge
   B. disguise aptitude items by achievement content
   C. emphasize local practice and reduce the weight of broad generalizations
   D. frame questions so as to avoid insularity in content and philosophy
   E. utilize the names of schools, localities, and persons generally known by candidates

7. The following practices have been recommended at various times to the board of education as ways to increase the number of applicants for licenses who are not residents of the city.
Of these, the practice that is likely to be MOST feasible is that the board of examiners should
   A. change the character of its written tests so as to make it possible for out-of-town candidates who have not been coached for these tests to have an advantage over local candidates who have been coached
   B. conduct and complete in July and August of each year license examinations especially designed for out-of-town teaches who are taking summer session courses in the city
   C. conduct its experience tests in such a manner as to give more weight to regular teaching experience outside of the city than to local experience as substitute teacher
   D. conduct its written and other tests in any city or college center in the United States at which twenty or more persons apply
   E. schedule examinations during vacation periods and plan each examination so that out-of-town candidates can complete all examination procedures during a single two-day stay in the city

8. The board of education should increase its efforts to induce persons residing outside of the city to apply for teaching licenses in the city MAINLY because
   A. an increase in the number of applicants will of itself make it possible to enforce higher standards of competence
   B. diversification within any teaching staff with respect to the general background, training, and experience of its members is salutary
   C. out-of-towners are less likely to have "crammed" for the license examinations and, as a result, their ratings would tend to be more valid than those achieved by local applicants
   D. the available local supply of competent applicants is inadequate for most licenses
   E. there is a strong presumption that any person who wishes to teach in a community other than the one in which he was reared or trained is possessed of enterprise, adaptability, and other qualities desirable in a teacher

9. The board of education is about to conduct interview tests for applicants for a certain teaching license.
   To meet the requirement of competitiveness, the MOST important consideration to observe is that the
   A. entire record of the tests must be open to public inspection so that any interested party may satisfy himself that the same standards were applied to all applicants
   B. number of examining panels employed be reduced to a minimum, that, so far as possible, all applicants be asked the same questions, and that, if this is not possible, the test material used be of comparable difficulty for all applicants
   C. qualities measured by the test must be reasonably relevant to the position sought and must be precisely defined
   D. ratings on each item must be justified by objective data duly recorded by each of the examiners
   E. tests must conform to measures or standards which are sufficiently objective to be capable of being challenged or reviewed by other examiners of equal ability and experience

10. Of the common reasons which may disqualify a candidate for a teaching license in a physical and/or medical examination, the LEAST important is:
    A. The possibility that the health or safety of students may be endangered
    B. Inability to complete the normal period of service
    C. Undesirable or unsettling influence on children
    D. Inability to render the quality of service normally required
    E. The possibility of frequent or prolonged absences

11. Interview tests are being conducted for license as teacher of common branch subjects in elementary schools. Each examining panel consists of two elementary school principals and a speech expert. All of the examiners have had considerable experience in interviewing applicants and are known to be competent in this work. The topic that the applicants are asked to discuss is an aspect of the teaching of the language arts in the present elementary school program. Each test is scheduled to least from 15 to 20 minutes. Each member of the examining panel is to rate all aspects of the applicants' performance. Under the circumstances, the factor for which the test is likely to achieve a MOST valid appraisal is that of the applicants'
    A. general fitness
    B. knowledge of subject matter
    C. overall personality
    D. reasoning ability
    E. speech

12. Many precautions must be taken in order to assure a reasonably accurate demonstration of a candidate's teaching ability through direct work with learners.
    The LEAST important of these is to make certain that the candidate has an opportunity to
    A. observe the class he is to teach several times prior to his teaching
    B. learn a day in advance the area of work for which he will be responsible
    C. review the textbook which the class has been using
    D. learn what area has already been covered by the teacher whose place he is taking
    E. study the lesson plan of the teacher whose work he is to take

13. In devising a test to determine the competence of teachers, the one of the following skills with which you would be LEAST concerned is skill in
    A. directing discussion
    B. handling behavior problems
    C. identifying pupil needs
    D. providing for individual differences
    E. selection of instructional materials

14. A recommendation has been made that an agency be set up within the board of education, apart from the board of examiners, for the sole purpose of dealing with all appeals by candidates from examination ratings from inception to conclusion.
    Of the following comments for an against the acceptance of this recommendation, the one which is MOST valid is that it is
    A. *undesirable*, primarily because, before the appeal goes to a review body, the examiner responsible for the rating should be permitted to justify his rating
    B. *desirable*, primarily because no examiner will be in a position to pass upon an appeal from a rating he gave
    C. *undesirable*, primarily because the appeal process is an integral part of the selection process and should not, in the first instance, at least, be divorced from it

D. *desirable*, primarily because the handling of appeals will be expedited
E. *undesirable*, primarily because the handling of appeals will be needlessly complicated

15. Of the following administrative devices for preventing conflict within a board of examiners with respect to the extent of the authority of each of the examiners, the MOST effective, as far as is practicable, is to
    A. assign all related work to the same examiner
    B. have the chairman of the board administratively responsible for resolving all disagreements
    C. set up a committee of senior members of the board to determine policy
    D. have the chairman of the board review examiners' assignments periodically
    E. assign wok to the examiners on a rotation basis

16. Of the following, the MOST effective method of interesting qualified persons not already employed in the city public school system to apply for the directorship of a special subject, e.g., home economics, music, health education, in the city school system, would be for the board of examiners to
    A. obtain from the Office of Education at Washington, D.C. a list of directors and supervisors of the special subject throughout the United States, and to mail circulars of announcement directly to such persons
    B. place advertisements in appropriate professional journals, giving full details concerning the scope of the examination and making it clear that applications from out-of-town applicants will be especially welcome
    C. request local universities specializing in offering graduate courses for out-of-town educators to furnish the board of examiners with lists of the names of persons preparing for supervisory positions in the specialty, and to circularize such persons
    D. send a representative to an appropriate professional convention to provide publicity for the examination and to search out and talk to prospective applicants
    E. send letters to the school superintendents in other cities, asking them to call the attention of qualified persons in their schools to the city's need and to the prospective examination to be held for the position

17. In analyzing the discriminatory power of a test, one item shows that equal proportions of high-scoring and low-scoring persons have succeeded on it. In general, this indicates that the item
    A. contributes to the reliability of the test
    B. has a high discriminatory coefficient
    C. does not contribute to score differentiation
    D. has no validity because it is of doubtful reliability
    E. is probably ambiguous

18. A board of qualified persons is to assist an examiner by conducting oral examinations of a group of candidates.
Of the following, the examiner's BEST procedure with the board members would be to
    A. provide each member of the board with a detailed description of the duties of the position and a list of specific subject-matter questions which cover the entire field
    B. allow them to structure each interview s they wish in order to stimulate optimum interaction between candidates and interviewers
    C. provide each member of the board with a statement of the behaviors he should observe and suggested standard questions designed to provide opportunities for observing these behaviors
    D. call them together for an advance briefing at which the correct answers the examiner wants them to elicit from each candidate will be discussed and provide them with a rank-order listing of the candidates on the written test
    E. provide the board with a detailed list of specific questions to fit into any situation so the interviews will not lag or be open to possible interviewer bias

18._____

19. On a test consisting of 200 items, taken by 80 persons, an individual scored at the 60th percentile.
This means, in general, that
    A. he answered 120 questions correctly
    B. his score surpassed those attained by 48 persons
    C. higher scores than his were attained by 48 persons
    D. his score was more than six-tenths of one standard deviation from the mean
    E. he answered 80 items correctly

19._____

20. In order to achieve objectivity in the selection of education personnel, it is MOST important that
    A. only those dimensions be tested which are known to be related to teacher effectiveness
    B. testing for factual knowledge only be avoided
    C. the attributes deemed essential be clearly set forth
    D. the candidates be tested for factual knowledge as far as possible
    E. the types of tests to be used be clearly set forth

20._____

21. Skill in written test construction is BEST demonstrated by the
    A. ability to apply knowledge of scoring techniques
    B. manner in which statistical techniques are applied
    C. ability to maintain a constructively critical attitude toward the facets of the area to be covered
    D. manner in which the materials to be tested are converted into test items
    E. ability to standardize test items

21._____

22. It has been proposed that a curvilinear relationship be set up between varying lengths of similar experience and credit for that experience. This proposal would tend to be acceptable if it is true that
    A. a single formula for scoring different kinds of experience could be developed
    B. people benefit more from some kinds of experience than from other kinds
    C. experience cannot be scored objectively and, consequently, corrective factors must be introduced
    D. people benefit more from their initial years of experience than from later experience
    E. prediction of job success should be based on recent experience

22.____

23. After two sessions of preliminary training, six panels, each consisting of three assistant examiners, interviewed applicants for the license of teacher of mathematics in junior high schools. Each panel interviewed six applicants. All applicants were rated numerically with a maximum of 20 points and with 12 as a passing grade. The results were:

23.____

Panel	Passed	Rejected	Rated Doubtful
A	4	2	0
B	6	0	0
C	2	3	1
D	5	1	0
E	2	4	0
F	3	3	0
	22	13	1

Of the following, the MOST suitable procedure for the examiner-in-charge to follow would be:
   A. Arrange for re-examination by new panels of all applicants who failed or were rated doubtful
   B. Compare the interview test ratings of these applicants with their ratings in the written test and with the official reports on the quality of their services, if any, and recall for a second interview test those applicants in whose cases the examiner-in-charge discovers obvious discrepancies
   C. Personally retest the applicants who were not passed by Panels C, E, and F to make sure that these panels were not unduly severe, and make appropriate revisions of their ratings if justified by the performance of the applicants in the retests
   D. Present these figures to the assistant examiners for appropriate discussion and consideration, and, unless there is a disposition on the part of one or more panels to reconsider their ratings, he should accept all ratings as final for that test
   E. Statistically work out a coefficient reflecting the degree of leniency or severity of each panel. Apply these coefficients to the ratings of all applicants.

24. Of the following test parts of an examination for teachers, the type of test for which rating on a qualifying, rather than competitive, basis can be BEST justified is the _____ test.
    A. classroom teaching
    B. interview
    C. medical
    D. speech
    E. written essay

25. When an applicant has been rated "unsatisfactory" in a personal test, such as an interview or a teaching test, it is the practice of some examining officials to prepare for the applicant, as part of the record of the test, a separate statement setting forth in detail the reason for his rejection.
    Such a statement is MOST worthwhile if it serves the purpose of
    A. indicating to the applicant the areas in which self-improvement is desirable
    B. protecting the examining authority in the event of litigation
    C. providing the applicant with a concrete basis for formulating an appeal
    D. requiring the examiner who conducted the test to crystallize his thinking and justify the rating
    E. satisfying the applicant that his rejection was justified

26. For the board of examiners to plan its work schedule so as to provide a constant backlog of work would be
    A. *undesirable*, primarily because it is almost impossible to plan for this type of backlog
    B. *desirable*, primarily because the board would be in a better position to change its plans if no deadlines were involved
    C. *undesirable*, primarily because lists of persons eligible for appointment would not be ready when required
    D. *desirable*, primarily because the procedure would tend to insure continuity of work flow
    E. *undesirable*, primarily because the board would be under constant pressure to get work out

27. Of the following statements, the one which BEST describes factory analysis is that factor analysis
    A. is a means of determining the abilities which cover the whole range of human capacity
    B. applied to a group of variables indicates the degree to which they are independent of each other
    C. is a method which has been suggested to replace present methods employed for purposes of prediction
    D. applied to complex processes such as organization and integration of materials, yields valid evaluations
    E. provides an adequate substitute for the psychological analysis of mental processes

28. In the preparation of valid examinations for selection or advancement of teachers, the MOST essential ingredient among the following is:
    A. Careful and detailed administrative review within the examining agency of the final draft of the questions to be used in the examination
    B. A job analysis or description of duties of the positions involved
    C. Collaboration of persons in the preparation of examinations who are thoroughly familiar with the types of jobs being filled
    D. Preliminary trial and statistical analysis of the questions to be used in the examination by persons administratively responsible for filling the positions
    E. Production of standard directions and copy for administration of examinations to the candidates

29. To ascertain the probability with which the assignment of papers to two raters, A and B, represents a random or chance allocation of the papers. the MOST suitable of the following statistical measures to use is the
    A. average standard error of each of the distributions of ratings of the two raters
    B. closeness of fit to the normal curve of the combined distributions of the scores given by the two raters
    C. coefficient of correlation between the scores given by the two raters
    D. critical ratio of the difference between the distributions of the ratings of the two raters
    E. skewness of the combined distribution

30. You have only one form of a test of 200 items to be used in selecting teachers.
    In experimenting with it to determine its reliability, the BEST method to use would be to
    A. obtain the bi-serial correlation of each item with the total score on the test
    B. correlate scores of a norm group on the first 100 items with those obtained on the second 100 items (second half)
    C. rank the items in order of difficulty, split into odd-numbered and even-numbered, and correlate scores thus obtained
    D. correlate the scores from two administrations to a control group a week apart
    E. split the items according to odd-numbered ones and even-numbered ones, and correlate the two scores thus obtained

31. Observed teaching performance should not be the determining factor in teacher selection PRIMARILY because
    A. effectiveness in teaching can vary greatly according to size of class, level of student intelligence, and other factors not always properly weighted
    B. one or two "perfect" or "near perfect" performances do not reveal potentialities as to skill, understanding, or personality
    C. many teachers do not demonstrate their most effective teaching when under observation by administrators or examiners

D. one or two teaching performances cannot possibly include all or most of the important facts of good teaching for a term or semester
E. temporary illness or incapacity may prevent best performance at the time of observation

32. A young woman about to graduate from a state teachers college in a nearby state applies to an examiner for advice. She states that her family will soon move to the city. She would like to apply for a license as teacher of common branch subjects in elementary schools for which applications are being accepted at present. However, she is concerned over the fact that, as a condition of her admission to the state teachers college, she subscribed to an agreement to teach in that state for a minimum of two years.
Knowing that the license is usually valid for three years and that it normally takes a year to publish the eligible list, the examiner should
   A. advise her to obtain a position in the schools of the state in which she now resides and to apply for the city license in the examination to be held a year hence
   B. explain to her that she may apply at once for the city license
   C. make it clear to her that the agreement she entered into is no longer binding since, as soon as she is graduated, it will not be enforceable
   D. suggest that she serve the two years required as she agreed, and to apply in the city after completing her obligation
   E. urge her to seek a release from her agreement and to return to the board of examiners to file an application if she is successful

32._____

Questions 33-34.

DIRECTIONS: Questions 33 and 34 are to be answered on the basis of the following situation.

An examiner is puzzled by the fact that when two of his most trusted assistant examiners work together in conducting an oral examination, they agree much better in their ratings for most candidates than do other pairs of assistant examiners, but that, nevertheless, they give widely divergent ratings to a few candidates. In making their ratings, all assistant examiners employ rating guide sheets which the examiner has recently prepared himself after thorough study of more than twenty different rating sheets and review of some seventy books and articles on techniques of rating in the oral interview.

33. Of the following, the MOST probable explanation for the divergent ratings is:
   A. One of the assistant examiners is reacting to certain of the candidates much more subjectively than the other assistant examiner.
   B. The format of the rating guide sheets does not make adequate provision for careful checking by the assistant examines.
   C. The general agreement is due to chance and the rating guide sheets do not, in general, promote objectivity.
   D. The ratings of one or both of the assistant examiners are affected by some circumstances external to the interviews themselves, such as fatigue, anxiety over home problems, dissatisfaction with job outlook, etc.
   E. The two assistant examines are interpreting their rating guide sheets differently on some points which are crucial in rating some candidates.

33._____

34. Of the following steps, the one which is MOST likely to be profitable for the examiner to take in an effort to correct this situation is:
    A. Assign a third assistant examiner to work with the pair so as to identify which one of them deviates most often from his usual standards and why these deviations occur.
    B. Confer with each of the assistant examiners separately, take careful notes while each gives in detail his reasons for his rating of a candidate on whom the two were in marked disagreement, and then compare the notes taken to identify discrepancies.
    C. Hold a conference with the two assistant examiners, describe the situation to them frankly and objectively, and tell them to resolve their differences.
    D. Recall the candidates in whose ratings the disagreements have been found and examine them himself in order to resolve the disagreements.
    E. Rewrite the rating guide sheets after having examined them carefully to discover the possible causes for the disagreements which have been noted.

34.____

35. Fewest candidates would probably be discouraged from applying to take a scheduled examination for an elementary school license by the statement that
    A. background knowledge as well as the fields of knowledge taught in the elementary school will be tested in the examination
    B. poor speech has been the major cause of failure on the examination in the past
    C. teaches who can meet high standards are preferred
    D. the examination will be composed entirely of objective test questions
    E. the examination will include a competitive performance test in music and art

35.____

36. In the development of standards for evaluation of non-teaching work experience of candidates, the one of the following on which MAJOR emphasis should be placed is the
    A. closeness of relationship between non-teaching experiences and the teaching position under consideration
    B. elements of persistence and dependability in these work experiences
    C. relationship between scholastic preparation and types of employment obtained
    D. social status of such non-teaching experiences
    E. variety of non-teaching experience

36.____

37. In the selection of teacher personnel, the personal interview should be structured so as to reveal PRIMARILY
    A. the ability of the candidate to stand up under emotional tensions
    B. the candidate's degree of insight into himself
    C. whether or not the candidate has any emotional problems
    D. the candidate's native intelligence
    E. the candidate's personal biases and prejudices

37.____

38. In the course of an examination for license as principal of a vocational high school, a total of 14 applicants appear before the entire board of examiners for interview tests in a period of three successive days. The examiners make running notes of the substance of the applicants' presentation and responses. In addition, wire recordings are made.
Of the following, these wire recordings are likely to be of GREATEST value in
   A. aiding the member of the board designated to draft an official statement of the reasons for the rejection in the case of any applicant who failed in the test
   B. determining the accuracy of any allegations made by an applicant as to the substance and manner of his responses
   C. helping any member of the board who is not able to recall the details of a specific interview
   D. justifying the action of the board in granting a licenses to an applicant in the event that this action is questioned by other educational authorities
   E. settling disagreements among the members of the board as to how an applicant should be rated

38.____

39. The group oral test has been increasingly utilized during recent years in examinations MAINLY because
   A. the applicants come away from the examination with a greater degree of confidence in the operation of the merit system
   B. it has been found possible by this method to examine a larger number of applicants per time unit
   C. the group test has been found to be a valuable means of checking on the reliability of the individual interview test
   D. it is believed that, by this type of test, certain traits may be more accurately evaluated than by any other form of examination
   E. the situation provided in the group test is more realistic and more natural than in the case of an individual test

39.____

40. A significant trend in aptitude and achievement tests is
   A. allowing a choice of questions rather than having all examinees answer all questions
   B. the arrangement by different publishers to use the same norms population
   C. the inclusion of a larger number of shorter questions to increase reliability
   D. setting time limits so that most examinees can finish
   E. the use of scores on fewer items as a basis of separate interpretation

40.____

41. To determine appropriate training and experience qualification requirements for elementary school principals at the entrance level, the MOST effective of the following methods is to
   A. get questionnaire responses from representative samples of successful and unsuccessful elementary school principals as to their status in these items at the time when they became principals
   B. check national surveys of characteristics of persons employed in such positions and from these make the necessary determinations

41.____

C. have a committee of principals meet with the board of examiners and, through discussion, arrive at acceptable standards
D. check the membership roster of the National Education Association's division of elementary school administrators to determine norms for acceptable training and experience
E. seek the judgments of professors of education engaged in the preparation of school administrators

Questions 42-43.

DIRECTIONS: Questions 42 and 43 are to be answered on the basis of the following information.

An examiner reviews the scores achieved by 260 candidates on an objective test of teaching methods composed of 15 five-choice items. The test has been scored by the standard formula to correct for guessing. The examiner finds that the highest raw score attained is 147, and the lowest raw score is 58. The mean raw score is 100.2, the standard deviation is 14.3, and the distribution is not significantly skewed. The examiner is aware that most candidates have completed their pre-service preparation in institutions which give course marks or grades on a percentage scale for which 70 is passing. His review of the candidates' credentials and his judgment on their raw score performance convinces him that about 80 percent of the candidates should pass the objective test. The examiner has responsibility for determining the form in which individual performance on the test will be reported to each candidate.

42. The formula used to score this test was: Raw Score equals Rights minus
    A. 1/5 Wrongs
    B. Wrongs
    C. Omits minus 1/5 Wrongs
    D. Wrongs plus 30
    E. 1/4 Wrongs

43. The examiner should set the passing mark at a raw score of APPROXIMATELY
    A. 70   B. 78   C. 85   D. 93   E. 100

44. During a meeting of the board of examiners, the chairman stated that it is of utmost importance that we communicate to assistant examiners the desirability of achieving our goals and the importance of the jobs they are performing toward reaching these.
    In general, the MOST important result of adopting this point of view would be that
    A. assistant examiners would be better prepared to take over the duties of an examiner when necessary
    B. avenues of communication would be more clearly defined
    C. assistant examiners would be in a better position to evaluate the objectives of the board
    D. less supervision of the work of an assistant examiner would be required
    E. assistant examiners would know what the general objectives of the board are

45. It has been decided to set up a special license for the principalship of elementary schools located in high delinquency areas. In the rating of candidates for this license, special attention should be given to the candidate's
    A. emotional stability, as measured by one of the better-known paper-and-pencil tests of personality adjustment
    B. performance on some type of projective technique
    C. reaction in a stress interview
    D. record of experience in a similar situation
    E. score on the Minnesota Attitude Inventory Test

45.____

46. The distribution of scores on the written test for a teacher of common branches in the elementary schools is skewed considerably in the direction of low scores. Of the following, the SOUNDEST interpretation of this finding is that the
    A. candidates were not able, for the most part, to finish the test
    B. correlation between test score and teaching performance will probably be low
    C. reliability of the test was attenuated by outside influences
    D. test did not discriminate among the best candidates, probably because the test was too easy
    E. test is not homogeneous in nature, either with respect to difficulty or with respect to content

46.____

47. During a periodic review of appeal procedures, the question is raised as to whether either representative answers or perfect answers should or should not be shown to candidates.
    This question should be decided in favor of
    A. *showing* this information to candidates primarily because many appeals would not be made if candidates knew what had been expected of them
    B. *not showing* this information to candidates primarily because candidates tend to interpret their answers on the basis of the representative answer in order to make a case
    C. *showing* this information to candidates primarily because the time examiners spend reviewing papers with candidates would be sharply reduced
    D. *not showing* this information to candidates primarily because candidates may question the correctness of the representative answers
    E. *showing* this information to candidates primarily because, without something with which answers can be compared, a meaningful appeal cannot be made

47.____

48. In the conduct of speech tests, the MOST important of the following considerations is that
    A. applicants be given the opportunity of silently reviewing in advance of the test the material on which they are to be tested
    B. a record be made in phonetic script of the applicant's errors and shortcomings in speech
    C. provision should be made for an unrehearsed talk or free conversation with the examiner

48.____

D. standardized speech tests be employed
E. the test material used include a substantial number of words frequently mispronounced

49. The BEST way to reduce the errors caused by variations in the marking standards of raters of essay questions is for the supervising examiner to
   A. arrange for sessions at which marking keys may be developed, applied, and discussed
   B. instruct the raters beforehand as to the number of papers to be passed by each rater on each question
   C. read and re-grade any papers for which ratings appear to be out of line
   D. reduce the distribution of the scores given by each rater to the form of the normal curve through the use of the T score or one of the other standard score techniques
   E. transmute the raw scores into percents of maximum score

50. In the process of appraising a teacher candidate, LEAST consideration should be given to
   A. his character and personality ratings
   B. the quality of his professional experience
   C. the extent of his participation in community activities
   D. the quality of his professional preparation
   E. his understanding of and interest in children

KEY (CORRECT ANSWERS)

1. C	11. E	21. D	31. A	41. A
2. A	12. E	22. D	32. B	42. E
3. B	13. A	23. D	33. E	43. C
4. A	14. C	24. C	34. B	44. D
5. E	15. A	25. A	35. D	45. D
6. B	16. D	26. D	36. B	46. D
7. E	17. C	27. B	37. B	47. E
8. B	18. C	28. C	38. B	48. C
9. E	19. B	29. D	39. D	49. A
10. B	20. C	30. C	40. D	50. C

BASIC PRINCIPLES AND PRACTICES IN EDUCATION
THE NEW PROGRAM OF EDUCATION
CONTENTS

	Page
I. PHILOSOPHY AND OBJECTIVES	1
A. Philosophy	1
B. Concepts of Education	1
C. Objectives	1
D. Methods of Achieving These Objectives	2
E. Organismic Psychology	2
F. Underlying Tenets of the Program	2
G. What Does the New Program Mean?	3
H. Advantages and Disadvantages	3
I. Traditional vs. Progressive Education General Principles	4
J. in Any Modern Philosophy of Elementary Education	5
II. THE CURRICULUM	5
A. Definitions	5
B. General Considerations	5
C. Conditions that Compel Curricular Changes	6
D. Changes that Result From Curriculum Improvement	6
E. Main Problems in Curriculum Development	7
F. Factors Affecting Curriculum Programs	7
G. Considerations for Curriculum Programs	7
H. Questions Related to Curriculum Development	7
III. GROUPING AND COMMITTEE WORK	8
A. Organizing Groups for Instruction	8
B. Criteria for Group Work	8
C. Committee Work	9
IV. EVALUATION	10
A. Items to be Evaluated	10
B. Reasons for Evaluating	10
C. Who Evaluates?	10
D. Evaluation in a Unit of Work	10
V. DISCIPLINE	12
A. Meaning	12
B. Discipline vs. Order	12
C. The Difference Between Conduct and Behavior	12

	Page
V. DISCIPLINE (cont'd)	12
D. Planes of Discipline	12
E. General Principles of Classroom Discipline	13
F. Positive vs. Negative Discipline	13
G. Why Some Teachers Have Disciplinary Troubles	13
H. Class Morale as a Factor in Classroom Discipline	13
I. The Use of Incentives	14
J. Classroom Punishments	16
K. Some Practical Suggestions for Teachers (Characteristic of Transition from Order to Discipline)	17
VI. BASIC FUNDAMENTALS OF EDUCATIONAL PSYCHOLOGY	17
A. Conditioning	17
B. Learning by Trial and Error (Connectionism)	18
C. Learning by Insight: Gestalt Psychology	18
D. The Field Theory (Organismic, Holistic Theory)	19
E. Transfer of Training	19
F. Habit	20
G. Individual Differences	21
VII. HISTORY OF EDUCATION	22
A. Leaders	22
1. Socrates	22
2. Plato	22
3. Aristotle	22
4. Comenius	23
5. Locke	23
6. Rousseau	23
7. Basedow	23
8. Pestalozzi	23
9. Herbart	24
10. Froebel	24
11. Spencer	24
12. Mann	24
13. Barnard	24
14. Dewey	24
B. Conceptualized Definitions and Aims of Education	24

156

BASIC PRINCIPLES AND PRACTICES IN EDUCATION
THE NEW PROGRAM OF EDUCATION

I. PHILOSOPHY AND OBJECTIVES

A. PHILOSOPHY
1. An analysis of the aims and purposes of education
2. An appraisal of current educational practices
3. A statement of the "ideal" to be attained
4. A justification of the means to be employed

B. CONCEPTS OF EDUCATION
1. Education as knowledge
    a. Emphasis on factual learning
    b. Transmitting the past heritage
    c. Excessive use of texts
2. Education as discipline
    a. Training the memory, imagination, etc.
    b. Emphasis on rote memory, drill, frequent tests, etc.
    c. Reliance on theory of transfer of training
3. Education as growth
    a. Developing latent capacities and realization of child's potentialities
    b. Experiential and functional learning
    c. Emphasis on attitudes, appreciations, and interests
    d. Child-centered curriculum
    e. Stress on social relationships and democratic living procedures

C. OBJECTIVES
1. Character - ethical living in a society promoting the common welfare
2. American Heritage - faith in American democracy and respect for dignity and worth of the individual regardless of race, religion, nationality or socio-economic status
3. Health - sound body and wholesome mental and emotional development
4. Exploration - discovery and development of individual aptitudes
5. Thinking - develop ability to reason critically, using facts and principles
6. Knowledges and skills - command of common integrating knowledges and skills
7. Appreciation and expression - appreciation and enjoyment of beauty and development of powers of creative expression
8. Social relationships - develop desirable social relationships at home, in school, in the community
9. Economic relationships - appreciation of economic processes and of contributions of all who serve in the world of work

MNEMONIC DEVICE FOR REMEMBERING THESE OBJECTIVES

T hinking
E xploration
A merican heritage
C haracter
H ealth

K nowledges and skills
A ppreciation
S ocial relationships
E conomic relationships

D. METHOD OF ACHIEVING THESE OBJECTIVES
1. Former emphasis on content with limited worthwhile, real experiences. Present stress on experiences with content used as a means to an end rather than as an end in itself.
2. This calls for a reorganization of our courses of study. Organization will now be in related areas rather than in separate isolated syllabi. These areas include:
   a. Pupil participation - to include planning, routines, and housekeeping, responsibilities, exploring school and community activities.
   b. Health - to include health instruction and guidance, safety education, rest, recreation, emotional adjustment, nutrition.
   c. Art - to include experimenting, use of various media as means of expression, practical applications in home, school, and community.
   d. Music - vocal, instrumental, rhythmic for enjoyment, expression, and understanding.
   e. Language Arts - reading, literature, composition, spelling, penmanship, speech, listening, dramatization.
   f. Social Studies - history, geography, civics, character, family relationships, consumer problems, intercultural education, citizenship and concepts of democracy.
   g. Science - nature study, weather, plants and soil, animals, earth and sky, food and water, tools and instruments, simple machines and electrical devices, flightcraft.
   h. Arithmetic - size, space, distance, time, weight, concepts, computations, problem solving.

MNEMONIC DEVICE FOR THESE AREAS

H ealth	L anguage Arts
A rithmetic	A rt
S ocial Studies	M usic
	P upil participation
	S cience

E. ORGANISMIC PSYCHOLOGY *(our current program is based chiefly on these principles)*
1. The principle of continuous growth - This emphasizes the flexible, experimental, emergent nature of the individual and of society; it stresses the continuity of experience. (Aspects: continuous progress plan; constant curriculum revision.)
2. The principle of experience as the method of learning - This emphasizes learning through functional, real experiences as opposed to memorization, drill, dictated assignments, etc. (Aspects: excursions; planning; research; reporting.)
3. The principal of integration - This emphasizes the wholeness and unity of individuals and of society. It stresses the interaction between the learner and the learning situation and demands maximum life-likeness in learning situations. (Aspects: units; use of community resources; large areas of instruction; larger time-blocks.)

F. UNDERLYING TENETS OF THE PROGRAM
1. Education of the whole child - social, civic, intellectual, ethical, vocational
2. Learning through real, functional experiences (activity vs. passivity)

3. The "intangibles" as an important end of education (interests, attitudes, character, etc.)
4. The concept of the child-centered school as opposed to the subject-centered school
5. The inclusion of the nine objectives of education as a part of educational planning at every step

G. WHAT DOES THE NEW PROGRAM MEAN?
1. These things are basic:
   a. Socialization of procedures
   b. Integration of personality (before integration of subject matter)
   c. Increased pupil-teacher participation in planning and evaluating the educative process
   d. Group procedures
   e. A program to meet the individual's time-table of growth as well as a general development time-table
   f. First-hand experiencing as a "must" in education
   g. A mental hygiene viewpoint for the teacher
   h. Closer relationship between school-life and life in the world outside
   i. An acceptance of the view that concomitant learnings can sometimes be more important than the original learnings to be taught
2. It is NOT merely:
   a. Unit development
   b. Correlation of subject matter
   c. Working through committees
   d. Provision for research activities
   e. Emphasis on reporting and discussion
   f. Planning for a culmination
   g. Keeping diaries and logs

H. ADVANTAGES AND DISADVANTAGES
1. Proponents of the New Program maintain that this program:
   a. Provides a flexible content
   b. Encourages individual aptitudes
   c. Permits much practice in social behavior
   d. Encourages independent learning
   e. Encourages creative expression
   f. Provides a vitalized curriculum
   g. Permits greater integration of subject matter
   h. Provides for leisure-time activities
   i. Provides a success program for each child
   j. Makes greater provision for diagnosis, guidance, and individual remedial treatment
   k. Contributes abundantly towards the development of good character
2. Opponents of the New Program maintain that:
   a. There is no gradation of the difficulties of different units of work
   b. It is not true to life (since life is not a series of activities)
   c. Too much reliance is placed on incidental learning
   d. There is no provision for participation by every child
   e. Teachers have not been trained sufficiently
   f. Equipment is underemphasized

g. The interests of children are not sufficient as a guide for subject matter
h. The superficial aspects are overemphasized
i. Many important "learnings" are omitted
j. No provision is made for duplication in the case of pupils who are transferred or admitted

I. TRADITIONAL VS. PROGRESSIVE EDUCATION

TRADITIONAL *PROGRESSIVE*

1. PHILOSOPHY

a. School is a preparation lor life	a. School is "life itself" life
b. Emphasis on social heritage	b. Development of whole personality-knowledge, attitudes, morals, health
c. Adjust pipil to society that arises	c. School aims to improve society

2. CURRICULUM

a. Factual curriculum laid out in advance for all	a. Subject matter -vital, purposeful, integrated, flexible, follows child's interests
b. Subjects clearly separated and isolated	b. Long units, integration and correlation of subject matter
c. Emphasis on memorization	c. Learning through experiences
d. Slavish use of text books	d. Use of a variety of reference and source materials

3. ROLE OF TEACHER

a. Dominant factor in the learning process	a. Teacher is a guide and helper
b. Pupil passivity	b. Socialization and maximum pupil participation

4. METHODS

a. Stressed mastery of subject	a. Adjustment of curriculum to matter needs, interests, and capacities of each child
b. Isolated drills. Extrinsic	b. Functional learning. Individualized drill at the point of error. Intrinsic
c. Rigid, formal discipline	c. A hum of activity. Self-discipline. Social adjustment
d. Inside of schoolroom	d. Excursions and field trips

5. SUPERVISION

a. Dictatorial and inflexible	a. Democratic, scientific, creative
b. Teachers rated according to ability in achieving grade standards (standardized ap-tests)	b. Teachers judged on basis of their ability to promote desirable attitudes - interests, preciations, etc. (attitude tests and case histories)

J. GENERAL PRINCIPLES IN ANY MODERN PHILOSOPHY OF ELEMENTARY EDUCATION
1. Education must be democratic, universal, and compulsory
2. There must be a unifying philosophy for the school system as a whole
3. This philosophy must be essentially a social philosophy; the school must adjust children to a changing social order
4. The curriculum must be flexible and must be subject to frequent (continuous) revision
5. There must be flexibility in classroom procedures
6. Adequate equipment must be provided
7. Adequate provision must be made for the mentally and physically handicapped

II. THE CURRICULUM

A. DEFINITIONS
1. The CURRICULUM consists of all the experiences, including all the subject matter and skills, which are utilized and interpreted by the school to further the aims of education. These experiences result from interaction between persons, influences, and material facilities. Some of the factors which effect the curriculum are:
   a. The political, economic, and social structure of the surrounding society
   b. The public opinion toward education
   c. The aims and philosophies of those operating the educational system
   d. The decisions concerning methods and materials, teacher selection, sarlaries, and physical plant
   e. The course of study, or, more properly, the documents made available to the teachers
2. Early COURSES OF STUDY usually consisted only of a subject-matter outline; later ones included also some suggested learning activities, teaching procedures, diagnostic devices, and evaluation techniques. The emphasis, in all instances, was on "prescribed" subject matter to be covered, and some courses of study even specified the number of minutes per day to be devoted to each of the segments and the specific fact questions to be used.
3. Modern GUIDES for teachers are not usually called courses of study. They suggest a wealth of materials and experiences; far from minimizing subject matter, they suggest more of it better adapted for use with varying levels of abilities and interests. They include bulletins on:
   a. the teaching of various subjects
   b. the organization of experience units with subject lines disregarded
   c. the characteristics of children
   d. varied learning experiences
   e. teaching procedures
   f. ways of using different types and amounts of subject matter
   g. sources of instructional aids
   h. evaluational techniques
   i. bibliographies, etc.

B. GENERAL CONSIDERATIONS
1. A curriculum develops in answer to the needs of a group of learners and to the demands of a given society.

2. A curriculum is made by a teacher and her pupils as they work together in the school.
3. The development of a specific curriculum is a cooperative activity in which many persons participate (superintendents, principals, teachers, subject-matter specialists, consultants, school psychologists, pupils, parents, social agencies, advisory commissions, etc.)
4. A program of curriculum improvement involves a study of:
   a. the political, economic, and social structure of the surrounding society
   b. public opinion toward education
   c. advice or information for the public
   d. the aims and philosophy of current educational practice
   e. the abilities, needs, purposes and individual differences among the learners
   f. the origin and nature of subject matter
   g. the development of present curriculums
   h. the nature of modern outcomes of learning i. the many new techniques of evaluation
5. A program of curriculum improvement is far broader than the writing of a course of study or series of teachers' guides; it is concerned with the improvement of living and learning conditions in the school and in the community of which it is a part.
6. A program of curriculum improvement should result in changes of attitudes, appreciations, and skills on the part of the participants and in important changes in the learning situation.

C. CONDITIONS THAT COMPEL CURRICULAR CHANGES

1. Technological developments - In a society where most people work for someone else, it is important that the curriculum emphasize the attitudes and skills of cooperation.
2. International problems - The curriculum must emphasize international understanding as well as the defense of America and other freedom-loving nations.
3. Social change - The curriculum must prepare children for living in a complex and changing world, and must emphasize moral responsibility for one's acts both as an individual as well as a member of a group.
4. Educational progress - The increase of available materials of instruction and the expanding role of the teacher call for a redistribution of teachers' time and energies in terms of a new set of values.

D. CHANGES THAT RESULT FROM CURRICULUM IMPROVEMENT

1. In the professional staff-cooperative planning; working together on educational problems; experimentation with promising procedures; study of human growth and development.
2. In the teaching-learning situation - improvement in the school plant, equipment, and supplies; use of community resources; available community services; opportunities for children to participate in community life.
3. In improved pupil behavior - ability to define and solve meaningful problems: development of new interest; self-evaluation; skill in communication; skill in human relations; initiative; creative-ness .
4. In community relationships - participation by lay citizens; public support; public relations.
5. In school organization - plan of organization; staff selection procedures; school size; class size; daily schedules; district services; faculty conferences.

6. In instructional materials - cooperative production of instructional materials; more effective use of commercial materials; better selection of teaching aids; establishment of a "materials center"; development of a professional library.
7. In ways of working together - teacher-pupil planning; group dynamics; sociometric techniques; intergroup education.

E. MAIN PROBLEMS IN CURRICULUM DEVELOPMENT
1. The determination of educational directions
2. The selection of experiences comprising the educational program
3. The selection of a pattern of curriculum organization
4. The determination of principles and procedures by which the curriculum can be evaluated and changed

F. FACTORS AFFECTING CURRICULUM DEVELOPMENT
1. The existing political, economic, and social structure
2. Pressure exerted by minority groups or vested interests
3. Legislation
4. Tradition
5. Influence of logically organized subject matter and compartmen-talization
6. Textbooks

G. CONSIDERATIONS FOR CURRICULUM PROGRAMS
1. The improvement program is to be developed with the aid of supervisors, teachers, pupils, parents, and community.
2. The curriculum should be readily adaptable to individual differences, needs, and interests and to the special needs of groups, schools and communities.
3. There should be provision for articulation between and among the various divisions and levels of the school system.
4. There must be provision for continuous experimentation and research.
5. There must be flexibility and allowance for interpretation and change to meet new situations and conditions.
6. There must be provision for evaluation of principles, practices, and outcomes, as well as for appraisal of the curriculum improvement program itself.
7. The curriculum must provide conditions, situations, and activities favorable to the continuous growth and progress of each individual.
8. Curriculum policies and practices should encourage friendly understanding and democratic relations among supervisors, teachers, pupils and parents.
9. The success of a curriculum is dependent on competent leadership. (Supervision interprets and implements the curriculum and seeks to improve teaching and learning; teachers' attitudes and understandings determine the effectiveness of the curriculum; community aims, purposes, and resources exert an important influence on the curriculum; pupils help in developing a wholesome pattern of democratic living in which the curriculum operates most effectively.)

H. QUESTIONS RELATED TO CURRICULUM DEVELOPMENT
1. Why is the traditional curriculum, used with seeming success for years, now under such criticism, analysis, and change?
2. Is the curriculum an instrument of social progress?
3. Should the aims of education and the content of the curriculum be determined with some definiteness in advance of actual teaching-learning situations?
4. Is all, none, or a given part of the curriculum to be required of all learners - regardless of origin, present status, and very probable destiny?
5. How shall the curriculum be organized - scope and sequence determined?
6. How shall the curriculum content be selected?

7. What are the desired outcomes of learning experiences?
8. How much of the curriculum can be formulated by the pupils?
9. What stand shall the curriculum take on "indoctrination?"
10. What procedures should be used in reconstructing the curriculum?
11. What are the criteria for evaluating a curriculum?

III. GROUPING AND COMMITTEE WORK

A. ORGANIZING GROUPS FOR INSTRUCTION
 1. Know the children before you group
    a. General level of achievement (standardized tests)
    b. Individual problems in the area (everyday performance)
    c. Capacity to achieve (expectancy)
    d. Personal and social adjustment (sociogram)
 2. Develop a "readiness" for grouping
    a. Teach the techniques that will be the basis for independent activity later
    b. Be familiar with the types of exercises to be used for group work later; anticipate some of the skills which will be required
    c. Develop work-skills (choosing something, sharing materials, working independently, etc.)
 3. Launch the best group first
    a. The first group will be those children most advanced intellectually and socially
    b. The remainder of the class learns to work independently as the teacher works with the first group
    c. As both these groups learn to work simultaneously, the teacher notes the point at which further subdivision becomes necessary (for example, the slower group may be broken down into a normal and slow group)
 4. Group standards should be set cooperatively by the teacher and class
 5. Some abilities to aim for:
    a. Working alone
    b. Working quietly
    c. Completing a job
    d. Moving to the next job when the present one is completed
    e. Finding and correcting one's errors
    f. Evaluating one's own work
 6. Arrangement of pupils
    a. Reduce to a minimum the interference of one group with another (through location of groups in the room, allocation of blackboard space, etc.)
    b. Have a group's materials placed near to where that group works

B. CRITERIA FOR GROUP WORK
 1. Are the procedures used in accordance with the techniques advocated in the program of education?
    a. What is the basis on which the groups are set up? (Common weaknesses, sociogram, etc.)
    b. Is the goal for each group set and understood?
    c. Have these goals been set by cooperative planning?
    d. In what type of activity is the group engaged - individual or group? Is there a free interplay of minds at all times?

e. Are there evidences of evaluation within the group - by individuals and by the group?
f. What is the extent and variety of materials used?
2. Are there evidences of individual contributions by children in the group?
3. Are there evidences of committee work of children (charts, etc.)?
4. Are there evidences of teacher-supervision of group procedures?
5. Are there evidences of the growth of social skills, attitudes, and understandings of social living?

C. COMMITTEE WORK
1. Group dynamics as a factor in committee work
   a. Sociograms and friendship charts
   b. Place of the "stars"
   c. Working the isolates into the committee
2. As in grouping, the teacher starts with a single-committee and develops committee techniques with the members
3. Selection of a chairman and a secretary by the committee -importance of leadership and followership
4. Contributions of the members of a committee toward the solution of a problem - working together and all that it implies"
5. Place of the teacher
   a. She never "abdicates her position;" she advises and guides when indicated
   b. She watches closely those members with personal problems
   c. She anticipates difficulties in human relations
   d. She assigns a place for the committee to work comfortably
   e. She displays charts listing the committees, with leaders starred
   f. She makes available materials for research, including pictorial material and special materials for the non-reader or retarded reader
   g. She checks the progress of the group and of the individuals in the group regularly (before a reporting period, etc.)
6. Standards for group work periods

NOTE: These are suggestions for charts
   a. For a Group Leader
      a.1 Know what work to do each day
      a.2 Keep the group working
      a.3 Do not be too bossy
   b. For the Group
      b.1 We will speak softly
      b.2 We will talk only to our own group
      b.3 We will talk only about our own work
      b.4 We will try to find our own materials
      b.5 We will use our time wisely
      b.6 We will clean up when we have finished
   c. For Groups preparing a report
      c.1 Skim books for stories on the topic of your report
      c.2 Plan an outline of the whole topic
      c.3 Choose sub-topics for study
      c.4 Work on topics - make an outline, do some research, make something, etc.
      c.5 Give your report to the group for criticism c.6 Give the report to the class

IV. EVALUATION

A. ITEMS TO BE EVALUATED
1. Mental development *(traditionally, this has been almost the sole emphasis)*
2. Physical aspects
3. Social aspects
4. Emotional aspects

B. REASONS FOR EVALUATING
1. It is a means of discovering group and individual growth
2. It is a means of discovering whether children are developing at a rate commensurate with their general capacity (expectancy)
3. To discover children's strengths and weaknesses, and necessity for specific help (diagnostic) in particular cases
4. To indicate to the school how it can best provide the conditions of growth that make learning most economical and most effective
5. Children learn more effectively when they take part in evaluation
    a. As members of a group, they learn to become aware of group needs (through learning they must acquire for a specific purpose)
    b. They learn how to plan for group needs (through pratrtice in evaluating possible courses of action)
    c. They learn to take stock as they proceed with their tasks (through evaluating progress periodically)
    d. They learn ways of deciding when their project has reached a satisfactory conclusion (through practice in evaluating their achievements in the light of their original objectives)

C. WHEN TO EVALUATE
1. It is a continuing activity, taking place at every stage of the learning process *(Evaluation is not concerned solely with end products)*
2. The teacher evaluates situations as they occur
3. "The quality of living" that goes on in a classroom is evaluated as an indication of class morale
4. The amount of communication that takes place is, at all times, a significant evaluative factor
5. The need for recording social adjustments, emotional maturity, attention span, language development, interests, and enthusiasms of children makes continuous evaluation a necessity
6. Check lists and anecdotal records may be used to record what is observed

D. WHO EVALUATES?
1. Everyone concerned in the educative process should take part in evaluation
    a. The children, with or without the guidance of the teacher, make valid judgments
    b. The teacher evaluates herself, the effectiveness of her procedures, the progress of her class and the individuals therein, the climate of her room, and the classroom situation
    c. The school, as a composite of teachers and supervisors, evaluates its curriculum, its services to children, its growth of teachers and supervisors, and its relationship to the life of the community
    d. Members of the community, especially parents, evaluate the school, its program and its teachers (The school should provide such information so as to make possible an intelligent evaluation on the community's part)

E. EVALUATION IN A UNIT OF WORK
1. The unit should be evaluated in light of its objectives
2. The primary objective is not absorption of a mass of facts, but the development of attitudes, understandings, and appreciations
3. The evaluation of desirable social relationships, the development of good habits of work and thought, and the imparting of basic concepts are our major social studies goals
4. Measurement of the so-called intangibles, while admittedly difficult, is possible (Formal tests, such as the California Tests of Personality and Winnetka Behavior Rating Scale are not so valuable as teacher observation and judgment)
5. The teacher, by recording objectively significant behavior, can observe the developmental pattern of growth in chidren (anecdotal records, etc.)
6. Teacher-made checklists and tests are helpful in determining growth and progress
   a. Tests in ascertaining places where information is available (A test of this type may be administered before and after a unit is taken. Growth may be measured by comparing results)
      a.1 Whom would you ask where to find a certain building if you were downtown?
      a.2 How would you locate a certain book if you were in the library?
      a.3 If you weren't sure whether a word ended in "ant" or "ent," how could you find out?
      a.4 Where would you look to find out something about an explorer?
      a.5 How could you tell, by looking at a map, whether New York is closer to Connecticut than it is to Virginia?
   b. Tests involving the relevancy of data to particular problems and tests involving the relevancy of statements to a conclusion
      b.1 Does a person's race or religion have any bearing on his athletic or musical ability?
      b.2 Since your city uses great amounts of food, does that mean that your city produces huge amounts of meat, grain, etc.?
   c. Tests involving the reliability of various sources, the matching of persons with the fields of their probable competence
      c.1 Would Tiger Woods necessarily be an authority on international relations?
   d. Checklists of instances of voluntary cooperation (Does the child of his own accord clean up the area around his seat? Does the child bring materials from home?, etc.)
7. Methods of evaluation of a unit
   a. Objective tests *(prepared by teachers and pupils)*
   b. Teacher's written accounts and criticisms
   c. Teacher's anecdotal reports on individual and group work
   d. Matching achievement against predetermined objectives
   e. Comparison of activities and skills of this unit with those of preceding units
   f. Noting observations made by parents and community
8. Children's evaluation in a unit
   a. Charts: "Did I Do a Good Job?",etc.
   b. Evaluation "envelopes," in which children retain samples of their work and note-progress
   c. Children (and teacher) appraise:
      c.1 What have we learned?

c.2 What should we remember?
c.3 Did we do everything we set out to do?
c.4 What must still be done?
c.5 What could we have done better?
c.6 What questions should be included on a "test of all the important things we learned?"
c.7 How can we make further use of the things we learned?
9. Evaluation is a means of discovering:
   a. Group and individual growth
   b. Teacher-effectiveness or weakness
   c. Group needs
   d. Curriculum strengths or deficiencies
   e. Objectives realized
   f. Experience gained
   g. Subject matter acquired h. Skills mastered
   i. Evidences of creative expression
   j. Evidences of growth toward desirable habits, attitudes, and appreciations
   k. Activities not yet completed
   l. Subject matter not covered

V. DISCIPLINE

A. MEANING
1. Broad Meaning - The attainment by the individual of such knowledges, skills, habits, and attitudes as will promote the well-being of himself and of his social group.
2. Narrow Meaning - The creation of classroom conditions to provide a wholesome environment for the best functioning of the individual and the group.

B. DISCIPLINE VS. ORDER
1. Difference
   a. Discipline: Based on self-direction; maintained by building habits of self-control and by stressing the social need for desirable conduct. It aims at a self-directed class that works quietly and efficiently even though the teacher is temporarily too busy to supervise the class.
   b. Order: Based on instant obedience to commands emanating from above; depends on the teacher's ability to exercise constant surveillance and to use the pupils' fear of detection as a deterrent to undesirable action. Order reaches its height when the teacher can make the meaningless boast that she "can hear a pin drop."
2. As a means toward discipline, order is sometimes essential. It may be a legitimate aid to discipline. As a goal in itself, it has little justification.

C. THE DIFFERENCE BETWEEN CONDUCT AND BEHAVIOR
1. Conduct: The adult's reaction to the child's acts. It is considered "good" or "bad." Depends on adult's standards or values.
2. Behavior: The child's reaction to stimuli (physical, mental, or social). It is "normal" or "abnormal." Depends on child's personality.

D. PLANES OF DISCIPLINE
1. Obedience - military concept
2. Personal domination by the teacher - "good order" concept
3. Social pressure - living and working with others

4. Self-discipline - living and working alone

E. GENERAL PRINCIPLES OF CLASSROOM DISCIPLINE
1. Self-control is achieved through proper habit formation (psychological principles)
2. Desirable discipline is social control within the school group
3. Discipline should be positive and constructive, rather than negative and destructive
4. It should appeal to the highest motives of which the pupil is capable
5. It should impress pupils as being fair, reasonable, and socially necessary

F. POSITIVE VS. NEGATIVE DISCIPLINE
1. The essential difference is one of attitude and approach
   a. Present conformity to rule vs. cultivating motives for sound action in later years
   b. Getting children to do the right thing vs. preventing them from doing the wrong thing

2. Examples:

POSITIVE	NEGATIVE
a. Stimulating attention.	a. Coping with inattention. Scolding.
b. Creating desire to come to school because of meaningful activities.	b. Devising measures to curb truancy. Scolding
c. Encouraging children to come early by starting promptly with interesting work and duties.	c. Devising new procedures to curb lateness. Scolding,
d. Awakening the desire to do things for the good of the to the school.	d. Compelling observance of class and school rules. Punishment.
e. Giving children opportunity of participating in class and school administration.	e. Teacher does everything, school. Doing things for children which they can be trained ties to do for themselves,

3. Caution: It is impossible to dispense with negative discipline entirely, but the emphasis should be placed on the positive plane.

G. WHY SOME TEACHERS HAVE DISCIPLINARY TROUBLES
1. Pedagogical Reasons
   a. Failure to employ appropriate subject matter and materials
   b. Poor teaching techniques
   c. Failure to consider the individual pupil's capacities, talents, and interests
2. Classroom Management
   a. Failure to mechanize routines
   b. Unattractive, physically uncomfortable surroundings
3. Personality
   a. Lack of tact
   b. High strung manner
   c. Idiosyncrasies in dress
   d. High pitched voice e. Lack of a sense of humor

4. Psychological
   a. Lack of sympathy with children
   b. Procrastination in handling cases (not facing the issue)
   c. Lack of a fair disciplinary policy

H. CLASS MORALE AS A FACTOR IN CLASSROOM DISCIPLINE
1. Meaning of morale or class spirit
   a. "Morale is the feeling among members of a group that stimulates them to work happily together toward the realization of shared aims"
   b. "The personality of the group born of common attitudes"
2. How Developed

L a. *Leadership* of the teacher - she sets the tone
   a.1 Her personality - ability to fire others with enthusiasm for ideals and service; to arouse faith of pupils in her
   a.2 Her educational qualifications
   a.3 Her understanding of children

A b. Stressing of strong social *attitudes* - work of the group more important than that of the individual - team work of pupils

C c. Situations arousing *common* loyalties - participation in joint efforts
   c.1 Class projects - making things for the class or the school (posters, art objects, Christmas gifts to soldiers or destitute children, class newspaper, class party, help with parents' bazaar)
   c.2 Assembly programs, pageants
   c.3 Athletic teams
   c.4 Friendly competition with other classes (attendance records, contributions to the Red Cross)

P d. Situations arousing *pride* as a result of achievement and recognition
   d.1 Service to the class and school
   d.2 Records - attendance, punctuality, neatness, cleanliness, etc.
   d.3 Good deeds and accomplishments of classmates
   d.4 Accomplishment of learning goals (New Program)

S e. Attractive *surroundings* - contribution of pupils to the appearance of the room

(Mnemonic - S C A L P)

I. THE USE OF INCENTIVES
1. Distinction between incentives and motives
   a. Incentive - An environmental object or condition, the attainment or avoidance of which motivates behavior (external) -praise, blame, reward, punishment, rivalry
   b. Motive - The process within an organism which energizes or directs it toward a specific line of behavior (internal) -interest, need, urge, drive, desire
   c. Incentive is the stimulus; motive is the reaction, though the terms, including "motivation," are used loosely and interchangeably.
2. Real vs. Artificial Motivation (intrinsic vs. extrinsic)
   a. Real Motivation - Gives purpose and direction to the learning process, is part of the task, arises from the value of the task for its own sake, is related to the life of the child (aroused by problems or challenges to which the child desires the answer or solution)

b. Artificial Motivation - attempts to make uninteresting material attractive by sugarcoating; is based on traditional attitude that every lesson is a unit in itself; is usually unrelated or only slightly related to the task (stores, games, marks, rewards)
c. The new program vs. the traditional program from the point of view of motivation
d. Some examples of real and artificial motivation:

REAL	ARTIFICIAL
1. Arithmetic: Learning percents through computing class averages in attendance or the standing of athletic teams	1. Learning by reference to father's bank account
2. Spelling: Learning words by writing a real letter	2. Learning through the desire to get a better mark
3. Geography: Learning t?he geography of the city through trips and excursions	3. Learning in order to do well on a quiz
4. Science: Learning about plants through growing them	4. Learning through a reference to the flower shop around the corner or to a picture
5. Social Studies: Learning the industries of a country through a study of how people live and work	5. Learning through reference to the work children's "parents do
6. Art: Learning color and perspective through illustrating a unit by murals	6. Learning in order to get a good mark, to have work displayed, or to obtain the approval of the teacher

(NOTE: Extrinsic motivation is sometimes justifiable or desirable, but it should be subordinated to intrinsic drives wherever possible.)

3. Incentives in the Classroom
   a. Principles
      a.1 The best incentive is one which makes a task significant to the child
      a.2 It should influence future as well as present actions and attitudes
      a.3 It should make doing an act a satisfying process
      a.4 It should encourage the social point of view
   b. Motives to which the teacher can appeal
      b.1 The desire to do the right for its own sake should always be the ultimate goal even with very young children
      b.2 The desire for self-respect - knowledge of progress, recognition of abilities or status
      b.3 The desire to win the approval of one's fellow - displaying good work, posting lists of children doing well, monitorships
      b.4 The desire to gain the approval of the teacher or one's parents - praise succeeds better than blame, recognizing the good better than scolding the bad, letters to parents

b.5 The desire for new experiences - problems, excursions, class clubs, projects

b.6 The desire to win a reward - need not be of material value -praise, exhibition of work, monitorships should be within reach of all - avoid bribery

(NOTE: The lowest form of incentive is better than the best form of punishment.)

J. CLASSROOM PUNISHMENTS
1. The Basis for Punishment
   a. What should be the aim? Retributive, deterrent, or corrective?
   b. Punishment may be justified if it is *corrective*
      b.1 It must be a means of removing a tendency to unsocial behavior
      b.2 It must not be a separate entity, but part of the education process
      b.3 It must aid in the process of adjusting behavior in a positive direction
   c. Criteria of effective punishment
      c.1 The child should be shown that he is being punished for a social transgression
      c.2 The teacher's personal feelings must not be a consideration
      c.3 Punishment is to be used only when the child fails to respond to intentives
      c.4 It should be adapted to the child (not uniform)
      c.5 It must not be unduly severe
      c.6 It must not leave a residue of antagonism or resentment
      c.7 It must not constitute the complete treatment for problem behavior
2. Punishment by Natural Consequence
   a. It is sound in theory but difficult in practice in the classroom (copying, cheating, failing to do work, obscene language)
   b. The principle can be followed, by making punishment seem to be a natural consequence wherever possible
3. Punishment by Fear
   a. Fear is an inhibiting rather than a stimulating force. It has a paralyzing harmful effect on development. It should rarely be used
   b. Corporal punishment is the lowest form of the use of fear. If ever administered, it should be for its shocking effect, rather than for punitive or corrective reasons
4. Evaluation of Classroom Punishments
   a. Minor punishments, such as staring at a child or calling his name - effective in nipping trouble in the bud
   b. Deprivation of position - effective if the door is held open for reinstatement
   c. Reprimands - effective, if given unemotionally and child is shown how his act interferes with others (must be used sparingly)
   d. Doing a written task - ineffective because it avoids the true causes of the trouble (I must come to school on time) and builds wrong associations (writing spelling words twenty five t imes)
   e. Picking up papers, etc. - effective if used as a means of making up for an offense, doing a positive deed in place of a negative
   f. Detention - generally ineffective because it leads to wrong associations with school

- g. Isolation - of doubtful value. The practice of having a child stand in a corner or in the corridor has no justification
- h. Social disapproval - effective if public humiliation does not result
- i. Saturation - ineffective and dangerous (it may backfire)
- j. Sarcasm - dangerous because mistaken for humor, builds resentment instead of cooperation (of doubtful value even with "smart alecks")
- k. Epithets - unjustified
- l. Sending for parent - effective if designed to understand causes and to devise program for cooperation between home and school

K. SOME PRACTICAL SUGGESTIONS FOR TEACHERS *(CHARACTERISTIC OF TRANSITION FROM ORDER TO DISCIPLINE)*
1. Give pupils the impression that you expect perfect order
2. Learn the names of all pupils as soon as possible
3. Give no unnecessary orders or directions - no repetitions
4. An explanatory statement, preparatory to giving a direction or order, reduces the possibility of confusion or disobedience
5. Insist upon a reasonable compliance with those directions which are given
6. Don't let little things go *(Nip disorder, in the bud)*
7. Keep the machinery of class management simple
8. Plan lessons and all work well
9. Keep the class busy on worthwhile work and activities
10. Use rewards and punishments judiciously - watch for and reward desirable actions
11. Avoid punishing in anger (It's the child, not the offense, that must be considered)
12. Don't punish the group for the offense of an individual
13. Don't make threats
14. Severe penalties should not be used for minor offenses
15. The teacher should never give the impression that she has exhausted her supply of punishments or rewards
16. Avoid forcing an issue with a disobedient pupil before the class
17. When a child is punished, keep the door open for him to return to the good graces of the class and the teacher
18. Have a sense of humor
19. Be fair and consistent in your decisions
20. Have an element of surprise - something new - in class work
21. Seat pupils so that opportunities for infraction are lessened
22. The voice should be subdued, but audible enough to be heard clearly throughout the room
23. Primarily, the handling of discipline cases is the responsibility of the teacher
24. In handling discipline cases, the teacher may have reasonable recourse to the parents
25. When a teacher has exhausted her own resources, or in the cases of emergency, she should call upon the supervisor for help

VI. BASIC FUNDAMENTALS OF EDUCATIONAL PSYCHOLOGY

A. CONDITIONING

Learning takes place as a result of experience with outside stimuli.
Responses are established by means of fixed associations.

1. Principles of Conditioning *(for use by teachers)*
   a. Learners' responses must be systematically studied
   b. Records of progress indicate need for change of pace, concentration on difficult parts, return to basic skills, new motivation, variations in use of cues
   c. Learner should make own records of progress
   d. Unlearning takes place rapidly; support and repeated reinforcement are required to consolidate and maintain habitual performance
   e. Teacher must control stimulating conditions (motivation)
   f. Teacher must help learner by providing varying conditions and extended practice
   g. Forced pacing methods are a poor substitute for adequate motivation

B. LEARNING BY TRIAL AND ERROR (CONNECTIONISM)
Learning involves the making of new mental and neural connections and the discarding or strengthening of old connections.

1. Concerned with what takes place between S-R to the neural connections
   a. Atomistic analysis of behavior
   b. Development is from hereditary instincts and reflexes to acquired habits
   c. Intellect and intelligence are quantitative
2. Thorndike's Laws of Learning
   a. Readiness - When a conduction unit is ready to act, conduction by it is satisfying and failure to conduct or being forced when not ready is annoying.
   b. Exercise - (Use and Disuse) Repetition with satisfaction strengthens the connection; disuse weakens the connection.
   c. Effect - Satisfaction strengthens the connection which it follows and to which it belongs. *(Importance of motivation)*
3. Thorndike's Five Characteristics of Learning
   a. Multiple responses to the same external situation pervade nine tenths of learning.
   b. The responses made are the product of the "set" or "attitude" of the learner. The satisfaction or annoyance produced by a response is conditioned by the learner's attitude.
   c. Partial Activity: One or another element in the situation may be prepotent in determining the response.
   d. Law of Assimilation or Analogy: If one element in the situation resembles another, it will call forth a corresponding response.
   e. Associative Shifting - Omitting elements of a situation and still getting the same response. *(Conditioned response)*
4. The Significance of "Cues" in Learning
   a. The learner tends to respond to loud sound, intense, brilliant or rapidly changing cues.
   b. Conspicuous stimuli may receive undue attention. Important stimuli may thus be overlooked.
   c. Cues help emphasize important stimuli.
   d. The teacher must discover when to use proper cues, and how much guidance to give the learner.

C. LEARNING BY INSIGHT: GESTALT PSYCHOLOGY
   1. Constant striving to make sense out of a situation

2. The learner's efforts are not purely random
3. Understanding is enhanced by responding to total patterns, to relation between things
4. Motivation helps create perception of the problem
5. The learner's background of experience aids in insight, in perceiving figurations, in seeing the relationships of the parts to the whole, and in acquiring meaning and value

D. THE FIELD THEORY (ORGANISMIC, HOLISTIC THEORY)
1. Derived from the Gestalt theory
2. Insight is the alteration of organic structure within an area of the "whole organism"
3. Significances
   a. Breakdown of atomistic views
   b. Importance of chemical function of neural mechanisms
   c. Fundamental role of "feelings and emotions" in learning
   d. Muscular coordination of the complete organism is a factor in skill acquisition
   e. Recognition of the principle of maturation
   f. Best motivation derives from needs of learners

E. TRANSFER OF TRAINING
1. Recognized as significant in educational theory and practice
   a. Traditional Concept - Doctrine of Formal Discipline: the mind gains strength through use, and this strength is automatically available in all situations. (Faculties of the Mind)
   b. Current Concept - No faculties as such. Transfer is a fact of mental life occurring under certain mental conditions, not because of external causes.
2. Factors Influencing Transfer
   a. Methods of procedure in learning and teaching
   b. Attitude of readiness set up by instructions given
   c. Degree of mastery of the material learned
   d. Integration of the initial learning - as to content and method
   e. Extent to which generalization and application are applied -"psychological organization"
3. Current Theories of Transfer
   a. Theory of Identical Elements (Thorndike)
      a.1 Identity of content
      a.2 Identity of procedure
      a.3 Identity of aims or ideals
      These identical elements make use of the same neural bonds.
   b. Theory of Generalization or Abstraction or Relationship Transfer takes place to the extent that one generalizes his experiences and is able to apply general principles to different situations. (Scientific method)
4. Implications for the Supervisor
   a. Materials used should have real value for children, not for mental discipline.
   b. A subject which has slight transfer value in a large field may be of more value than a subject which has a greater transfer value, but in a very limited field.
   c. The difficulty of a subject is not any indication of its transfer value.
   d. Recognition of child growth and development is the basic aim.

e. The position accorded any subject in the school curriculum should be decided by the value of the special training it affords and by the social significance of its content rather than by its promise to develop general intellectual capacities.
5. Implications for the Teacher
   a. The most effective use of knowledge is assured, not through acquisition of any particular item of experience but only through the establishment of associations which give it general value.
   b. Transfer is most common at the higher levels of intellectual activity.
   c. Children should receive training in methods of memorizing, acquiring skills, and in solving problems.
   d. If transfer value is slight, then it is most economical to practice directly those habits and skills we wish to develop.
   e. An individual's ability to apply knowledge is not in proportion to his knowledge of facts.
   f. The teacher should know what it is that she wants the children to transfer to other fields, and she must learn by experience or experiment how to teach for transfer.
   g. The theory of transfer is recognized by all schools of psychology. More research is necessary before teachers can be guided by the theory to any great extent.

F. HABIT
   1. Meaning - A learned response made automatically to the appropriate stimulus.
   2. Principles of Habit Formation (Bagley)
      a. Focalize consciousness (Motivation)
         a.1 Give clearest possible idea of habit to be formed
         a.2 Use demonstration
         a.3 Make it vivid
         a.4 Arouse motivation.
         a.5 Give instruction in how habits are formed a.6 Multiple sense appeal
      b. Attentive repetition
         b.1 Vigorous, short, definite drill
         b.2 Use devices
         b.3 Have a definite goal (focalization)
         b.4 Watch for lag in attention
         b.5 Vary the number of repetitions
         b.6 "Practice makes perfect" only if with attention
      c. No exceptions
         c.1 Analyze habit in advance to prepare for likely slips
         c.2 Give special drill on difficult parts
         c.3 Put child on his guard c.4 Remove opposing stimuli
         c.5 Avoid forming similar habits at the same time
         c.6 Punishment, if necessary, should follow wrong act
      d. Automatization
         d.1 Attention to weak elements
         d.2 Distribution of practice (optional length)
   3. Values and Limitations
      a. Diminishes fatigue because habit mechanizes reactions so that they accomplish their function with directness and minimum time and effort
      b. Releases consciousness for the guidance of other activities

        c. Makes responses reliable and accurate
        d. Complete domination, however, retards progress
        e. Sensibilities often deadened, lessening normal emotional tones
        f. Difficult to break bad habits
    4. Breaking Bad Habits
        a. Avoid the situation which will result in the undesirable habit
        b. Avoid opportunity for its practice
        c. Concentrate on one or two bad habits at a time
        d. Follow the principles of habit formation for developing the reverse of the bad habit (Substitution)
        e. Attach unpleasant feeling tone
    5. Significance for Teaching
        a. Dependence of habit on sensory stimulation *(Habits never initiate themselves)*
        b. Importance of gradation of subject matter to develop mechanical habits
        c. In skills, improvement is very rapid at first
        d. Attention to physical and psychical conditions (time of day, length of period, etc.)
        e. Recognition of possible periods of lapse and plateau
            e. 1 Need for rest
            e. 2 Attention and interest misdirected
            e. 3 Conflict in habits
            e. 4 Minor causes - indisposition, irritation
        f. Recognition of individual differences in habit formation
        g. Rate of forgetting high at first
        h. Consideration of Speed vs. Accuracy
        i. Recognition of three sets of habits (Mechanical; Subject Matter; Mental)
G. INDIVIDUAL DIFFERENCES
    1. Principles
        a. Pupils differ in degree of ability, not in the ability itself
        b. Individuals differ in degree of difficulty of tasks which they can learn; also in the method of learning
        c. Pupils of the same age and grade differ greatly - there is considerable overlapping of successive grades
        d. No one class can ever be entirely homogeneous - variations are continuous
        e. There are no readily available and fixed categories which the school can employ for the purpose of differentiated instruction
        f. Provision for individualization presents teaching and administrative difficulties
        g. Chronological age alone cannot be the determinant of an individual's capacity
    2. Conclusions for the School
        a. Administrative
            a. 1 Vary the time element
            a. 2 Flexible grouping
            a. 3 Testing programs
            a. 4 Modification of the curriculum
            a. 5 Provision for educational guidance
            a. 6 Flexible promotions

                a. 7   Supervision of proper teaching practices
            b.   Curricular
                b. 1   Individualization of instruction
                b. 2   Diagnostic testing and remedial teaching
                b. 3   Provision for individual methods of learning
                b. 4   Grouping within the class
                b. 5   Record of needs, progress, and evaluation

<u>VII. HISTORY OF EDUCATION</u>

A. LEADERS
1. Socrates (5th century B. C.)(469-399 B. C.)(Athens, Period of Sophists)
    (1) Writings - Left no writings, is studied in works of Plato and Xenophon.
    (2) Emphasis-Highest formulation of principles of moral life up to his time.
    (3) Contributions - His starting point:"Man is the measure of all things" (Protagoras).
    (4) Developed opinion into true or universal knowledge.
    (5) Aid of education: Not sophist brilliancy of speech, but knowledge arising from power of thought, analysis of experience.
    (6) Method: Dialectic, skillful questioning, distinguishing between permanent form and changing appearance, forming concepts from percepts.
2. Plato (4th century B.C.) (429-348 B.C.) (Athens, Academy)
    (1) Writings - "Republic," "Dialogues."
    (2) Three social classes: philosophers, warriors, workers.
    (3) Six major concerns of life: psychology, knowledge, soul, state, politics, ethics.
    (4) The ideal *State,* which exists for the realization of *justice,* consists of three classes of people: philosophers, soldiers, and workers.
    These classes of society correspond to the soul (or *psychology)* of the individual: intelligence or reason; the passions, spirit, or will; and the desires, appetites, or sensations.
    The *ethics of* the classes embraces the traits of character which they should exhibit: wisdom, or correctness of thought; honor, courage, energy of will, or justice of the heart; and temperance, self-control, or justice of the senses. *Politics* indicates the duties of the classes: the philosophers are to rule, the soldiers to protect and defend the State, and the workers to obey and support those above them.
    (5) Aim of education: To discover and develop individual qualifications to fit into classes of society; harmony of individual and social motives.
3. Aristotle (3rd century B.C.) (384-322 B.C.)(Athens, Lyceum)
    (1) Writings - "Organon," "Politics," "Ethics," "Metaphysics."
    (2) Like Plato, he believed the highest art of man to be to direct society so as to produce the greatest good for mankind.
    (3) Education is subject to politics, each kind of state having its appropriate kind of education.
    (4) Education is a life activity.
    (5) Method: Objective and scientific; used inductive method, and thus founded practically all the modern sciences.
    (6) Education democratic, although all could not reach the same high point.
    (7) Greatest systematizer of knowledge.

(8) Formulated deductive reasoning; dialectic given form and universal influence.
(9) Gave vocabulary of reasoning to the world.

4. Comenius (17th century)' (1592-1670)
   (1) Writings - "Orbus Pictus," "Vestibulum,""Janua,""School of Infancy," "The Great Didactic"
   (2) Sense - realist
      a. The teacher should appeal through sense-perception to understand the child
   (3) Contributions
      a. Forerunner of 18th and 19th century educational theory
      b. Reformed Latin textbooks

5. John Locke (17th century) (1632-1704)
   (1) Writings - "Essay on Conduct of the Human Understanding," "Thoughts"
   (2) Founder of modern psychology; advocate of faculty psychology
   (3) Empiricism; induction
   (4) Conception of the child's mind as a "tabula rasa" (blank slate)
   (5) His influence strong up to the middle of the 19th century

6. Rousseau (18th century) (1712-1778)
   (1) Writings - "La Nouvelle Heloise," "Emile"
   (2) Education is life, not preparation for life
   (3) Importance of the child
   (4) Functional education
   (5) Individual differences

7. Johann Bernard Basedow (18th century)(1723-1790)
   (1) Writings - "Elementarwerk," "Book of Method"; established school called Philanthropinum, at Dessau.
   (2) Belongs to the line of Sense-Realists following Eousseau and forerunner to Pestalozzi.
   (3) Made first attempt since Comeniums to improve the work of the school through the use of appropriate textbooks.
   (4) Ideas embodied:
      (a) Children to be treated as such, not as adults.
      (b) Each child taught a handicraft for educational and social reasons.
      (c) Vernacular rather than classical languages chief subject matter of education.
      (d) Instruction connected with realities rather than with words.
      (e) Rich and poor educated together.
   (5) Contributions
      (a) Trained teachers.
      (b) Milder form of discipline.
      (c) Broader and more philanthropic view of man's duty to his fellow-man.

8. Pestalozzi (18th and early 19th century)(1746-1827)
   (1) Writings - "How Gertrude Teaches Her Children/" "Leonard and Gertrude"
   (2) Sense impression
   (3) Respect for the individuality of the child
   (4) Discipline based upon love
   (5) Education for the subnormal
   (6) Normal schools

9. Herbart (19th and first half *of* the 19th century)(1776-1841)
    (1) Writings - First to write a textbook on psychology,"Testbook of Psychology"; Psychology as a Science"
    (2) Rejected the faculty psychology of Pestalozzi
    (3) Substituted his own method - the Five Formal Steps:
        (a) Preparation
        (b) Presentation
        (c) Comparison
        (d) Generalization
        (e) Application
    (4) Organization and technique of classroom instruction
    (5) Emphasis on environment in education
10. Froebel (first half of 19th century)(1782-1852)
    (1) Writings - "Education of Man," "Mutter," "Kose Lieder"
    (2) Founder of the kindergarten and the kindergarten idea
    (3) Education by doing
11. Spencer, Herbert (19th century) (1820-1903)
    (1) Writings - "Principles of Psychology," "Synthetic Philosophy," "Essays on Education"
    (2) Not originator but developer of the best in democratic education of his predecessors
    (3) Emphasis on scientific knowledge
12. Mann, Horace (19th century) (1796-1859)
    (1) Reference: Mary T.Mann, ed.,"The Life and Works of Horace Mann" (5 vols.-1891)
    (2) First secretary of the first Board of Education of Massachusetts (1817)
    (3) Conception of education as universal,secular,public,free, and compulsory
    (4) Outstanding organizer in education
13. Barnard, Henry (19th century) (1811-1900)
    (1) Writings - Edited "The American Journal of Education"(1855-1870)
    (2) Held positions in Connecticut and Rhode Island similar to that of Horace Mann in Massachusetts, i.e., Secretary of the Board of Education in Connecticut, 1838-1842, 1851-1855; and State Superintendent of Education in Rhode Island, 1845-1849.
    (3) First United States Commissioner of Education 1867-1870
14. Dewey, John (19th and 20th century) (1859-1952)
    (1) Writings - "The School and Society,""Democracy and Education," "Experience and Nature," "Freedom and Culture"
    (2) Education is life, not a preparation for life
    (3) Learning takes place by doing
    (4) The bases of education are psychological and sociological
    (5) Father of progressive education ("activity" program)

B. CONCEPTUALIZED DEFINITIONS AND AIMS OF EDUCATION
   1. Character, morality: Plutarch (Spartans), Herbart
   2. Perfect development: Plato,Rabelais,Montaigne,Comenius,Locke, Parker,Pestalozzi
   3. Happiness: Aristotle, James Mill
   4. Truth: Socrates
   5. Citizenship: Luther, Milton
   6. Mastery of nature: Bacon, Huxley

7. Religion: Comenius
8. Mental power, discipline: Locke, Van Dyke, Ruediger
9. Preparation for the future: Kant
10. Habits: Rousseau, William James
11. Unfolding: Froebel, Hegel
12. Holy life: Froebel
13. Interests: Herbart
14. Knowledge: L.F. Ward
15. Complete living: Spencer
16. Culture, liberal education: Dewey
17. Skill: Nathaniel Butler, E.G. Moore
18. Inheritance of culture: N.M. Butler
19. Socialization: W.T. Harris, Dewey
20. Social efficiency: Dewey, Bagley
21. Adjustment: Dewey, Ruediger, Chapman and Counts
22. Growth: Dewey
23. Organization of experience: Dewey
24. Self realization: Dewey and Tufts
25. Satisfying wants: Thorndike and Gates
26. Insight: Gentile

www.ingramcontent.com/pod-product-compliance
Lightning Source LLC
Chambersburg PA
CBHW082038300426
44117CB00015B/2524